Translated Texts for Byzantinists

The intention of the series is to broaden access to Byzantine texts from 800 AD, enabling students, non-specialists and scholars working in related disciplines to access material otherwise unavailable to them. The series will cover a wide range of texts, including historical, theological and literary works, all of which include an English translation of the Byzantine text with introduction and commentary.

Liverpool University Press gratefully acknowledges the generous support of Dr Costas Kaplanis, alumnus of King's College London, who suggested the idea of the series to Professor Herrin and has underwritten the initial expenses.

General Editors
Judith Ryder, Oxford
Elizabeth Jeffreys, Oxford
Judith Herrin, King's College London

Editorial Committee
Michael Angold, Edinburgh
Mary Cunningham, Nottingham
Charalambos Dendrinos, Royal Holloway
Niels Gaul, Edinburgh
Liz James, Sussex
Tim Greenwood, St Andrews
Anthony Hirst, London
Michael Jeffreys, Oxford
Costas Kaplanis, King's College London
Marc Lauxtermann, Oxford
Fr Andrew Louth, Durham
Ruth Macrides, Birmingham
Rosemary Morris, York
Leonora Neville, University of Wisconsin-Madison
Charlotte Roueché, King's College London
Teresa Shawcross, Princeton
Paul Stephenson, Lincoln
Mary Whitby, Oxford

AF720720

Translated Texts for Byzantinists
Volume 3

The Laws of the Isaurian Era

The *Ecloga* and its Appendices

Translated with introduction and commentary by
MIKE HUMPHREYS

Liverpool
University
Press

First published 2017
Liverpool University Press
4 Cambridge Street
Liverpool, L69 7ZU

Copyright © 2017 Mike Humphreys

The right of Mike Humphreys to be identified as the author of this book has been asserted by him in accordance with the Copyright, Designs and Patents Act 1988.

All rights reserved. No part of this book may be reproduced stored in a retrieval system, or transmitted, in any form or by any means, electronic, mechanical, photocopying, recording, or otherwise, without the prior written permission of the publisher.

British Library Cataloguing-in-Publication Data
A British Library CIP Record is available.

ISBN 978-1-78694-007-0 cased
ISBN 978-1-78694-008-7 limp

Typeset by Carnegie Book Production, Lancaster
Printed and bound by CPI Group (UK) Ltd, Croydon CR0 4YY

CONTENTS

Preface vii

List of Abbreviations x

Introduction 1

The Ecloga 34

The Decision Concerning Soldiers Who are Sons-in-Law 78

The Soldier's Law 80

The Appendix Eclogae 89

The Rhodian Sea Law 113

The Farmer's Law 129

The Mosaic Law 140

The Novels of Irene 164

Bibliography 169

Index 176

PREFACE

The present work is one of a pair, as is immediately obvious from a glance at my footnotes. Indeed, it was while working on the project that would become *Law, Power, and Imperial Ideology in the Iconoclast Era, c.680–850* (Oxford Studies in Byzantium, Oxford, 2015) that I realised the need for a new translation of the legal texts which I was studying. Translations do exist for most of those texts, in particular due to the early twentieth-century efforts of Walter Ashburner and Edwin Freshfield. However, while the former's editions, translations and commentaries are still entirely valid and useful, the latter's are more dated. Their works are scattered and often difficult to access, nor did they translate everything. Furthermore, nearly all the texts have received new critical editions. More importantly, it became my conviction that one reason why these texts lay mostly abandoned by Byzantine studies was the lack of a good translation. Hence the present work. Inevitably, there is some overlap between the two books, and I would like to thank the respective boards of Translated Texts for Byzantinists and Oxford Studies in Byzantium, along with Liverpool University Press and Oxford University Press, for permitting this.

Given that I have set out my arguments extensively elsewhere, as well as engaging with the scholarship, I have been wary of overly repeating myself in the present work, and would respectfully point interested readers to the monograph *Law, Power, and Imperial Ideology* for more details. As it is, I have tried to recycle only those arguments that are most pertinent as to why I have included a certain text, why I have placed it in the work as I have, and why and how I believe these texts are connected. Indeed, it is in those connections that I am most interested, and it is with listing and partially explaining those connections that the footnotes are predominantly concerned. I have also attempted to provide the most immediate source basis of these laws, but any reader searching for an exhaustive commentary mapping the development of Roman law in these texts will be disappointed. Such a work would become unmanageably long and would drown in detail. Instead, commentary has only been provided as an aid to explain or highlight aspects of the text. Moreover, it is in part due to the off-putting nature of dense legal terminology that Roman law has receded into the margins of Byzantine scholarship. Therefore, with my apologies to Roman and Byzantine law specialists, discussion of Roman law terms and ideas has been kept to a minimum, and is only encountered when felt necessary to explain a feature of the text.

Even relatively small books like the present volume are only possible through the aid of many, and much that is good in it is due to others, while of course all the mistakes are my own. As such, I would like to give sincere thanks to the following, in no particular order: my two readers, whose comments were exceedingly helpful; the editors and board of TTB, Judith Ryder, Elizabeth Jeffreys, Mary Whitby, James Howard-Johnston, Mark Whittow, Jonathan Shepard, Rosamond McKitterick and Danica Summerlin. Special thanks are due to Ingrid Rembold, Fraser McNair and Jane Humphreys for reading considerable portions of the text. As ever, I give my eternal thanks to my family, in particular my wife Beth. Furthermore, given that one reason I wrote this book was to provide an aid for teaching, I would like to thank two of the most important teachers in my life, Richard Tillett and Peter Sarris, who at different times and in different ways nurtured my passion for history. Finally, I would like to give thanks for the life of my Grandad, George Humphreys, who sadly passed away during the completion of this work. His curiosity, love of argument and boundless generosity were a constant inspiration, and it is to his memory that this work is dedicated.

St John's College, Cambridge
March 2016
Mike Humphreys

To the memory of George Humphreys

LIST OF ABBREVIATIONS

AE	*Appendix Eclogae*, ed. L. Burgmann and S. Troianos, *FM* III (Frankfurt, 1979), 24–125.
Avotins	I. Avotins, *On the Greek of the Novels of Justinian* (Hildesheim, 1992).
Berger	A. Berger, *Encyclopaedic Dictionary of Roman Law* (Philadelphia, 1953).
C	*Codex Iustinianus*, ed. P. Krüger, vol. 2 of *Corpus iuris civilis* (11th ed., Berlin, 1929).
Coll. Trip.	*Collectio Tripartita*, ed. N. Van der Wal and B. Stolte, *Collectio Tripartita: Justinian on Religious and Ecclesiastical Affairs* (Groningen, 1994).
D	*Digest*, ed. P. Krüger and T. Mommsen, vol. 1 of *Corpus iuris civilis* (16th ed., Berlin, 1928).
E	*Ecloga*, ed. L. Burgmann, *Ecloga: Das Gesetzbuch Leons III. und Konstantinos V.* (Frankfurt, 1983).
FM	*Fontes Minores*
I	*Institutes*, ed. P. Krüger and T. Mommsen, vol. 1 of *Corpus iuris civilis* (16th ed., Berlin, 1928).
JHS	*The Journal of Hellenic Studies*
MS(S)	Manuscript(s)
N	*Novellae*, ed. R. Schöll and G. Kroll, vol. 3 of *Corpus iuris civilis* (6th ed., Berlin, 1928).
NG	*Nomos Georgikos*, ed. I. Medvedev et al., *Vizantiĭskiĭ zemledel'cheskiĭ zakon* (Leningrad, 1984).
NM	*Nomos Mosaikos*, ed. L. Burgmann and S. Troianos, *FM* III (Frankfurt, 1979), 126–67.
NN	*Nomos Rhodion Nautikos*, ed. W. Ashburner, *The Rhodian Sea-Law* (Oxford, 1909).
NS	*Nomos Stratiotikos*, ed. W. Ashburner, 'The Byzantine Mutiny Law', *JHS* 46 (1926), 85–109.
ODB	A. Kazhdan et al. (eds), *The Oxford Dictionary of Byzantium*, 3 vols (Oxford, 1991).

INTRODUCTION

The texts translated in this work were chosen based on my belief that they were published during the Isaurian dynasty (r. 717–97/802). Moreover, I argue that these texts were not independent legislative statements whose only association with each other is temporal proximity, but were designed to be read together as a whole. In particular, I maintain that the *Ecloga*, promulgated in 741 by Leo III (r. 717–41) and Constantine V (r. 741–75), was supplemented over the succeeding half-century by a collection of texts deliberately designed to augment it. Some of those texts were meant as true appendices, in that they were crafted to be appended directly onto the body of the *Ecloga*. Others were what I have called 'associated codes', always intended to be separate texts concerned with a declared topic but meant to supplement the *Ecloga*, and which together formed a (relatively small) corpus of law as it existed by the end of the eighth century. That corpus, I argue, was part of an Isaurian-led campaign to reformulate the empire in the wake of defeat at the hands of the Islamic Caliphate. Through it the Isaurians sought to reaffirm shaken imperial authority by recasting imperial identity along Old Testament lines, the gathered laws perceived as the successors to the laws of Moses and Solomon. Furthermore, I argue that these laws were not mere ideological posturing, the Isaurians only talking to their subjects, to themselves, or to God. Rather, they are evidence of a continuing legal order and discourse, and of an Isaurian programme to reinvigorate as well as reimagine the late antique inheritance and imperial government in general.[1]

The reader should be aware that none of this is uncontroversial, and that it is far from incontrovertibly proved. Indeed, given the fact that apart from the *Ecloga* and the novels of the Empress Irene (r. 797–802), none of the texts in this present work contain any sort of dating formula, and that their manuscripts only survive in any numbers from c.1000 onwards—as is sadly

1 M. Humphreys, *Law, Power, and Imperial Ideology in the Iconoclast Era, c.680–850* (Oxford, 2015).

true not only of Byzantine law in general but all Byzantine manuscripts—it is impossible to arrive at certain dates.[2] Here it is neither appropriate nor is there the space to engage with the entirety of scholarship on the matter, and the enterprise is superfluous given I have set out my views in depth elsewhere. What the reader should note, though, is that the majority, though not uncontested, opinion of Byzantine legal scholarship is that all the present texts, whatever and whenever their origins, had by c.800 come to form a coherent corpus of law, both in practice and as a textual grouping.[3] Therefore, it is not necessary for the reader to accept my ideas about when these texts were composed, by whom and for what purpose. Instead, they can be read as witnesses to the eighth century, or the Isaurian era as I have called it. Difficult witnesses, it is true, for no law can ever be simply read as an accurate description of the society that produced it. But the same can be said of all sources, and given that the period is hardly over-endowed with material, and what survives is frequently distorted by the iconoclast controversy, the present texts offer a precious window onto a little understood age.[4] Before examining these texts in more detail a brief historical introduction is necessary to place eighth-century law in its proper context.

2 For a collection of all Byzantine legal manuscripts see L. Burgmann et al. (eds), *Repertorium der Handschriften des byzantinischen Rechts: Teil I Die Handschriften des weltlichen Rechts* (Frankfurt, 1995); A. Schminck and D. Getov (eds), *Teil II Die Handschriften des kirchlichen Rechts I* (Frankfurt, 2010).

3 See for instance L. Burgmann, 'Ecloga', in A. Kazhdan et al. (eds), *The Oxford Dictionary of Byzantium* (Oxford, 1991), vol. 1, 672–73. For an introduction to Byzantine law and the legal texts see H. Scheltema, 'Byzantine law', in J. Hussey (ed.), *The Cambridge Medieval History Vol. IV* (Cambridge, 1967), pt. 2, 55–77; P. Pieler, 'Byzantinische Rechtsliteratur', in H. Hunger (ed.), *Die hochsprachliche profane Literatur der Byzantiner* (Munich, 1978), vol. 2, 341–480; N. Van der Wal and J. Lokin, *Historiae iuris Graeco-Romani delineatio: les sources du droit byzantin de 300 à 1453* (Groningen, 1985); S. Troianos, *Oi Pēges tou Vyzantinou dikaiou: eisagōgiko voēthēma* (Athens, 1986).

4 For the iconoclast era see M.-F. Auzépy, 'State of Emergency', in J. Shepard (ed.), *The Cambridge History of the Byzantine Empire c.500–1492* (Cambridge, 2008), 251–91; L. Brubaker and J. Haldon, *Byzantium in the Iconoclast Era, c.680–850: The Sources* (Aldershot, 2001); L. Brubaker and J. Haldon, *Byzantium in the Iconoclast Era, c.680–850: A History* (Cambridge, 2011).

Roman Law after Justinian

When talking about Roman law there is one figure who is impossible to avoid, namely Justinian I (r. 527–65).[5] Justinian's impact on Roman law was so great that it forever changed legal discourse. After Justinian, the entirety of Roman law was operating from his legacy, a fact explicitly and repeatedly acknowledged in the texts translated here. Justinian began by codifying the manifold forms of imperial legislation, collecting and editing laws stretching from the first emperor, Augustus, right up until his own reign. The result was the *Codex Justinianus*, first issued in 529 and subsequently given a definitive second edition in 534.[6] The even vaster discourse of Roman jurisprudence was similarly collated and condensed into the *Digest*, promulgated in 533.[7] Published alongside the *Digest* was the *Institutes*, an introduction to the overhauled law and a primer for law students that was granted the full force of law.[8] Together, these effectively transformed centuries of accumulated legal and political discourses, the quintessential language of Roman power, identity and civilisation, into the voice and will of Justinian. This newly purified tool was then utilised in Justinian's attempts to reform the empire through a stream of novels and edicts.[9] The totality of Justinian's works would later be called the *Corpus iuris civilis*, or 'Body of Civil Law', and it stands alongside the Bible and the Qur'an as one of the most influential texts produced in Antiquity.[10] Whatever the practical impact of these changes in Justinian's own time, they indelibly imprinted the name and memory of Justinian on Roman law,

5 For the image of Justinian for later Byzantines, and in particular his position in the legal imagination, see G. Prinzing, 'Das Bild Iustinians I. in der Uberlieferung der Byzantiner vom 7. bis 15. Jahrhundert', *FM* VII (Frankfurt, 1986), 1–99, esp. 54–67. For an overview of his law reforms see T. Honoré, *Tribonian* (London, 1978). For an overview of Justinian's reign see M. Maas (ed.), *The Cambridge Companion to the Age of Justinian* (Cambridge, 2005).

6 *Codex Iustinianus*, ed. P. Krüger, vol. 2 of *Corpus iuris civilis* (11th ed., Berlin, 1929).

7 *Digest*, ed. P. Krüger and T. Mommsen, vol. 1 of *Corpus iuris civilis* (16th ed., Berlin, 1928).

8 *Institutes*, ed. P. Krüger and T. Mommsen, vol. 1 *of Corpus iuris civilis* (16th ed., Berlin, 1928).

9 *Novellae*, ed. R. Schöll and G. Kroll, vol. 3 of *Corpus iuris civilis* (6th ed., Berlin, 1928). For Justinian's use of the novels as part of his campaign of reform see M. Maas, 'Roman History and Christian Ideology in Justinianic Reform Legislation', *Dumbarton Oaks Papers* 40 (1986), 17–31.

10 For the comparison see, *inter alia*, G. Fowden, *Before and After Muhammad: The First Millennium Refocused* (Princeton, 2013), 166.

and his works became and remained the bedrock and ultimate repository of Roman law for the remainder of Byzantine history.

Justinian's achievement was indubitably great. Yet it was not total, and it had unintended consequences.[11] Justinian may have codified all Roman law produced before his own reign, but he bequeathed to his successors a discourse split between three codes—the *Code*, *Digest* and *Institutes*—and more than a hundred novels and edicts that were never officially gathered or incorporated into a new *Code*. The sheer size and complexity of this corpus also made it more difficult to access, as did the fact that the bulk of it was written in Latin in an empire where Greek was now predominant. These difficulties prompted a series of sixth-century legal scholars, called *Antecessores*, to produce commentaries, translations and paraphrases in Greek to aid the teaching of law students.[12] Over the course of time, it was these shorter, simpler, thematic texts written in Greek that became the living law of the empire rather than the complex and remote Latin of Justinian, and it would be these texts that formed the source basis for the Isaurian texts translated here. Meanwhile, the wellspring of new imperial legislation in the form of novels, already reduced to a trickle in the later years of Justinian's reign, finally ran dry under Heraclius (r. 610–41).[13]

This did not mean that Roman law was dead and forgotten. The fact that seventh-century emperors, in stark contrast to their late antique predecessors, do not seem to have legislated either at all or to any great degree is indicative of a change in the nature of imperial government and the markedly different circumstances of the times.[14] However, it does not mean that Justinianic law was abandoned. Furthermore, though the evidence is murky, throughout all the many trials and tribulations of the seventh century, the legal machinery of the Roman state did not suddenly vanish or cease operating.[15] Courts still sat, cases were tried and lawyers trained. Indeed, law students were rowdy enough in Constantinople that one of the canons of the Council in Trullo in 691/92 threatened them with excommunication.[16] Thus, when the Isaurians came to produce the *Ecloga* in 741 they were not operating within a legal vacuum, nor reanimating the

11 Humphreys, *Law, power, and Imperial Ideology*, 25.

12 Scheltema 'Byzantine Law', 55–60.

13 Heraclius, *Novels*, ed. J. Konidaris, 'Die Novellen des Kaisers Herakleios', *FM* V (Frankfurt, 1982), 33–106.

14 Humphreys, *Law, Power, and Imperial Ideology*, 26–36.

15 Humphreys, *Law, Power, and Imperial Ideology*, 86–88.

16 *The Council in Trullo*, ed. H. Ohme, *Das Konzil Quinisextum* (Turnhout, 2006), c.71.

corpse of law. Rather one should view them as reinvigorating a discourse and a legal system that had declined and abated in intensity since its Justinianic heyday. At the same time, one should not doubt that there had been decline, for it is evident that both Roman law and the imperial legal order suffered in parallel with the material decline and dislocation of the empire.

The Seventh-Century Crisis

Certainly the wave of crises and problems that beset the empire in the seventh century was unprecedented in magnitude.[17] In 600 the empire remained largely as Justinian I had left it: a superpower centred on the Eastern Mediterranean, endowed with a complex, late antique, Christian, Roman culture. This was an empire that was hardly free of problems, from debilitating bouts of plague, elite obstructionism and confessional in-fighting, to aggressive and powerful neighbours. However, it was also not an empire on the verge of collapse. The sheer weight of Roman history, the empire having dominated the Near East since before the birth of Christ, which providential act had been woven into imperial narratives that reinforced Rome's centrality and eternity, militated against any notion that things might fundamentally change. As such, the shock of defeat would be even greater.

First the Persians and then the Arabs overran Syria and Egypt, the richest and most populous provinces of the empire. In the Balkans, Avars, Slavs and finally Bulgars undermined Roman control and essentially confined the empire to enclaves along the littoral. In Italy, the Lombards dominated the peninsula while nominally imperial territory was increasingly autonomous in practice, with the papacy in particular growing in authority. The remaining imperial heartlands of Asia Minor were incessantly ravaged, by both the battalions of 'barbarians' and plague. Together these encouraged the collapse of urban life outside Constantinople, which was sheltered by its formidable fortifications. The classical city had been the locus of Roman power and culture, and so the transformation of the empire from a matrix

17 See J. Haldon, *Byzantium in the Seventh Century: The Transformation of a Culture* (rev. ed., Cambridge, 1997); J. Howard-Johnston, *Witnesses to a World Crisis: Historians and Histories of the Middle East in the Seventh Century* (Oxford, 2010); P. Sarris, *Empires of Faith: The Fall of Rome to the Rise of Islam, 500–700* (Oxford, 2011), esp. 226–306; M. Whittow, *The Making of Orthodox Byzantium* (Basingstoke, 1996), esp. 38–193.

of cities into one of villages—begun, it is true, before the seventh century but completed during it—constituted a fundamental shift in the nature of imperial power and Roman society in Anatolia.[18] Given that the city was also home to the lowest rungs of the imperial judicial order, this must also have negatively impacted on the workings of Roman law.[19]

Although in serious straits, the empire was neither doomed to defeat, nor did the Roman state collapse.[20] Taxes continued to be collected, coins minted and the army paid, all organised by an extensive bureaucracy both in Constantinople and the provinces. For our purposes, we should also note that the provinces and their governors, the most important cog in the Roman legal order, survived, as did palatine officials who acted as the empire's highest judges.[21] Indeed, the Roman Empire not only survived but for much of the century actively competed with the Arab Caliphate for hegemony over the Near East. It was only when North Africa finally fell in 698 that the writing was truly on the wall.[22] The next quarter-century would see the empire start to unravel. Seven emperors would come and go in a series of coups, plots and rebellions. All the while, Arab armies drove deeper and deeper into Anatolia. By 717 an Arab army besieged Constantinople. The empire that declared itself eternal and without limits, that thought it played the central role in providential history, finally seemed on the cusp of annihilation.

That the chief foe and cause of imperial decline was a rival monotheist faith whose reality and permanence it was increasingly difficult to ignore or imagine being reversed, made things even harder for the Romans to accept.[23] How was one to interpret God's punishment of the Romans, and

18 Brubaker and Haldon, *History*, 531–72; W. Brandes and J. Haldon, 'Towns, Tax and Transformation: State, Cities and their Hinterlands in the East Roman World, ca. 500–800', in N. Gauthier, (ed.), *Towns and their Hinterlands between Late Antiquity and the Early Middle Ages* (Leiden, 2000), 141–72.

19 For late antique courts see A.H.M. Jones, *The Later Roman Empire, 284–602: A Social Economic and Administrative Survey*, 2 vols (Oxford, 1964), 479–84.

20 For a good overview of the continuities that allowed the empire to survive see Whittow, *Making of Byzantium*, 96–133.

21 For the late antique provincial and palatine judiciary see Jones, *Later Roman Empire*, 479–84. For the survival and adaptation of this administration see Brubaker and Haldon, *History*, 665–79.

22 Howard-Johnston, *Witnesses to a World Crisis*, 499–501.

23 For the multiplicity of ways Byzantines saw Islam see R. Hoyland, *Seeing Islam as Others Saw It: A Survey and Evaluation of Christian, Jewish, and Zoroastrian Writings on Early Islam* (Princeton, 1997). For the emergence and development of the Caliphate in this period see F. Donner, *Muhammad and the Believers at the Origins of Islam* (London, 2010).

how was one to quell the divine wrath? These were the questions that framed the imperial response to the crisis in the seventh century and beyond.

The Isaurian World

It was at this moment of existential crisis that Leo III seized power.[24] In part due to his resolute leadership, Constantinople weathered the Arab siege, and while the capital endured so would the empire. Yet after the 717–18 siege, several truths were now impossible to avoid. The world of Justinian and Heraclius had gone for good. The empire was now in essence an Anatolian one, with scattered remnants in the Balkans and the West. Facing it across its eastern frontier was a foe that was infinitely larger, richer and more powerful. It was also now evident that the Caliphate was permanent, and that Islam was more than a Jewish or Christian heresy. A triumphant, Islamic superpower challenged every article of faith on which the Christian Roman Empire had been built. To cope, the empire needed to adapt. It needed to find a formula for survival, at both the practical and ideological level, and it needed to find an explanation for what had happened, and what was the empire's role in its diminished state.

Over the next eight decades Leo III and his Isaurian dynasty would largely achieve this, and in the process laid the foundation for the Medieval Byzantine world.[25] Militarily, the Arabs were slowly constrained, and an equilibrium of raid and counter-raid emerged over a no man's land frontier that ran along the Taurus Mountains.[26] In part this was the result of the slow decline of the Damascene Umayyad regime, which culminated in the 'Abbasid Revolution of 750. This disruption of Arab power and the more eastern focus of the Baghdad Caliphate gave the Isaurians a breathing space for reform. However, the role of the Isaurians should not be downplayed. Leo III was a successful general whose prestige, leadership and personal connections—in particular, he made his son-in-law Artabasdos commander of the Opsikion theme, the largest and previously most rebellious of Byzantium's armies—united the army behind the new

24 For the significance of this moment, see M. Angold, 'The Byzantine Political Process at Crisis Point', in P. Stephenson (ed.), *The Byzantine World* (London, 2010), 5–21.

25 See in particular Auzépy, 'State of Emergency' and her collected works in M.-F. Auzépy, *L'Histoire des iconoclastes* (Paris, 2007).

26 For this and Isaurian military affairs in general see Brubaker and Haldon, *History*, 163–76, 552–54, 729–43.

regime. The latent flaws in this arrangement came to the surface after Leo's death in 741, when Artabasdos managed to seize the throne. Leo's son Constantine V only secured his throne after a civil war c.741–43.[27] Constantine then proceeded to curtail the over-powerful Opsikion theme by breaking it in three.[28] He also created new, full-time, professional military corps called the *tagmata*, which were based in Constantinople and paid directly from the imperial treasury.[29] These served to reduce the opportunity for future thematic commanders to make a bid for the throne, and considerably increased the military power of the empire. Constantine V used this to good effect in his, mostly successful, campaigns against the Bulgars.[30] Although the empire's military fortunes would darken again in the 780s with the renewal of more aggressive campaigning against Byzantium by the Arabs, the Isaurians left an empire that had a powerful army and broadly stable frontiers.

Underpinning their military success, the Isaurians ensured the continued provision of supplies and taxes that paid for war by overhauling the administrative system. The details of these reforms do not concern us here, but in essence, Byzantium had muddled through the seventh century by adding *ad hoc* extra layers to the Justinianic edifice rather than comprehensively reforming it. The Isaurians set about reorganising the system into something more coherent, aligning provincial fiscal structures with those of the military. In particular, a set of interrelated reforms to the fiscal administration occurred around 730.[31] It is against this background of a state renewing its control over and contacts with its provinces that the *Ecloga* would be produced. Nor did reform stop, for under Constantine V the new separate department of the *dromos*, an amalgam of postal, foreign and spy services, emerged.[32] Moreover, c.769 there is (much-disputed) evidence for commutation of some tax revenues into cash.[33] Whatever the

27 Brubaker and Haldon, *History*, 156–63; P. Speck, *Artabasdos, der rechtgläubige Vorkämpfer der göttlichen Lehren: Untersuchungen zur Revolte des Artabasdos und ihrer Darstellung in der byzantinischen Historiographie* (Bonn, 1981).

28 Brubaker and Haldon, *History*, 740–43.

29 J. Haldon, *Byzantine Praetorians* (Bonn, 1984). These should not be confused with the *tagma*, the standard military unit of the *Soldier's Law*.

30 Brubaker and Haldon, *History*, 163–66.

31 Brubaker and Haldon, *History*, 695–705.

32 Brubaker and Haldon, *History*, 705–09.

33 N. Oikonomidès, 'The Role of the Byzantine State in the Economy', in A. Laiou et al. (eds), *The Economic History of Byzantium* (Washington D.C., 2002), vol. 3, 973–1058, esp. 981.

truth, it is evident that the Isaurian regime engaged in serious reform of the machinery of imperial government with the aim of reaffirming central authority and maintaining the steady supply of resources that was the foundation stone of Byzantine military power. One should also note that the Isaurians continued the process towards the specialisation of public office that would distinguish Byzantine administration from the more generalist Roman system.[34] In particular, judicial and fiscal matters were largely separated.[35]

These changes to the practicalities of the state were important but, as we have noted, the Isaurians did not start from scratch; they did not need to. The apparatus of the late antique empire—the army and navy, the tax and coinage system, palatine and provincial administration, the court and Constantinople—all largely survived the crisis of the seventh century, with adaptations. Indeed, the remarkable continuity of the Roman state was an essential factor in the survival of the empire. What the Isaurians achieved was to simplify and realign the state apparatus for the retrenched world of the eighth century.

As important as, and perhaps more important than, these practical changes were changes in how the state perceived and portrayed itself, and how it answered the questions raised by defeat, in particular defeat to a superpower that proclaimed its own monotheist faith. The imperial office itself had seen its prestige and authority shrivel with the borders of the empire and the frequent turnover of emperors. For their own dynasty's continued occupation of the throne, the Isaurians needed to boost the prestige and centrality of the office. Of course, this was in part achieved by administrative and military reforms, and by the glory garnered by successful leadership in war. But it is also notable that from the beginning the Isaurians placed a considerable emphasis on their own dynasty. Leo III not only made his son co-emperor at the tender age of two, but broadcast the fact on his coins and seals.[36] These depicted Constantine as a miniature Leo, and indeed all portraiture was abandoned in Isaurian iconography in favour of a unified image of imperial power shared and manifested in the dynasty. Constantine V went even further by retaining

34 See P. Magdalino, 'Justice and Finance in the Byzantine State, Ninth to Twelfth Centuries', in A. Laiou and D. Simon (eds), *Law and Society in Byzantium: Ninth–Twelfth Centuries* (Washington D.C., 1994), 93–115.

35 Brubaker and Haldon, *History*, 676–77.

36 P. Grierson, *Catalogue of the Byzantine Coins in the Dumbarton Oaks Collection and in the Whittemore Collection, III: Leo III to Nicephorus III, 717–1081* (Washington D.C., 1973), vol. 1, 226–32.

his dead father's image on his coins, even after he associated his own son Leo IV in the purple. By the time of Constantine VI, Leo IV's son, no fewer than three deceased Isaurian antecedents, alternating the imperial names of Leo and Constantine, appeared on the reverse of Byzantine coins. Never before in Roman history had dynasty and imperial power been so closely and repeatedly associated.

However, the central plank of the Isaurian reimagination of imperial ideology in response to the shock of defeat encountered again and again in this era is the trumpeting of Byzantium as the New Israel. Rather than glorying in Classical civilisation and finding legitimation in the trappings of Roman imperial power, the Isaurians modelled themselves on Moses and Solomon, and imperial history was made to correspond with the biblical past.[37] In the stories of the trials and tribulations of the Old Testament Israelites, constantly surrounded by heathen powers and punished for transgressing God's law, eighth-century Byzantines found a mirror of and an explanation for their own position. Byzantium could still be God's Chosen People, occupying the central role in providential history, while it was being punished and diminished on earth. Moreover, this almost total correspondence between eighth-century Byzantium and the Old Testament Hebrews offered a prescription for how the empire could flourish once again. The old Israelites had been punished for failing to adhere to the law given to Moses, falling away into idolatry and sin. Therefore, the way to propitiate divine wrath was to purge those sins and live up to the covenant with God.

Iconoclasm

The most famous manifestation of this ideological and cultural shift is known as 'iconoclasm'.[38] The traditional narrative has the Isaurian emperors leading the charge against icons, orchestrating a campaign of destruction

37 For the significance of the Old Testament in Byzantium see P. Magdalino and R. Nelson (eds), *The Old Testament in Byzantium* (Washington D.C., 2010).

38 The best studies now are Brubaker and Haldon, *History* and Auzépy, *L'Histoire des iconoclastes*. See also C. Barber, *Figure and Likeness: On the Limits of Representation in Byzantine Iconoclasm* (Princeton, 2002); A. Bryer and J. Herrin, *Iconoclasm: Papers Given at the Ninth Spring Symposium of Byzantine Studies, University of Birmingham, March 1975* (Birmingham, 1977); S. Gero, *Byzantine Iconoclasm during the Reign of Leo III with Particular Attention to the Oriental Sources* (Louvain, 1973), and idem, *Byzantine Iconoclasm during the Reign of Constantine V with Particular Attention to the Oriental Sources* (Louvain, 1977).

and oppressing icon supporters, especially monks. Iconoclasm was seen as the defining struggle of the age, and the iconoclasts largely condemned as aberrations within the grander narrative of Byzantine and Orthodox history. Recent scholarship has poured significant quantities of cold water on these ideas.[39] Almost every literary source from the period—the legal sources standing out as a major exception—has been tried and found wanting for iconophile bias and reworking after the event. Substantial doubt now reigns over the extent, nature and significance of iconoclasm, and the role of the Isaurians within it. Whatever the truth, it is clear that there was considerable debate concerning the legitimacy of religious figural imagery, and that much of the debate was conducted through the prism of Scripture, the iconoclasts in particular arguing that the Second Commandment against worshipping graven images condemned icons as idols, and that the people's idolatry explained the empire's travails.[40]

What can also be agreed is that however fascinating this controversy is, and however significant one thinks it was in Byzantine history, iconoclasm has fundamentally distorted our understanding of the age. In the first instance, our literary sources were normally written, and indeed rewritten, with an anti-iconoclast agenda, deliberately denigrating the Isaurians as heretics and downplaying their successes while focusing on their religious policies and magnifying their impact and sinfulness. Moreover, the vast bulk of these sources were written after the Isaurian dynasty had ended, and when icon veneration had been restored as official policy, first in 787–815 and then after 843.[41] While these authors sought to refashion the narrative of the eighth century into that of the 'iconoclast era', there is little evidence that this was how the Isaurians presented themselves or that the majority of eighth-century Byzantines saw things this way.

Following the sources' lead, modern scholarship has repeatedly examined every facet and nuance of iconoclasm, and the society that created it is more often explored for information about iconoclasm than vice versa. Indeed, so dominant has been the hold of this controversy that the eighth century—rather than being described on its own or after its dominant dynasty, as is normal with every other period in Byzantine history—is normally subsumed within a broader period, the 'iconoclast

39 Apart from Brubaker and Haldon, *History* and Auzépy, *L'Histoire des iconoclastes*, see P. Speck, *Ich bin's nicht, Kaiser Konstantin ist es gewesen: die Legenden vom Einfluss des Teufels, des Juden und des Moslem auf den Ikonoklasmus* (Bonn, 1990).

40 Barber, *Figure and Likeness*, 39–60.

41 Brubaker and Haldon, *History*, 787–99.

era', starting sometime in the seventh century and continuing until the Triumph of Orthodoxy of 843, when icon veneration was declared once and for all a legitimate part of Orthodox Christianity. The implicit assumption in this is that this debate over the validity of religious imagery within Christian worship so dominated the times and set the political, cultural, religious, intellectual and social agendas that it characterised almost two centuries of Byzantine history. Although attempts have been made both to downgrade the significance and re-think the nature of iconoclasm, and to contextualise it within broader and, arguably, more important shifts in Byzantine society, government and culture, the old paradigm is persistent.

Law and the Legal Sources

Where then does this leave law and the legal sources translated in this work? It is my view that the law of the period was neither separate to the processes described above, nor of peripheral importance, but rather was intimately interwoven with them and stood at the heart of the Isaurian world. For a variety of reasons, law as a focus of study, and the legal texts themselves, have largely receded to the margins of historical scholarship.[42] In mainstream Byzantine studies this lack of interest has become quite stark, especially for this period.[43] This is despite a wave of (mostly German) scholarship in the 1970s and 1980s that has transformed our understanding of the texts, and in particular provided new critical editions for nearly all of them. That wave has rendered previous translations obsolete, to differing degrees. Furthermore, those previous translations are also scattered across multiple books and articles, some of which are difficult to access.

These, then, are the reasons why this set of translations has been compiled. It is hoped that a new translation that brings together all the texts of the period for the first time will stimulate renewed interest in Byzantine law. Furthermore, if I am correct in ascribing these texts to the Isaurians, then they represent by far the most extensive source set to have emanated directly from the regime. For a period that is so dominated by the works of their iconophile enemies, this is highly significant. Even if the reader concludes that not all the works translated here are the direct products

42 J. Crook, 'Legal History and General History', *Bulletin of the Institute of Classical Studies* 41 (1996), 31–36.

43 B. Stolte, 'Not New but Novel: Notes on the Historiography of Byzantine Law', *BMGS* 22 (1998), 264–79; and idem, 'Balancing Byzantine Law', *FM* XI (Frankfurt, 2005), 57–75.

of the Isaurian regime, one can confidently assert that they offer unique and substantial insights into an age that is as murky as it is fundamental to Byzantine history. Finally, in declaring that this book deals with the 'Isaurian' rather than the 'iconoclast' era, it is hoped that another small step can be taken towards relativising the significance of iconoclasm, and seeing the period and its rulers on their own merits rather than as part of another paradigm.

The Texts

The scene set, the legal sources can now take centre stage. What follows are summaries of the texts translated in this work. These are intended as introductions, not as exhaustive commentaries or analyses. A brief survey of each text's (often disputed) date, content and significance is given, alongside a justification for its inclusion in this collection. The reader should be reminded again that much about these texts, in particular their posited relationship to the *Ecloga* and dating to the eighth century, is not universally agreed. The reader should also be aware that the sequence of texts given in the translation is found in no extant manuscript. For instance, the *Mosaic Law* along with several titles[44] of the *Appendix Eclogae* normally precede the *Ecloga*, rather than following it as they do here. Overall there is considerable diversity within the manuscript tradition, a tradition that only survives from the very end of tenth century onwards, that is, some 250 years after the publication of the *Ecloga*. No certain significance should be imputed to the proffered ordering. However, there is reasoning behind the sequence followed, and it is briefly explained for each text.

i) *The Ecloga*

The foundational text of this whole book is the *Ecloga*.[45] It is the only text in this study that has a precise date, and even that has been debated due to conflicting evidence.[46] The *Ecloga*'s title declares it to be the work of

44 A 'title' is a subdivision of a book devoted to a particular theme.

45 *Ecloga*, ed. L. Burgmann, *Ecloga: Das Gesetzbuch Leons III. und Konstantinos V.* (Frankfurt, 1983). Old edition by A. Momferratos, *Ecloga Leonis et Constantini cum appendice* (Athens, 1889); trans. E. Freshfield, *A Manual of Roman Law, The Ecloga* (Cambridge, 1926).

46 For relevant literature on the dating and the argument for March 741 see Burgmann, *Ecloga*, 10–12, 100–04.

Leo III and Constantine V, issued in March of the ninth indiction, in the year of the world 6248. The indiction was a 15-year cycle associated with tax assessment, running from 1 September to 31 August, and was the principal dating formula for imperial documents.[47] However, while every year within the cycle was numbered, the entire cycle was not, necessitating extra information to identify the year. There were two ninth indiction years during the joint reign of Leo III and Constantine V, so the March mentioned could be that of 726 or 741. The Anno Mundi date, calculated from when the Byzantines thought the world was created, equates to 740. The nineteenth-century Momferratos edition of the text, which was the basis for the Freshfield translation, was based on a manuscript that gave an Anno Mundi date of 726. This is one reason why that dating was preferred by many early scholars, another being the utter inconsequence of iconoclasm in the text, which was explained away as due to publication prior to Leo III's first moves against icons, traditionally dated to 727. However, the Burgmann edition demonstrates the superiority of the 6248 Anno Mundi date and the preference of using the indiction as the basis of the date. It is now commonly agreed, therefore, that that the *Ecloga* was published in March 741.

Ecloga literally means a 'selection', and that is broadly what it is. It is a selection—a self-declared concise and utilitarian one—of Roman law. More specifically, its title declares it to be a brief compendium drawn from the listed works of Justinian I. From both the body of the text and the *Ecloga*'s prologue it is evident that the compilers were not, in the main at least, working directly from the Justinianic texts. Instead the *Ecloga* was compiled from the works of the *Antecessores*, about whose fragmentation of Roman law into many texts the *Ecloga*'s *prooimion* or prologue complains.[48] The precise extent to which the *Ecloga* is derivative is impossible to establish, and probably ranges considerably from significant reworking to almost verbatim copying. There are also elements that are new, and on occasion the text refers to previous legislation by the Isaurians that was then incorporated into the *Ecloga*.[49] Overall though we can be

47 N. Oikonomidès, 'Indiction', in A. Kazhdan et al. (eds), *The Oxford Dictionary of Byzantium* (Oxford, 1991), vol. 2, 993.

48 E.pr., 35, complains that: 'the laws enacted by previous emperors have been written in many books, and for some the meaning contained in these is hard to understand, and to others is utterly incomprehensible, especially to those who live outside this God-guarded and imperial city of ours'.

49 E.g. E.2.3 and 2.9.

broadly certain that the *Ecloga* is not merely derivative but represents a significant degree of editorial input.[50]

The *Ecloga*'s *prooimion* reveals at least some members of the commission empowered by Leo and Constantine to produce the text. Its most prominent official, and presumably its head, was the *Quaestor*. This post, established (probably) by Constantine I, had been and remained that of the pre-eminent legal officer in the empire, an amalgam of imperial spokesman and spin doctor, high court judge and legal draftsman.[51] The *Quaestor* was assisted by his deputies, the *Antigrapheis* (s. *Antigraphēs*), the heads of secretarial bureaux that had a (somewhat ill-defined) role in preparing legislation and court cases and in answering legal questions and petitions.[52] The commission also included unnamed patricians, the highest contemporary dignity granted to all the major offices of state, and, most sweepingly and illuminatingly, 'those others who fear God'.[53] This commission tells us three things. First, that there was wide input from across the Isaurian regime in the creation of this text. Second, that there remained a significant legal hierarchy in the capital, inherited from late antiquity, which was utilised to create the *Ecloga*. And third, that whatever the legal or administrative credentials of the commission, it was defined, at least in part, by its godliness.

In broad terms, the overwhelming bulk of the *Ecloga* maintains Roman law as it was formulated by Justinian. Inevitably there are some changes, simplifications and omissions. Justinian's *Digest* alone is some 150,000 lines of Latin, while the *Ecloga* is under 1,000 lines of Greek.[54] Simple pressure of space demanded pith, compression and judicious exclusion of material deemed less important. But it was also the self-proclaimed goal of the *Ecloga* to present the law as clearly and concisely as possible. Its purpose was not to faithfully reproduce the entirety of Justinianic law in

50 See Humphreys, *Law, Power, and Imperial Ideology*, 88–93.

51 J.B. Bury, *The Imperial Administrative System in the Ninth Century, with a Revised Text of the Kletorologion of Philotheos* (London, 1911), 73–75; N. Oikonomidès, *Les Listes de préséances byzantines des IXᵉ–Xᵉ siècles* (Paris, 1972), 321.

52 Bury, *Administrative System*, 75–76; Oikonomidès, *Listes de préséances*, 321–22. The *antigrapheis* were the *magistri scriniorum* of late antiquity, now renamed and directly under the authority of the *Quaestor*. For their late antique role, see Jones, *Later Roman Empire*, 504–07. The name clearly comes from their responsibilities in replying to rescripts (petitions about legal questions), which was rendered into Greek as *antigraphē*.

53 E.pr., 35; For more on the commission see Brugmann, *Ecloga*, 3–4; Humphreys, *Law, Power, and Imperial Ideology*, 86–87.

54 For its proclaimed length see *Digest, Constitutio Tanta*, 1.

all its vastness, complexity and occasional self-contradiction, but to select from it those elements that were considered most pressing, and then to convey them in a form that was easy to understand. It also declared that its goal was more than repetition, but correction 'to be more humane'.[55] Therein lies much of the *Ecloga*'s utility to scholars. For in its choices, its 'corrections', what was left out and how those choices were presented, lie considerable insight into what the Isaurians considered important.

This is not the place to examine these insights in depth,[56] but I wish to briefly highlight the following aspects. First, both in the commission empowered to compile it and in references throughout the text, there appears an operational legal order essentially inherited from late antiquity. Judges and magistrates are frequently mentioned, cajoled, given instructions and salaried.[57] Courts are referenced in passing, as are notaries. Indeed, the principal audience envisaged in the prologue of the *Ecloga* is members of the legal order, and judges above all. It is they who are barraged with Scripture exhorting them to judge wisely and not to accept gifts. It was for judges that this concise, easy to use and comprehensible text was produced. The *Ecloga*, then, was not a text talking to itself or to God, but one created by a legal order for a legal order. The fact that this order was never fully described in the *Ecloga* or elsewhere does not indicate its absence. Rather, the passing references to courts and judges more likely reflect the assumption that it was not necessary to spell out who and what constituted the Byzantine legal order, for its existence was taken for granted as an ordinary, unremarkable part of Byzantine life.

Second, the rhetoric of the *Ecloga*'s prologue is by far the longest statement we possess from the regime as to how it saw itself and the world. That world was one suffused with Scripture, in particular dominated by ideas and phrases from the Old Testament. The Isaurians are presented as heaven's appointed guardians and rulers of the Christian people, who are the new elect and who, like the old Chosen People of Scripture, are to be governed by law. Leo III and Constantine V were the successors of Moses and Solomon, while another model is adduced in the last title of the *Ecloga*, that of the Maccabees. This was a model that could maintain the Christian

55 E.pr., 34. For the importance of this concept of *philanthropia* see Humphreys, *Law, Power, and Imperial Ideology*, 94–95.

56 For more see Humphreys, *Law, Power, and Imperial Ideology*, 81–129.

57 For the importance of the last, found in E.pr., 37–38, see D. Simon, 'Legislation as Both a World Order and a Legal Order', in A. Laiou and D. Simon (eds), *Law and Society in Byzantium: Ninth–Twelfth Centuries* (Washington D.C., 1994), 1–25, esp. 14.

empire as the epicentre of God's providential plans while explaining its recent travails. The Christian empire would only be secure if it ensured that law and justice were upheld, and the new covenant was strikingly similar to the old.[58]

Third, the bulk of the *Ecloga* consists of a concise restatement of Roman private law on all those matters that had always interested it: marriage, inheritance, property, contracts. Of these the only truly significant alterations involve marriage. Indeed, the *Ecloga* highlights that marriage law was one of the few areas where the Isaurians had produced new legislation.[59] In particular, the Isaurians sharply limited the grounds for divorce and justified their changes along expressly biblical lines.[60] Moreover, it is illuminating that some of the few extended pieces of rhetoric in the *Ecloga* outside the *prooimion* buttress these alterations to marriage law. Evidently the Isaurians considered these changes to be a fundamental part of their moral mission.

Fourth, although the majority of the *Ecloga* is concerned with private law, there is a marked rise in the prominence of criminal law. By far the longest title, E.17, is dedicated to it. There one finds penalties for crimes as diverse as treason, murder and theft. More surprising is the sustained attack on sexual immorality: E.17.19–39 deal with adultery, illicit fornication, rape, bigamy and forbidden marriages, incest, homosexuality and bestiality. Some of this is well grounded in Roman law, while other aspects, such as the punishment for bestiality, are entirely novel. Indeed, in keeping with the rhetoric, the inspiration underlying much of this stems more from the Old Testament than the Roman past. This probably also lies behind another notable variation: the rise of corporal punishment relative to the decline of more traditional Roman punishments of execution, exile and fine. Not that the cutting off of limbs and more gruesome forms of punishment were unknown in late antiquity; far from it.[61] But in the *Ecloga* corporal punishment takes centre stage.[62]

Finally, the *Ecloga* innovated through its format. Its utilitarian selection of law stands in marked contrast to the grand codifications of Justinian, augmented by his novels. These rich texts were often difficult to understand and access. The *Ecloga*'s brief compendium is, and was meant to be, easily

58 See Humphreys, *Law, Power, and Imperial Ideology*, 93–105, 127.

59 E.2.3 and 2.9.

60 E.2.9.

61 R. MacMullen, 'Judicial Savagery in the Roman Empire', *Chiron* 16 (1988), 147–66.

62 See Humphreys, *Law, Power, and Imperial Ideology*, 118–25.

understandable and portable. It was successful enough to spawn a range of imitators, from the parallel selection of the *Mosaic Law* and the thematic anthologies of the *Farmer's Law* and *Rhodian Sea Law*, to imitators in Arabic, Slavic and Coptic, and finally to the Macedonians' *Prochiron* and *Eisagoge*, which attempted to replace the *Ecloga*.[63] The fact that, despite this, the *Ecloga* continued to be reproduced in multiple manuscripts for the remainder of Byzantine history is an indication of just how successful and useful the text was and remained.

ii) *The Decision Concerning Soldiers Who Are Sons-in-Law*

The *krisis peri gambrōn stratiōtōn* or *Decision Concerning Soldiers Who Are Sons-in-Law* is attributed by its editor to the joint reign of Leo III and Constantine V.[64] This is due to the reference to the imperial plural—which would not be appropriate again until 751, when Constantine V crowned his son Leo IV co-emperor—and the fact that the text nearly always appears as an adjunct to the *Ecloga*, and indeed was frequently described in the manuscripts as a nineteenth title of that text. Moreover, the *krisis* deals with a very similar problem to E.16.2, namely how to deal with disputes over property between soldiers and the households that, at least in part, supported them, and compensation for outlays of the latter to the former.[65] As such, it is plausible that the *krisis* represents either a case or a point of law raised in response to the changes in the *Ecloga*, and should be dated

63 *Prochiron*, ed. K. Zacharia von Lingenthal, *Ὁ Πρόχειρος Νόμος* (Heidelberg, 1837); trans. E. Freshfield, *A Manual of Eastern Roman Law: The Procheiros Nomos* (Cambridge, 1928); *Eisagoge*, ed. K. Zacharia von Lingenthal, *Collectio librorum juris Graeco-Romani ineditorum* (Leipzig, 1852), 61–217. For these texts' relationship to the *Ecloga*, see T. Van Bochove, *To Date and Not to Date: On the Date and Status of Byzantine Law Books* (Groningen, 1996), esp. 57–81. For the novelty and impact of the *Ecloga*'s format on its derivatives and imitators see Burgmann, 'Ecloga'; Humphreys, *Law, Power, and Imperial Ideology*, 92.

64 *Krisis peri gambrōn stratiōtōn*, ed. D. Simon, 'Byzantinische Hausgemeinschafts-verträge', in F. Baur, K. Larenz and F. Wieacker (eds), *Beiträge zur europäischen Rechtsgeschichte und zum geltenden Zivilrecht: Festgabe für J. Sontis* (Munich, 1977), 91–128, text at 94.

65 For discussion of the *krisis* and its importance for information about the Byzantine army see N. Oikonomidès, 'Middle Byzantine Provincial Recruits: Salary and Armaments', in J. Duffy and J. Peradotto (eds), *Gonimos: Neoplatonic and Byzantine Studies* (Buffalo, 1988), 121–36, esp. 134; R.-J. Lilie, 'Die zweihundertjährige Reform: zu den Anfängen der Themenorganisation im 7. und 8. Jahrhundert', *Byzantinoslavica* 45 (1984), 27–39, 190–201, esp. 196–97; J. Haldon, 'Military Service, Military Lands, and the Status of Soldiers: Current Problems and Interpretations', *Dumbarton Oaks Papers* 47 (1993), 1–67, esp. 21–23.

to some time between the publication of the *Ecloga* in March 741 and the death of Leo III on 18 June that year.[66]

The importance of this text is twofold. First, it substantiates the impression given by the *Ecloga* that a substantial portion, though by no means all, of the Byzantine army was supported by households in return for certain privileges. This was an important part of how Byzantium managed to field an army sufficiently large to guard against the much more powerful Caliphate without bankrupting itself. In essence, part of the costs of equipping the army fell directly to households, who were then compensated with claims against the soldier's property and income, and probably with some tax breaks. This not only relieved the cash-strapped state of some of its burden but enmeshed the interests of the state with those of soldiers and military families. Second, the *krisis* is evidence of the Isaurians' legal activism, or the activism of the legal order they encouraged in the *Ecloga* or, most likely, both. The *Ecloga* was not left alone but added to, and if I am correct about the dating, added to remarkably quickly.

iii) *The Soldier's Law*

The text most commonly called the *Nomos Stratiotikos* or *Soldier's Law* appears in its earliest versions not as a *nomos* (i.e. a separate law book), but rather as a title—that is, a subdivision of a book devoted to a particular theme—which is given the heading *peri stratiōtikōn epitimiōn ek tou Rophou kai tōn taktikōn*, 'concerning penalties for soldiers taken from Rufus and the Tacticians'.[67] This is exactly how the *Ecloga* is organised, and the texts known as the *Appendix Eclogae*, and as such the *Soldier's Law* reads as a continuation of the *Ecloga* and as another title amidst the *Appendix Eclogae*. Indeed, in numerous manuscripts the *Soldier's Law* follows directly on from Title 18 of the *Ecloga*, with the *krisis peri gambrōn stratiōtōn* frequently found in between.[68] This arrangement makes sense, forming as it does a coherent block of military law beginning with E.17.53 on punishing deserters, and E.18 on the division of war spoils, then moving onto the *krisis* concerning soldier's property when supported by a father-in-law, and culminating in this new title on soldiers. This is the reason why it is found here in the present work, rather than with the

66 See Humphreys, *Law, Power, and Imperial Ideology*, 135–38.

67 *Nomos Stratiotikos*, ed. W. Ashburner, 'The Byzantine Mutiny Law', *JHS* 46 (1926), 85–109. For analysis see Humphreys, *Law, Power, and Imperial Ideology*, 152–65.

68 Humphreys, *Law, Power, and Imperial Ideology*, 139–43.

other *nomoi* with which it is more usually paired, viz. the *Rhodian Sea Law* and the *Farmer's Law*.[69]

Of all the texts translated in this work, the *Soldier's Law* is the one in most need of a new critical edition. Walter Ashburner's 1926 version, while still workable, is based on only a fraction of the extant manuscripts; nor did he provide any translation or commentary, which helps to explain why the text is also one of the least studied in Byzantine legal history. More oddly, Ashburner decided to base his edition on what he deemed to be the oldest manuscript despite its patently odd ordering of chapters compared to the other manuscripts. My translation follows the order of a different manuscript—Rome *Biblioteca Vallicelliana* F 47 (identified as V in Ashburner's edition)—a manuscript probably as venerable but whose ordering is much better supported in the wider manuscript tradition.[70] To aid the reader a reference to Ashburner's numbering has been added in a footnote for every chapter.

The text as reconstructed from Ashburner's description of this manuscript is divided into four sections which probably reflect multiple recensions of the text.[71] The first section has 15 numbered chapters taken from the *Strategikon*, a late sixth-century handbook on military matters attributed to the Emperor Maurice.[72] It is to this that the title 'Rufus and the Tacticians' seems to be referring, though who this Rufus was is unknown. The extracts are mostly repeated verbatim, but there is a degree of editing and reordering, with repetitious phrases excised. One order in the *Strategikon* concerning the allowance for soldiers to purchase their own weapons is not included, giving a plausible *terminus post quem* of 616 for the section, when Heraclius abolished the allowance.[73] These first fifteen chapters focus on various aspects of martial discipline, such as insubordination and breaking ranks in battle. The second section is headed

69 For critical discussion of the relationship between these three oft-associated texts and their manuscripts see L. Burgmann, 'Die Nomoi Stratiotikos, Georgikos und Nautikos', *Zbornik Radova Vizantološkog Instituta* XLVI (2009), 53–64.

70 For this problem and the preferred use of this manuscript, as reconstructed from Ashburner's extensive critical apparatus, see Burgmann, 'Die Nomoi Stratiotikos, Georgikos und Nautikos', 59–60; Humphreys, *Law, Power, and Imperial Ideology*, 153–55.

71 Burgmann, 'Die Nomoi Stratiotikos, Georgikos und Nautikos', 60; Humphreys, *Law, Power, and Imperial Ideology*, 155–59.

72 *Strategikon*, ed. G. Dennis and E. Gamillscheg, *Das Strategikon des Maurikios* (Vienna, 1981); trans. G. Dennis, *Maurice's Strategikon: Handbook of Byzantine Military Strategy* (Philadelphia, 1984).

73 Humphreys, *Law, Power, and Imperial Ideology*, 156.

poinalios stratiōtikos, 'martial penalties', just as E.17, which normally precedes it in the manuscript tradition, is entitled 'Penalties for criminal cases'. This section contains 14 articles normally prefixed with a rubric referencing their derivation from the *Corpus*, similar to several titles of the *Appendix Eclogae*. These articles cover a varied range of topics, drawn from across the *Corpus*. A third section entitled 'Concerning the status of soldiers' heads two chapters restricting soldiers' employment by others. A final section, 'Further concerning the status of soldiers from the 49th Book of the Digest Title 16', has 22 chapters dealing with issues ranging from soldiers who attempted suicide to adulterers' ineligibility for service.

I have argued that the *Soldier's Law* as it stands was probably created during the reign of Constantine V, though including elements that had been assembled in the seventh century.[74] Certainly, as noted, in its earlier version as the *peri stratiōtikōn epitimiōn*, the *Soldier's Law* often appears as an appendage to the *Ecloga*, usually following it immediately and comprising a nineteenth title. Moreover, Constantine's military reforms, such as the creation of the *tagmata* and the break-up of the politically unreliably *Opsikion* theme, would represent a propitious time for such a text. If this dating is correct, then the text can be read as Constantine seeking to reaffirm martial discipline, moral correctness among the soldiery and imperial control over the army.

iv) *The Appendix Eclogae*

Like the *Nomos Stratiotikos*, the *Appendix Eclogae* is a misnomer.[75] The 14 titles gathered under this name by its editors do not constitute a uniform text, a coherent, single appendix that was added to the *Ecloga*. No manuscript contains all 14 titles, and there is distinct variation in the order in which they appear. For instance, AE.1 and 2 most commonly precede the *Ecloga* in the manuscript tradition. While AE.3–6 are a recurring block, sometimes extended with AE.7–8, they are most often followed by AE.10, not AE.9. The popularity of these titles, to judge by their frequency in the manuscript tradition, also varies wildly, from the very common AE.9 to the incredibly rare AE.14. Their association with the *Ecloga* is also inconsistent. For example, the unit AE.3–6 and 10 is a very common companion, normally appearing after the *Soldier's Law*, while AE.12–14

74 Humphreys, *Law, Power, and Imperial Ideology*, 159–65.

75 *Appendix Eclogae*, ed. L. Burgmann and S. Troianos, *FM* III (Frankfurt, 1979), 24–125.

are more distantly related in the manuscript tradition. They also differ in format, some titles' chapters being headed by rubrics that describe (with various degrees of accuracy) their ultimate source in the *Corpus*, while others do not have such rubrics. Some titles display a degree of editing and compilation; others are copy-and-paste affairs.[76]

However, there are good reasons why these texts have been associated with each other and with the *Ecloga* since the nineteenth century. First, the majority of the titles of the *Appendix Eclogae* are very strongly associated in the manuscript tradition with the *Ecloga*, and with its derivatives and successors. Second, the form of these texts, comprising titles that begin with a thematic heading 'Concerning …', makes them read as direct continuations of the text to which they are appended, the earliest of which in the manuscript tradition is the *Ecloga*, which is similarly organised into titles. It is for these two reasons that the *Appendix Eclogae* is included at this point in the work though, in order to aid the reader, it is translated in the order found in its critical edition rather than in any more common arrangement found with the *Ecloga*.

Third, the wide-ranging content and interests of the *Appendix Eclogae* distinctly overlap with the *Ecloga*. The various titles deal with issues as diverse as marriage, adultery, inheritance, border markers, securities, witnesses, and enumerating the penalties for heretics, pagans, Jews and sorcerers. This is a list that coincides in interest, but not in detail with the *Ecloga*. That the *Appendix Eclogae* does not repeat the exact same ground as the *Ecloga* but rather expands upon it is probably reflective of a deliberate intent to supplement the *Ecloga*, which is reflected in its physical attachment to the *Ecloga* in numerous manuscripts. Finally, the *Appendix Eclogae* is drawn from the same sources as the *Ecloga*. The overwhelming majority of its content comes ultimately, and often explicitly, from the Justinianic *Corpus*. As with the *Ecloga*, that process was not direct, but filtered through intermediary texts. Indeed, several rubrics in the *Appendix Eclogae* actually tell us which *Antecessor* they were taken from.[77] The most popular source was the *Collectio Tripartita*, a sixth-century work that had translated and rearranged many of Justinian's laws pertaining to ecclesiastical and religious matters.[78] Overall, the *Appendix Eclogae* is probably a more derivative work than the *Ecloga*, and there is little reason why it could

76 For all this see Humphreys, *Law, Power, and Imperial Ideology*, 138–52.

77 See for example, AE.13.

78 *Collectio Tripartita*, ed. N. Van der Wal and B. Stolte, *Collectio Tripartita: Justinian on Religious and Ecclesiastical Affairs* (Groningen, 1994).

not have been compiled quickly soon after the *Ecloga*, and then published as appendices to it. As such, it is plausible to imagine, at the least, large tranches of the *Appendix Eclogae* having been issued under Constantine V, which would also help explain why there is no attribution to an emperor, for these texts were appended to a text, the *Ecloga*, that already bore the ruling emperor's name.[79]

What then was the purpose of the *Appendix Eclogae*, and what can it tell us about the eighth century? First, it is further evidence that the *Ecloga* was not a one-off event but rather initiated a process of legal reform. Like the majority of the *Ecloga*, the intention was not primarily to legislate anew, and certainly not to replace the Roman law fundamentally reshaped by Justinian. Indeed, the *Appendix Eclogae* continued the *Ecloga*'s specified intention of gathering and sifting through the detritus of legal works that had emerged after Justinian, which confusing fragmentation of legal knowledge was given in the *Ecloga*'s prologue as one of the principal causes of the decline of imperial law and justice, which in turn had undermined the empire's covenant with God and was therefore a prime reason for overall imperial decline. Hence, the *Appendix Eclogae* is evidence of a continued programme of legal reform, a programme designed to collect, edit and repeat Justinianic legislation in a concise form. Moreover, the *Appendix Eclogae*, with its prominent use of rubrics explicitly citing their content's adherence to Justinianic law, served to further associate the legal world of the Isaurians with that of Justinian, and thereby legitimise the former.

One can also argue that if the *Appendix Eclogae* was published under Constantine V then it also served to underline Constantine's position as his father's legitimate successor, a claim which had been challenged by the civil war c.741–43 between Constantine and Artabasdos, Leo III's son-in-law. The notable prominence of penalties for heretics, Jews, pagans and magicians in the *Appendix Eclogae* would also plausibly fit the political situation of the early years of Constantine's reign, in which the empire was not only challenged by civil war but also by a plague in 746–47, which allowed iconophiles to challenge the regime's legitimacy, in particular questioning its divine backing.[80] This was also the period leading up to the iconoclast Council of Hiereia in 754, when Constantine

79 Humphreys, *Law, Power, and Imperial Ideology*, 145–53.

80 For the plague see D. Turner, 'The Politics of Despair: The Plague of 746–47 and Iconoclasm in the Byzantine Empire', *The Annual of the British School at Athens* 85 (1990), 419–34.

personally led iconoclast discussion and issued a document called the *Peuseis* that sought to demonstrate that the iconoclast argument was consistent with Orthodox tradition and Christology.[81] Reissuing laws of unquestioned tradition and legitimacy against heretics, pagans and Jews therefore had an ideological utility in presenting the Isaurians as orthodox, pious traditionalists.

v) *The Rhodian Sea Law*

Like the *Soldier's Law*, the *Rhodian Sea Law* is clearly a composite text.[82] It consists of three parts. Part 1 is a rare and manifestly legendary account of its origins that was almost certainly appended to the rest of the text at a later date, for which reason it is not translated here.[83] Part 2 contains 19 chapters, most of them exceedingly terse. The bulk of them are concerned with the division of profits among crewmen, and the regulation of space and behaviour on board ship. NN.2.14–19, though, deal with the more complex legal matters of deposits and loans. In this they generally follow Justinianic precedents, though it must be noted that the language is so concise that the meaning is not always clear. Part 3 is by far the longest section, and frequently preceded by a contents list or *pinax*. It contains 47 chapters with topics as diverse as fights on board ship, theft of anchors, deposits and jettison. By far the most frequent subject is assigning liability in various scenarios. Unlike the *Soldier's Law*, the *Rhodian Sea Law* was never organised as a title but always had its own, more concrete form as a *nomos*, a collection of law dedicated to a particular topic, in this instance the law concerning seafarers.

To a substantial degree, Roman law adopted pre-existing Hellenic customs that regulated marine commerce in the Mediterranean. These customs, in particular those concerning the jettison of cargo, came to be associated with the Rhodians, the leading mariners and merchants in the Mediterranean during Rome's rise to predominance over the sea. Hence the tag of the *Rhodian Law of the Sea* emerged, to which the present text refers.

Roman law recognised that marine travel entailed particular dangers

81 For the *Peuseis* and the run-up to the Council of Hiereia see Gero, *Constantine V*, 37–52; Brubaker and Haldon, *History*, 176–89.

82 *Nomos Rhodion Nautikos*, ed. W. Ashburner, *The Rhodian Sea-Law* (Oxford, 1909). Ashburner includes an extensive commentary that is still very useful. This has now been complemented by D. Letsios, *Νόμος Ῥοδίων Ναυτικός—Das Seegesetz der Rhodier. Untersuchung zu Seerecht und Handelsschiffahrt in Byzanz* (Rhodes, 1996).

83 See Ashburner, *Rhodian Sea-Law*, lxxi–lxxiv, 120.

that required special remedies. In particular, two complex issues were highlighted. First, considering the added risks of maritime commerce, marine loans (that is, loans of money or anything else either for maritime ventures or to be sent over the sea) were deemed different from loans made on land.[84] For normal loans the lender was without risk (i.e. whatever happened he should receive repayment of his loan), and could bring an action to recover it if this was not forthcoming. For maritime loans, however, the loan could be lost. However, the lender could charge a higher rate of interest, fixed by Justinian at 12% a year.[85] The second issue concerned losses that occurred on board ship or concerning a voyage. This issue was in turn divided into actions against the shipper for general damages or infringements of contract, and the particular liabilities caused by jettison.[86] The basic principle of the latter was that if cargo had to be thrown overboard for the sake of the ship everyone on board shared proportionally in the loss or, in the terms of the text and modern insurance, 'came into the contribution'.

The *Rhodian Sea Law* largely operates within these established concepts of Roman law. However, it embellishes its source material considerably by providing numerous scenarios and complicating circumstances, and then prescribing the correct response to each. In this it is acting in a similar manner to the other texts in this book. Rather than stating the principle, it prefers to enumerate fixed penalties for particular cases. Indeed, this recurrent tendency towards prescription is almost a leitmotif of these texts, and from this it can be inferred that the principal intended audience of the *Rhodian Sea Law*, just as with the other texts, was the judges who were expected to apply these rules.[87]

Ashburner, the *Rhodian Sea Law*'s editor, thought that it was produced between c.600–800.[88] He thought this due to the manuscript and linguistic overlap with the *Ecloga*, but deemed that this demonstrated little beyond a general contemporaneity. My main argument is not that there is similarity between the two, though there undoubtedly is, nor that the manuscripts prove a connection, though one could safely say that they strongly imply that an association had arisen between the two by the end of the eighth century. Rather, I argue that as the text stands it

84 D.22.2.

85 C.4.32.26.

86 D.14.1–2.

87 Humphreys, *Law, Power, and Imperial Ideology*, 192.

88 Ashburner, *Rhodian Sea-Law*, cxii–xiv.

not only requires an operative legal world to make sense, but requires one that is too similar to that of the *Ecloga* to be mere coincidence.[89] For instance, multiple complex cases of theft and homicide are included in the *Rhodian Sea Law*, which in itself informs us that the magistrates imagined in its texts had serious competences, but theft and murder in their simplest forms are not included, because they were already covered in the *Ecloga*.[90] Thus, like pieces of a puzzle, the *Rhodian Sea Law* states things and misses out others. This gives it a particular shape, which fits so neatly onto the *Ecloga* that it only makes sense to imagine that it was created with that text in mind, as a deliberate appendix to it. This does not mean that components of the *Rhodian Sea Law* did not exist before the *Ecloga*. Certainly it would seem plausible that Part 2 was an earlier text to which Part 3 was attached.[91] But I argue that the simplest explanation for the nature of the *Rhodian Sea Law* as it stands is that it was produced in the half-century after the *Ecloga*. However, the *Rhodian Sea Law* is also likely to have undergone another editorial process as, alone among the texts of this period, it was incorporated into the late ninth-century *Basilica*, the great reordering and translation of the Justinianic *Corpus iuris civilis* undertaken by the Macedonian emperors.[92] This is a plausible reason for the distinctly compressed and difficult state of the text. This makes the *Rhodian Sea Law* by far the most difficult text to translate in this study, its meaning often elusive. Yet, to judge by the text's huge popularity—around 50 manuscripts survive—this was evidently not a bar to its use by contemporaries.

vi) *The Farmer's Law*

Of all the texts in the present volume, the *Farmer's Law* is by far the most famous and studied.[93] Indeed, its 85 chapters have been manipulated to

89 Humphreys, *Law, Power, and Imperial Ideology*, 180–85.

90 For theft compare E.17.10–15 with NN.3.1–3, 38; for homicide compare E.17.45–48 with NN.3.6–7.

91 Humphreys, *Law, Power, and Imperial Ideology*, 188–91.

92 *Basilica*, ed. H. Scheltema et al., *Basilicorum libri LX*, Series A (Text) 8 vols, Series B (Scholia) 9 vols (Groningen, 1953–88). There is now a new edition of the *Rhodian Sea Law* as it appears in the *Basilica*: G. Rodolakes, *Apo to Nomo Rodiōn sto 53o Biblio tōn Basilikōn: sumbolē stē meletē tou Buzantinou nautikou dikaiou* (Athens, 2007).

93 *Nomos Georgikos*, ed. I. Medvedev et al., *Vizantiĭskiĭ zemledel'cheskiĭ zakon* (Leningrad, 1984). For the old edition see W. Ashburner, 'The Farmer's Law I', *JHS* 30 (1910), 85–108 (edition), 'The Farmer's Law II' *JHS* 32 (1912), 68–95 (commentary and translation).

support nearly every possible interpretation of Byzantine society. Although its centrality has slipped along with the remainder of Byzantine law in more recent decades, many of the great names of Byzantine scholarship from the nineteenth century to the post-war generation weighed in on its meaning, significance and date.[94] For the last, anything from contemporaneous with Justinian I in the mid-sixth century to a work of the patriarch Photius in the mid-/late ninth century has been suggested, though most opinions cluster around 600–800.

The reason why the *Farmer's Law* has generated so much commentary and dissent is its inescapable importance. No other legal text exists in such abundance. It is found in conjunction with every Byzantine legal handbook, beginning with the *Ecloga*, and was incorporated into multiple compilations. Moreover, it is almost the only textual evidence Byzantinists possess for what was going on in the countryside c.600–900. This means, given the prominence rightly accorded to agriculture and rural society in Byzantine studies, that the *Farmer's Law* is almost unavoidable territory for scholars of the period.

This centrality makes its insecure dating even more problematic. Like most other texts in this volume, the *Farmer's Law* contains no precise indication of either date or author. Considering the significant overlap of the manuscripts, style and interests the *Farmer's Law* has long been associated with the *Rhodian Sea Law*, the *Soldier's Law* and the *Ecloga*, and it would be uncontroversial, if not uncontested, to state that by c.800 it had joined these other texts to form an extended appendix to the *Ecloga*.[95] However, I argue that, like the *Rhodian Sea Law*, one can be more precise and definite in proposing a link between the *Ecloga* and the *Farmer's Law*. Several issues covered in the *Farmer's Law*, such as theft and arson, only make sense as they stand if they were written as extensions to points of law made in the *Ecloga*.[96] For instance, NG.41–42 and 46–47 all deal with various aspects of stealing cattle, but at no point deal with the crime of cattle rustling *per se*, because this was dealt with by E.17.13. This and multiple other cases can only mean that the *Farmer's Law* was written after the *Ecloga* and formulated deliberately as an associated code to the latter. Combining this with similarities in language, the manuscript evidence and known imperial policies, the half-century after 741, and

94 For an overview of the historiography, see Humphreys, *Law, Power, and Imperial Ideology*, 196–201.

95 Burgmann, 'Ecloga'; Humphreys, *Law, Power, and Imperial Ideology*, 202.

96 Humphreys, *Law, Power, and Imperial Ideology*, 207–18.

in particular the reign of Constantine V, seems a propitious time for the *Farmer's Law*'s publication.[97]

The vast majority of the *Farmer's Law* is, once again, working within a general Justinianic schema, providing concrete legal scenarios and prescribed penalties. Its title even announces that it was formed from extracts from the 'book(s) of Justinian'.[98] All the chapters of the *Farmer's Law* deal with property in some manner, whether it is about various forms of tenancy, the theft of tools, the construction of mills or the damage caused by the wandering of animals. The most prominent issue is delict law. A delict was a negligent or intentional act that gave rise to a claim for compensation by another without a contract being involved. The *Farmer's Law*, with its plethora of accidental damages caused by errant animals or careless humans, is overwhelmingly concerned such cases. This should hardly come as a surprise, for these are exactly the sorts of issues that have always occurred in agricultural societies, and lend the *Farmer's Law* a degree of universality, assuredly one reason why it could be so readily reused across multiple societies and times.[99]

The world revealed in the *Farmer's Law* is one dominated by private property that was interspersed with public land. Landowners, tenants, hired labour and slaves can be found cultivating the land and tending flocks. Fields, gardens and vineyards abut pasture and woodlands. In short, the world of the *Farmer's Law* is complex, variegated and socially stratified.[100] It is also a world where the state looms large. One can see its influence in the specifics, such as the impact of taxation on whether neighbours could cultivate an absentee farmer's lots (NG.18–19), or a judge adjudicating between villages over boundaries (NG.7). Moreover, the very existence of the *Farmer's Law* speaks of an operative legal order that was embedded within Byzantine society down to the village level, and which mediated the inevitable disputes of rural life. This would be true even if the *Farmer's Law* were a private work. But if, as I argue, the

97 Humphreys, *Law, Power, and Imperial Ideology*, 218–25.

98 Ashburner's edition had 'book' rather than 'books', leading to some speculation as to which book, but Medvedev et al.'s edition, based on far more manuscripts, demonstrates the marked variability in title given, some of which do not mention book(s) at all, some of which use the singular and others that use the plural. See Medvedev et al., *Vizantiĭskiĭ zemledel'cheskiĭ zakon*, 96.

99 Ashburner, 'Farmer's Law II', 87.

100 Humphreys, *Law, Power, and Imperial Ideology*, 205–207. For a broad picture of rural life in the period see Brubaker and Haldon, *History*, 564–72.

Farmer's Law was an official work designed to augment the *Ecloga*, then it would further the impression that the Isaurians used the reformulation and restatement of Roman law as a way to reassert central control over the empire down to its very roots.[101] Furthermore, the language of the *Farmer's Law* is suffused with imagery and phrases taken from Scripture, and contains considerable overlap with the *Mosaic Law*.[102] This is a mark of the ubiquity of scriptural and, in particular, Old Testament thought and language in the Isaurian world, and indicates further that the *Farmer's Law* should be located in the ideological and practical environment of the *Ecloga*.

vii) *The Mosaic Law*

The most overlooked law code produced by the Isaurians is also one of the most illuminating, the *Mosaic Law*.[103] The reason for the lack of interest among Byzantine legal scholars is obvious for the *Mosaic Law* is not a code of Roman law at all but, as its title proclaims, 'a selection from the Law given by God through Moses to the Israelites'. Such a title immediately alerts us to its intention, for it is self-consciously another *Ecloga*, this time of the law of Moses rather than of Justinian. Indeed, it is the mirror of the *Ecloga*, each channelling the laws of the two greatest lawgivers in the Byzantine world view. Its legitimising purpose can be summed up by one approving marginal comment in a manuscript: 'mark how all this corresponds with our legislation'.[104] Just as the emperor was legitimised through his closeness to and imitation of God, so Isaurian legislation was justified by its closeness to and imitation of the law of Moses. We have seen this repeated desire to align or buttress Isaurian law with reference to the Old Testament in the *Ecloga* and the texts that followed it. With the *Mosaic Law* that ambition was given concrete form. It is therefore unsurprising that within the manuscript tradition the *Mosaic Law* is frequently found preceding the *Ecloga*, constituting a form of ideological frontispiece. As Byzantine law became less closely associated with the Old Testament under the Macedonian emperors, the *Mosaic Law* lost its centrality and is

101 Humphreys, *Law, Power, and Imperial Ideology*, 229–31.

102 N. Svoronos, 'Notes sur l'origine et la date du code rural', *Travaux et mémoires* 8 (1981), 487–500; A. Schminck, 'Bermerkungen zum sog. "Nomos Mosaikos"', in *FM* XI (2005), 249–68; Humphreys, *Law, Power, and Imperial Ideology*, 218–23.

103 *Nomos Mosaikos*, ed. L. Burgmann and S. Troianos, 'Nomos Mosaikos', *FM* III (Frankfurt, 1979), 126–67.

104 Burgmann/Troianos, 'Nomos Mosaikos', 140.

not found with any frequency with their legal handbooks, the *Prochiron* and *Eisagoge*. Instead, the *Mosaic Law* became a standard element of canon law manuscripts.[105]

The *Mosaic Law* is extant in two versions.[106] In the most common and probably original version, 70 extracts from the *Pentateuch* are arranged under 50 thematic titles, preceded by a *pinax* or contents list. The second version adds an extract (NM.8.1) and significantly reorders the text. Its source text is the *Septuagint*, the Greek Old Testament.[107] While this inevitably means that the bulk of the *Mosaic Law* is derivative, for the word of God was conceived as immutable, the compilers of the *Mosaic Law* did not slavishly follow the *Septuagint*. Most obviously, the original text is broken down into extracts and rearranged under thematic titles, in a manner reminiscent of a Roman law text, including of course the *Ecloga*. But there are also occasions when clever editing and omission makes the text more applicable to the contemporary Byzantine audience. For instance, all mention of a high priest has been removed. Similarly, NM.46 enumerates the various Old Testament injunctions that refuges should be established for involuntary killers, but carefully leaves out the original instruction that three cities of refuge should be established, presumably because the Church now filled the role of sanctuary.

Naturally, considerably more novelty was possible in the rubric than the text itself. Indeed, it is the similarity of the rubrics' language to that of the *Ecloga*, even to the point of replacing the terms used in the *Septuagint* with the *Ecloga*'s terminology, which is the clinching argument in favour of a close association between the *Mosaic Law* and the *Ecloga*.[108] This impression is furthered by the manuscript evidence and the overlap of subject matter between the two texts. A final consideration is that the novels promulgated during the reign of Irene (r. 797–802) are distinctly hostile to the idea of the law of Moses being the desired foundation stone of Roman law and deliberately complain about oaths that were supported in the *Mosaic Law*, strongly implying that it predated Irene's reign.[109] Once again, it is the reign of Constantine V that seems most propitious for this text,

105 Humphreys, *Law, Power, and Imperial Ideology*, 231–32.

106 For discussion see Humphreys, *Law, Power, and Imperial Ideology*, 171–77.

107 *The Septuagint*, ed. and trans. L. Brenton, *The Septuagint with Apocrypha: Greek and English* (London, 1851).

108 Schminck, 'Nomos Mosaikos', 254–55; Humphreys, *Law, Power, and Imperial Ideology*, 173–75.

109 NM.12–13.

and that it was designed for the same purpose as many of the titles of the *Appendix Eclogae*, namely to deepen the legitimacy and further the policies of the Isaurian regime by demonstrating its allegiance to and enforcement of hallowed legal traditions.[110]

The subject matter of the *Mosaic Law* is as varied as that of the *Ecloga*. Exhortations to justice, the honouring of elders and protection of the poor are found next to punishments for arson, disputes over damage to and by animals, and loans. The two issues that loom largest in the text are precisely those that have repeatedly emerged in the other texts of this volume, namely property disputes and sexual immorality, the latter closely mirroring the concerns of E.17. The *Mosaic Law* thus acted as a work of legitimation, justifying the Isaurian legal programme in general by explicitly associating it with the Bible, the highest possible authority to the Byzantine mind. Moreover, by echoing concerns about property and sex, the *Mosaic Law* further informs us about the Isaurians' perceived mission: that the reimposition of good order, pleasing to God, needed the enforcement of correct contracts and the policing of personal morality.

viii) *The Novels of Irene*

The final two texts translated in this volume are distinctly different propositions from what has come before.[111] Most obviously, they are novels, the first issued, or at least the first to survive, since the reign of Heraclius. All the other texts are declared collections of existing law, whether they contain new material or not. Therefore, even in their form it is evident that Irene was breaking from the tradition of the family that she had married into. She had already shown great hostility towards the Isaurians. Irene had only risen to power in 780 following the early death of her husband Leo IV, and she became sole ruler in 797 after blinding her own son Constantine VI, following which mutilation he subsequently died.[112] Previously Irene had mutilated the other male members of the dynasty, the sons of Constantine V, who had plotted to overthrow her regency. Irene thus effectively extirpated the Isaurian dynasty. Irene also famously overturned what has been seen as the Isaurians' signature policy by returning to icon veneration

110 Humphreys, *Law, Power, and Imperial Ideology*, 178–79.

111 Irene, *Novels*, ed. L. Burgmann, 'Die Novellen der Kaiserin Eirene', *FM* IV (Frankfurt, 1981), 1–36. For further discussion of the novels and Irene's reign see Humphreys, *Law, Power, and Imperial Ideology*, 233–42.

112 For an overview of Irene's reign see J. Herrin, *Women in Purple: Rulers of Medieval Byzantium* (London, 2001), 51–129; Brubaker and Haldon, *History*, 248–94.

at the Second Council of Nicaea in 787.[113] Irene also favoured peace and the civilian bureaucracy rather than war and the army, who had formed the mainspring of Isaurian support. In short, Irene's reign can be seen as the deliberate antithesis of Isaurian policies.[114]

This is the context in which we should judge her two novels, dated only to her personal reign 797–802. The first concerns the use of oaths in judicial matters, the second marriages. Neither contains any great legal innovation, and both amend rather than fundamentally overturn the law of the *Ecloga*. But in rhetorical and ideological terms, they were a wrecking ball thrown at the heart of the Isaurian project.

Irene's first novel concerned oaths. Oaths were a central part of Byzantine political and judicial life.[115] In the *Ecloga* oaths are sanctioned to validate testimony and settle disputes, practices continued and supported in the other texts.[116] The Isaurians had also used oaths of loyalty to reinforce their hold on power. Irene and her son Constantine VI had engaged in a bidding war for oaths of loyalty from the army.[117] The problem with oaths was that Jesus had spoken against them.[118] This was thus a fruitful area in which to attack the Isaurians for being bad Christians who preferred the imperfect world of the Old Testament to the grace contained in the New. The actual changes in the novel are minor, with oaths of witnesses to be replaced by written documents and invocations to God. Yet they were couched in an extended piece of rhetoric woven from Scripture that condemned anyone who unthinkingly applied Mosaic Law (i.e. the Isaurians) as impious and uneducated. Rather than moral reformers, the Isaurians were, implicitly at least, portrayed as leading the people to the sin of oath-taking and oath-breaking.

The second novel bans third and further marriages, and marriages between masters and their female slaves. This returned to an issue dear to the

113 For II Nicaea see Brubaker and Haldon, *History*, 260–86.

114 Auzépy, 'State of Emergency', 277.

115 M. Nichanian, 'Iconoclasme et prestation de serment à Byzance? Du contrôle social à la Nouvelle alliance', in M.-F. Auzépy and G. Saint-Guillain (eds), *Oralité et lien social au Moyen Âge: Occident, Byzance, Islam: parole donnée, foi jurée, serment* (Paris, 2008), 81–102.

116 See for instance see E.6.4.3, 14.4, 14.7, 17.2; AE.12; NN.2.15, NN.3.12–14; NG. 26–28, 73; NM.8.1, 12.1–2, 13.

117 Theophanes Confessor, *Chronicle*, ed. C. de Boor, (Leipzig, 1883–85); trans. C. Mango and R. Scott, *The Chronicle of Theophanes Confessor: Byzantine and Near Eastern History, AD 284–813* (Oxford, 1997), 464–66.

118 Matthew 5:33–37.

Isaurians, and indeed the second title of the *Ecloga* is explicitly referenced. In practical terms, this novel made explicit what was already implicit in the *Ecloga*'s legislation rather than amending it. But by demonstrating that the Isaurians had failed to be rigorous enough even in their own pet projects the novel is a damning indictment. More importantly, this unambiguous prohibition of third marriages had obvious political benefits for Irene, for her position rested on her marriage to Constantine V's son by his first marriage, while several of her main rivals were the sons from Constantine's third marriage. Therefore, this legislation both legitimised her and delegitimised, figuratively and literally, her enemies, in particular Constantine V, who had dared to marry three times.

These two novels represent both a reaction to a legal period that had now closed – that of the gathering of law by the Isaurians and its republication in concise codes united by an ideological schema that placed great emphasis on the Old Testament – and the last legal products of the Isaurian dynasty. However, the vehemence of Irene's rhetoric is a backhanded compliment of the strength of the Isaurians' achievement, as is the need to focus on the same issues and justify changes through biblical exegesis. Despite their best efforts, these novels did not break the Isaurians' ideological hold over the law, and in their failure highlight several of the most important aspects of the Isaurian regime.[119] Therefore, they are a fitting way end to this volume.

119 Humphreys, *Law, Power, and Imperial Ideology*, 241–42.

THE ECLOGA[1]

A selection of the laws compiled in a concise form by Leo and Constantine, the wise and piety-loving emperors, from the Institutes, Digest, Code and Novels of Justinian the Great, and corrected to be more humane.
Issued in the month of March, in the 9th Indiction, in the year 6248 from the Creation of the Universe[2]

In the name of the Father, and of the Son, and of the Holy Ghost

Leo and Constantine, faithful Emperors

Our God, the Lord and Maker of all things, who created man and bestowed on him free will, 'gave', as the Prophet said, 'the Law to help' him,[3] and through it made known to him everything that should be done, and what should be abominated, so that he might choose the one as the bringer of Salvation, and spurn the other as the cause of chastisement; and no one who keeps or—let it not be so!—rejects His commandments shall be denied the appropriate repayment of their deeds. For it is God who announced both these outcomes beforehand, the power of whose words is immutable and measures the worthiness of each man by his deeds, and which, according to the Gospel, 'shall not pass away'.[4]

1 *Ecloga*, ed. L. Burgmann, *Ecloga: Das Gesetzbuch Leons III. und Konstantinos V.* (Frankfurt, 1983), with a parallel German translation. The previous edition was A. Momferratos, *Ecloga Leonis et Constantini cum appendice* (Athens, 1889). This edition was translated into English in E. Freshfield, *A Manual of Roman Law, The Ecloga* (Cambridge, 1926).

2 The various dating formulae equate to March 741. See Burgmann, *Ecloga*, 10–12, 100–104, and discussion in the Introduction, 13–14.

3 Isaiah 8:20.

4 Matthew 24:35.

Since, therefore, He has entrusted to us the rule of the empire, as it pleased Him, which made plain our love for Him in reverential fear, and since, according to Peter, the supreme head of the Apostles, He ordered us 'to be shepherds' of his most faithful 'flock',[5] we can think of nothing in return which ranks higher with Him or is more important than steering[6] 'in judgement and righteousness'[7] those entrusted to us by Him, so that thereby 'the bonds of all injustice are loosed, and the knots of violent dealings dissolved',[8] and the assaults of sinners beaten back, and thus we are crowned with victories over our enemies by His almighty hand, [a crown] more precious and worthy than the encircling diadem, and the empire is made peaceful for us and the state steadfast.

Wherefore, engrossed with such cares and having made with sleepless mind the discovery of those things pleasing to God and profitable for the common good, preferring Justice to all things terrestrial as the bringer of heavenly things, and as being sharper than any sword against enemies through the power of Him whom she [Justice] serves; and knowing that the laws enacted by previous emperors have been written in many books, and that for some the meaning contained in these is hard to understand, and for others is utterly incomprehensible, especially those who live outside this God-guarded and imperial city of ours, we called together our most glorious patricians, the most glorious *Quaestor*, and the most glorious consuls and *Antigrapheis*, and those others who fear God,[9] and we

5 I Peter 5:2. This is only the second time in imperial legal discourse that this imagery of the Good Shepherd is explicitly and significantly used. The first was at the Council in Trullo in 691–92, meaning that this is the first explicit use of this key biblical idea in Roman civil law. See H. Hunger, *Prooimion: Elemente der byzantinischen Kaiseridee in den Arengender Urkunden* (Vienna, 1964), 100–02; Humphreys, *Law, Power, and Imperial Ideology*, 49–50, 96–97.

6 'Steering' (*kubernēsis*) is a common metaphor for government, found, *inter alia*, in Plato, *Republic*, 1.341c; I Corinthians 12:28; Agapetus, *Ekthesis*, ed. R. Riedinger, *Der Fürstenspiegel des Kaisers Justinianos* (Athens, 1995), 2. For discussion of the metaphor and a translation of Agapetus see P. Bell, *Three Political Voices from the Age of Justinian* (Liverpool, 2009), 100 n. 7.

7 I Kings 10:9; Isaiah 9:7. Also cf. NM.1.

8 Isaiah 58:6.

9 In a later version of the *Ecloga*, 'those others who fear God' is replaced with 'the most learned legal experts' (*logiōtatoi scholastikoi*). See Burgmann, *Ecloga*, 3. The *Quaestor* was, as he had been in late antiquity, the emperor's chief lawyer, an amalgam of legal adviser, high judge, drafter of legislation and imperial spokesman. He was aided by (probably two) mid-ranking functionaries called *Antigrapheis*. On these posts see Bury, *Administrative System*, 73–76; Oikonomidès, *Listes de préséance*, 321–22. For further discussion of the

ordered that these books should be gathered together before us, and having examined them all with careful scrutiny for the useful content both in these books and in our own new decrees, we deemed it fitting that judgements on everyday matters and contracts, and appropriate penalties for crimes should be gathered up in this book in a clearer fashion and in greater detail, for the purpose of making the knowledge of the meaning of such pious laws easily comprehensible, for the solution of cases requiring fine judgement, for the just punishment of perpetrators, and for the restraint and correction of those favourably disposed towards sin.

And we exhort and at the same time command those appointed to the practice of law to abstain from all human passions[10] and by a sound understanding to give judgements of true Justice, neither disdaining a poor man nor letting a powerful man who has done wrong go unpunished, nor in appearance or word admiring justice and equality but in practice preferring injustice and greed as profitable, but when two men have a case before them, the one having made a gain at the expense of the other, [we exhort and command them] to bring equality between them and take away from the one who gained whatever amount they find the wronged man lost. For those who do not have true justice dwelling in their hearts, but are corrupted by money, or favour friends, or pursue enmity or defer to the powerful, cannot make straight judgements and show through their lives the truth spoken by the Psalmist, 'Do you truly speak righteousness, do you judge rightly, you sons of men? For in your hearts you practise lawlessness on the earth, your hands weave injustices'.[11] And as the wise Solomon, intimating in parables concerning the dispute over unfair measures, said, 'a weight great or small is abominable to the Lord'.[12]

These things have been laid down by us as advice and admonition for those who know what is just but pervert the truth. But for those who through a deficiency of good sense find it difficult to track down justice and

commission that compiled the *Ecloga* see Burgmann, *Ecloga*, 3–4; Humphreys, *Law, Power and Imperial Ideology*, 86–87.

10 This adheres to the Aristotelian concept that 'Law is reason free from passion'. See Aristotle, *Politics*, III.1287a 29–33; trans. S. Everson, *Aristotle: The Politics and the Constitution of Athens* (Cambridge, 1996). Here this is mediated through the ideas of Basil of Caesarea; indeed, the whole paragraph draws heavily on Basil of Caesarea, *In Principium Proverbiorum*, Patrologia Graeca 31 (Paris, 1857), 385–424, 400C5, 401B8–C6. See also Burgmann, *Ecloga*, 107.

11 Psalm 58:1–2.

12 Proverbs 20:10, 23. This entire paragraph is suffused with Old Testament thought concerning justice, for more of which see NM.1.

are completely incapable of apportioning to each what is fair, let them, in the words of Jesus son of Sirach, 'Seek not from the Lord pre-eminence, nor demand from the King the seat of honour, nor purpose to be judges having in no way the strength to remove injustice'.[13] Let those who possess intellect, sense and a clear knowledge of true justice see rightly in their judgements and dispassionately dispense to each according to their worth. For thus our Lord Jesus Christ, the power and wisdom of God, grants to them even more abundantly the knowledge of Justice and uncovers those things that are hard to discover; and He also made Solomon truly wise when he sought out what was just and granted him the ability to dispense rightly and correctly the judgement between the women concerning the child. For since what was said by each woman was not supported by witnesses, he commanded that resort be had to nature and prepared to use it to find out what was not known, for while the stranger accepted with equanimity the command concerning the slaying of the child, the true mother, because of her natural love, could not bear even to hear the order.[14]

Let those who have been appointed by our piety to judge cases and entrusted with the just weighing of our pious laws consider and understand these things, and conduct themselves accordingly. For by these things we endeavour to serve God, who entrusted us with the sceptre of the empire; with these weapons, by His power, we wish to firmly resist our enemies; in these things we trust to increase in goodness and prosper the flock branded by Christ, subjected by His authority to our clemency; and by these we hope to restore in us the ancient standard of justice of the state.

Since our Lord and Saviour Jesus Christ said, 'Do not judge by appearances, but judge with righteous judgement',[15] it is right to refrain from accepting gifts of any sort. For it is written, 'Woe to them who justify the ungodly for rewards,[16] and pervert the way of the humble,[17] and take away Justice from the righteous; their root shall be as chaff, and their flower shall go up as dust, for they were not willing to fulfil the law of the Lord.[18] For gifts and presents blind the eyes of the wise'.[19] Wherefore, being eager to utterly check such sordid love of gain, we have ordained that salaries

13 Ecclesiasticus 7:4, 6.
14 Cf. I Kings 3:16–28.
15 John 7:24.
16 Isaiah 5:23.
17 Amos 2:7.
18 Isaiah 5:24.
19 Deuteronomy 16:19.

should be provided from our pious purse[20] for the most glorious *Quaestor*, the *Antigrapheis* and all those who serve in judicial matters, so that they should not take anything at all from anyone who comes up before them, lest the words spoken by the prophet—'they sold Justice for money'[21]—be fulfilled by us, and that we thereby incur the wrath of God as transgressors of His commandments.

The Beginning of the Chapters of the New Legislation[22]

Title 1

1. Concerning the contraction of betrothal and its dissolution.
2. Concerning written agreements for betrothal.
3. Concerning fiancés who delay the marriage.
4. Concerning underage orphans who are betrothed and change their mind.
5. Concerning adult orphans [who are betrothed] who change their mind.

20 The *sakellion* or Treasury, had evolved from the personal treasury of the emperor into a department of general fiscal oversight, whose official was close to the emperor. See Haldon, *Seventh Century*, 180–86. For the judiciary to be paid directly from here should, therefore, as is clearly the intention, have tightened imperial control over imperial judges. For the importance of this change, see Simon, 'Legislation as Both a World Order and Legal Order', 14.

21 Amos 2:6.

22 This contents list, known in Greek as a *pinax*, is found in numerous MSS, including several of the oldest, and therefore was plausibly part of the original text, hence its inclusion here. Its existence might offer clues to the purpose of the text; a contents list, after all, is there to aid the reader in finding what he seeks in the document. This implies that the *Ecloga* was designed with real-world application in mind, as a reference work for repeated use, not just as some one-off pronouncement of imperial policy or power. Other texts in this work also appear on occasion in the manuscript tradition with a *pinax*, for instance the *Soldier's Law* (from here on NS) and the *Farmer's Law* (NG). But only those contents lists prefacing the *Mosaic Law* (NM) and the third part of the *Rhodian Sea Law* (NN) are so regular a feature of the manuscripts that one can feel relatively confident that they were produced simultaneously with the texts they catalogue. Therefore the *pinax* of the NN and of the NM are translated below, and can be found respectively on 115–17, 140–42. The comparison with the *Mosaic Law* is particularly illuminating, for in one manuscript where that text precedes the *Ecloga*, the NM's *pinax* is headed with the title 'the chapters of the old legislation', thereby deliberately mirroring the 'new legislation' of the *Ecloga*. See Burgmann/Troianos, 'Nomos Mosaikos', 138. Furthermore, this *pinax* introduces several technical terms which will be unfamiliar to many (e.g. *emphyteusis* and subject children). Puzzled readers should consult the passages below corresponding to the relevant numbered headings, where explanations are provided in the translated text and footnotes.

Title 2

1. Concerning permitted marriages.

2. Concerning forbidden marriages and betrothals.

3. Concerning written marriages and their contraction.

4. Concerning marriage and inheritance when either spouse dies without children.

5. Concerning the death of either spouse with subject children, and concerning second marriage and division of property.

6. Concerning unwritten marriage and union, and its dissolution.

7. Concerning marriage with a poor woman and what is due to her through inheritance.

8. Concerning second marriages and gifts between spouses, and concerning the time for mourning and the inheritance of the children of both.

9. Concerning the dissolution of marriage from causes due to the wife.

10. Concerning the dissolution of marriage from causes due to the husband.

Title 3

1. Concerning the contracting of the dowry and non-payment.

2. Concerning losses from misfortune that shall not adhere to the property of the dowry that the wife brought to her husband.

Title 4

1. Concerning the contraction of unwritten simple gifts.

2. Concerning the contraction of written gifts.

3. Concerning gifts made after death through wills.

4. Concerning the revocation of all gifts.

Title 5

1. Concerning persons prevented from making a will.

2. Concerning the creation of written wills.

3. Concerning the contraction of unwritten wills.

4. Concerning the number of witnesses found in a will.

5. Concerning children not mentioned in the will and born afterwards.

6. Concerning a child disinherited due to ingratitude and another who is a stranger and comes into it due to gratitude.

7. Concerning each heir who makes delays and postponements, and concerning legal shares.

8. Concerning wills made on the brink of death during wartime or on the road.

Title 6

1. Concerning intestate heirs.

2. Concerning inheritance when subject children and the rest [of the family] have died.

3. Concerning legacies.

4. Concerning inheritances and recovery of debts.

5. Concerning heirs or legatees who conceal the will.

6. Concerning intestate heirs and concerning those demanding legacies.

7. Concerning children who lose their lawful inheritance due to ingratitude.

Title 7

1. Concerning orphans who are left behind and their guardians.

Title 8

1. Concerning freedom and return to slavery.

2. Concerning a slave who wears the cap of liberty at a funeral.

3. Concerning a slave who marries a free woman or is sponsored in holy baptism by his master or his heirs.

4. Concerning the ransoming of free men from the enemy.

5. Concerning freedmen reduced to slavery again due to ingratitude.

6. Concerning slaves taken as prisoners of war who return from the enemy.

Title 9

1. Concerning sale and purchase.

2. Concerning deposits.

Title 10

1. Concerning loans and security.

2. Concerning creditors seizing and taking securities.

3. Concerning wives not being liable to their husbands' debts unless they agree to it.

4. Concerning written and unwritten partnership.

Title 11

1. Concerning all deposits.

Title 12

1. Concerning perpetual *emphyteusis* and those who render service who cause harm to the principal owner.

2. Concerning perpetual *emphyteusis* and its alienation.

3. Concerning reasonable ejection from *emphyteusis.*

4. Concerning holy houses prevented from making *emphyteusis*, and concerning the property not prevented, and concerning exchange.

5. Concerning limited *emphyteusis.*

6. Concerning those persons prevented from contracting perpetual or limited *emphyteusis.*

Title 13

1. Concerning written and unwritten leases.

Title 14

1. Concerning trustworthy and untrustworthy witnesses.

2. Concerning parents or children and slaves testifying.

3. Concerning not being compelled to produce evidence against oneself.

4. Concerning witnesses brought from far away.

5. Concerning those found to have made agreements before ordinary judges and not stood by them.

6. Concerning the non-admission of hearsay testimony.

7. Concerning *taboularioi* who testify.

8. Concerning witnesses in criminal cases.

9. Concerning the summoning of witnesses.

10. Concerning those who deny their own bond of debt or dispute the amount.

Title 15

1. Concerning settlements made by underage children.

2. Concerning fraudulent settlements.

Title 16

1. Concerning the property of soldiers who are subject [to parental power].

2. Concerning a soldier and a farmer who are brothers who, having entered into a joint property, then withdraw.

3. Concerning soldiers' profits.

4. Concerning clerics and others in state service through gifts.

5. Concerning dignitaries and other state servants who receive imperial salaries.

6. Concerning ordinary *peculia* of subject children.

7. Concerning property acquired by subject children from their own sweat, favour or inheritance.

Title 17
Penalties for Criminal Cases

1. Concerning those seeking refuge.

2. Concerning those who commit perjury.

3. Concerning conspirators.

4. Concerning anyone who lays hands on a cleric in a church or in a procession.

5. Concerning those who invade [another's property] and do not go to a magistrate.

6. Concerning those who renounce Christianity and convert to Islam.

7. Concerning a horse taken beyond its hired limit.

8. Concerning those who shut up another's animals.

9. Concerning rams and bulls that kill each other.
10. Concerning theft in camp.
11. Concerning rich and poor thieves.
12. Concerning a slave who is a thief.
13. Concerning cattle rustlers.
14. Concerning those who strip the dead.
15. Concerning temple robbers.
16. Concerning kidnappers.
17. Concerning those who corruptly procure others' slaves.
18. Concerning forgers.
19. Concerning married men who fornicate.
20. Concerning unmarried men who fornicate.
21. Concerning married men who copulate with their own female slave.
22. Concerning anyone who lies with another's female slave.
23. Concerning anyone who fornicates with a nun.
24. Concerning anyone who seizes a nun or secular virgin.
25. Concerning anyone who marries their godparent.
26. Concerning those who commit adultery with their godparent.
27. Concerning adulterers and adulteresses.
28. Concerning procurers.
29. Concerning corrupters.
30. Concerning anyone who forcibly corrupts a girl.
31. Concerning anyone who corrupts an underage girl.
32. Concerning anyone who corrupts another's fiancée.
33. Concerning those who commit incest.
34. Concerning anyone who has intercourse with a mother and daughter.
35. Concerning anyone who has two wives.
36. Concerning a woman who intentionally has an abortion.
37. Concerning those who after this legislation have illegitimate sex with relatives.
38. Concerning the wanton [i.e. homosexuals].

39. Concerning those who commit bestiality.
40. Concerning anyone who sets fire to another's wood.
41. Concerning those who commit intentional and unintentional arson.
42. Concerning anyone who gives a drink on whatever pretext that results in harm or death.
43. Concerning sorcerers and poisoners.
44. Concerning amulets.
45. Concerning intentional murder.
46. Concerning anyone who strikes someone with a sword.
47. Concerning homicide that occurs during a fight.
48. Concerning homicide caused by someone hitting with their hands.
49. Concerning the death of a slave due to a master's beating.
50. Concerning robbers.
51. Concerning slanderers.
52. Concerning Manichaeans and Montanists
53. Concerning deserters.

Title 18

1. Concerning the division of spoils.

Title 1: Concerning the contraction of betrothal and its dissolution

1.1. Betrothal of Christians can be contracted for minors from the age of seven upwards, based on the desires of the betrothed and the consent of their parents and kin, if the parties enter into the contract legally—and they do not fall into the category of those prevented from marrying—that is through a betrothal gift,[23] that is to say a *hypobolon*,[24] or through a written contract. And if the man who gave the betrothal gift should desire to renege and not marry, he shall lose the betrothal gift. However, if the desire to renege is on the girl's side, then she shall pay back the betrothal gift twice over, that is the betrothal gift and as much again.[25]

1.2. If a man makes a written agreement and wishes to renege, then he shall compensate the girl according to the contract. However, if it is on the part of the girl that the agreement is broken, without known accepted legal grounds, then the same sum which the man promised in the contract shall be given to him, along with anything else undertaken by him in the contract, and he shall be released from it.

1.3. If a man is betrothed to a girl and, either through animosity or on whatever grounds, delays the marriage, the girl is bound to wait for up to two years; and after this the party of the girl may summon him before witnesses to perform the marriage. Then either he shall accept this, or otherwise the girl has leave to marry whomsoever she wishes, and she will keep whatever she has received from her former fiancé.[26]

1.4.1. If orphan children, either male or female, should through the prompting of others become betrothed, and later change their mind, then

23 An *arrabōn* was in general contracts a deposit or down payment (see for example E.9.2), but had from the fourth century also gained the specific meaning of a betrothal gift from fiancé to fiancée. See M.-T. Fögen, 'Arrha Sponsalicia', *ODB*, vol. 1, 185–86.

24 *Hypobolon* would from the ninth/tenth-century novels of Leo VI onwards represent the Greek version of *donatio propter nuptias*, the bridegroom's gift to the bride on their marriage, the counterpart to the dowry. See M.-T. Fögen, 'Hypobolon', *ODB*, vol. 2, 965. However, in Justinianic legislation, *donatio propter nuptias* is rendered in Greek as *progamiaia dōrea*, the term used in E.2.3. Therefore, the meaning of *hypobolon* is here unclear. The answer that best fits the Greek is that the *arrabōn*, the 'betrothal gift', was here described as a *hypobolon* and only later did it gain a different meaning. Whatever the solution, the gist is clear: betrothal was brought into effect by payment of a gift or through a written contract.

25 Cf. C.5.1.5.

26 Cf. C.5.1.2.

up to the age of fifteen they may break the agreement with impunity, for as orphans they did not know what was to their advantage.

1.4.2. But if they have reached maturity they do not have permission to break the betrothal, for they had wit enough to know what they were doing.

Title 2: Concerning permitted and forbidden marriages, first and second marriages, written and unwritten marriages, and their dissolution

2.1. Marriage of Christians, whether written or unwritten, can be contracted between a man and a woman of marriageable age, that is fifteen for a man, and thirteen for a woman, both desiring it, and with the consent of their parents.[27]

2.2. Marriage is forbidden between those brought together in holy and salvation-bringing baptism, that is between a godfather and his god-daughter or her mother, or likewise between his son and his god-daughter or her mother;[28] and also between those known to be related to one another by blood, that is parents with children, brothers with sisters, and between their children, who are called cousins, and also between their children; and also between those who are known to be related by marriage, stepfathers with stepdaughters, fathers-in-law with daughters-in-law, brothers with sisters-in-law, that is their brother's wife, and likewise a father and son with a mother and daughter, or two brothers with two sisters. Betrothals between any of these people shall not be recognised.[29]

2.3. A written marriage is contracted through a written dowry contract, before three trustworthy witnesses, in accordance with our recent pious decrees, in which contract the man shall promise to keep and preserve the entire dowry properly and undiminished, along with, as is fitting, any additions made to it by him, with a fourth share recorded in the document issued by him as the portion in case of childlessness.[30] Three documents

27 Cf. I.1.10.pr.

28 Justinian in C.5.4.26 (530) was the first to introduce into Roman law restrictions on marriage due to a spiritual relationship, prohibiting men from marrying their god-daughters. *The Council in Trullo* (c.53) then prohibited marriage between a godfather and the mother of a god-daughter. That prohibition is here extended to the godfather's sons.

29 Cf. I.1.1–9; C.5.4.19, 26; *The Council in Trullo*, c.53–54; AE.4, 9; Irene Novel II.

30 See E.2.4.

shall be made between the parties, two identical ones concerning the dowry, and the third shall set down what the man gave the woman. And a nuptial gift from the man equal to the wife's dowry shall neither be stipulated[31] nor conveyed.[32]

2.4.1. And if it happens that a wife should die before her husband and they have no children, he shall receive only a fourth part of the whole [dowry], as has been said, having been granted possession of the profit of the dowry, and the remaining three-quarters of the dowry shall either go to her testamentary heirs, or if she dies intestate shall go to her next of kin.[33]

2.4.2. And if a husband dies before his wife and they have no children, then the entirety of the dowry shall revert to the wife, and a fourth part of all the man's property, up to the value of the dowry, shall also come to her for her own profit, and the remainder of his property shall either go to his testamentary heirs, or if he dies intestate to his next of kin.

2.5.1. If a husband dies before his wife and they have subject children,[34] then the wife, being the mother of the same children, shall be mistress over

31 *Stipulatio*, rendered in Greek as *eperōtaō*, was a fundamental form of contract in Roman law, where almost any form of exchange could be contracted through a question and answer format. See Berger, s.v. 'Stipulatio'; Avotins, s.v. 'ἐπερωτάω'. The originally oral nature of the contract is brought out with the combination with *katagraphō* ('to register/record'), the equivalent of the Latin *conscribo*, and the clause could be translated as: 'a nuptial gift from the man equal to the dowry shall neither be promised orally nor in writing'. However, *katagraphō* can also mean 'to convey/transfer by deed', which would make the distinction with *eperōtaō* a functional one: that an equal nuptial gift should neither be promised nor transferred. To my mind, this seems a more natural reading, but the other is a valid possibility.

32 Cf. N.97.1; 117.4. Justinian had introduced the requirement that a nuptial gift be equal to a dowry, so here the *Ecloga* is returning to the pre-Justinianic rule.

33 Cf. N.22.20.

34 *Patria Potestas* ('the power of the father') is one of the most prominent features of Roman law. Unless deliberately emancipated, children were subject to the power of their *paterfamilias* (the male head of the family), their eldest living male agnate—an ancestor along the male line who was most commonly their father—until the *paterfamilias*' death, regardless of their own age, marital status or rank. Although the scope of *patria potestas* had declined from the early era of Roman law, when fathers literally had the power of life and death over their children, it was still a significant factor in Roman law, especially in property law. In most cases, children subject to their father's power could not own property outright. Exceptions existed, such as in E.2.5.2, where a remarried father would have to hand over maternal property to his children if they were of age and they demanded it. Further exceptions can be found in E.16. For more see A. Arjava, 'Paternal Power in Late Antiquity', *Journal of Roman Studies* 88 (1998), 147–65.

her dowry and all her husband's property, and she shall have authority over and management of the entire household, and she shall manifestly make a public record, that is an inventory, of all the property and possessions left by her husband, and also in this record shall be included the property of her dowry and, if there is any, the property outside her dowry, and she must demonstrate through effective proofs how the same property came into her husband's household, and what remains after his death. Her children shall not have the power to oppose her or demand from her their father's property, but rather must show her all honour and obedience as their mother, according to the commandment of God.[35] And naturally the mother is bound, as is fitting for a parent, to educate her children, and provide for their marriages and give them dowries, as she thinks best. However, if it happens that she marries again, her children have leave to separate from her and receive all of their father's property without impairment, allowing her the dowry brought by her to their father, together only with the gift granted by him to her for augmentation of her dowry.[36]

2.5.2. If a wife dies before her husband and they have subject children, the husband, being the father of the same children, shall be master over her dowry and all her property not in the dowry, as his children are under his power, and he shall have authority and management of the entire household, and they shall not demand from him their mother's property, but rather show him all honour and obedience as is fitting to a parent, for as is written: 'Honour your father and mother in word and deed, so that a blessing may come upon you from them. For the blessing of the father establishes the houses of children, but the curse of the mother roots out the foundations. For you were begotten of them, and how can you repay them for what they have done for you?'[37] And the Apostle Paul confirms this when he says, 'Children obey your parents in the Lord, for this is right; and parents do not provoke your children, but bring them up in the training and instruction of the Lord'.[38] However, if it happens that he marries again and his children are still minors, he shall maintain their mother's property undiminished. But if they have reached legal maturity, if they desire it this property shall be given to them without reservation.[39]

35 Exodus 20:12; Deuteronomy 5:16; cf. NM.2.5.

36 Cf. N.22.23.

37 Ecclesiasticus 3:8–9; 7:28.

38 Ephesians 6:1, 4.

39 Cf. E.16.5.2.

2.5.3. If either one of the couple, whether the man or the wife, not having married again, wishes to be separated from their children, who happen to be minors, they shall not be allowed to do this, but must take care and provide for them, for as the Apostle says, 'a widow who has children or grandchildren should first learn to live piously in their own home; for this is pleasing to God'.[40] But if the children are of age, and they are capable of making a living and making their own home, and either of the parents wishes to be separated from them, they may, and such a person [i.e. the child] shall receive their property and the portion belonging to the children, according to the number of children.[41]

2.6. If, due to poverty or low standing, anyone is unable to make a written marriage, and an unwritten marriage contract is honestly made between the couple and their parents, it shall be made known either through a blessing in a church or before friends. And if anyone should take a free woman into their home, entrust her with the management of the household and have carnal intercourse with her, he shall have contracted an unwritten marriage with her. And if due to childlessness he attempts to banish her from cohabiting with him, without acknowledged legal causes, she shall be given the property she brought into the house, as is fitting, and in addition a fourth part of his property.[42]

2.7. If a man legally marries a woman without means and dies without children and intestate, then the wife shall receive a fourth part of her husband's estate, as there are no children, if the estate of the husband is worth up to ten pounds [of gold]. And if the man is worth more than ten pounds, she shall not have permission to receive anything more, and the rest shall go either to the husband's next of kin or, if it is found that there is no next of kin, it shall go to the Treasury.[43]

2.8.1. A second marriage can be contracted, either in writing or orally, between people who are not prohibited from marriage; if they have no

40 I Timothy 5:4.

41 Under Roman law, except in extraordinary circumstances such as ingratitude (see E.5.6), legitimate children were automatically entitled to a share of their parents' inheritance, determined by the number of siblings. Justinian fixed the rate as a third, shared between the children, if there were up to four children, and half if more than four (N.18; a summation is given at E.5.7). Here the text is saying that if a parent wished to emancipate a child they had to give them their legal share of the inheritance then and there.

42 Cf. N.74.5.

43 Cf. N.53.6.

children, then without further ado it shall be agreed according to the rules set down above. However, if the man marrying for the second time has children, then he shall not be allowed to grant to his second wife in whatever form of gift any more than a child's share of his own property. The same shall likewise be observed by a woman intending to marry a second time, who naturally must wait twelve months from the death of her first husband. If she marries again before twelve months, she shall be infamous and shall in no way benefit from her first husband's estate.[44] But if she does keep the appointed time, she shall receive her dowry and, as is fitting, any additions made to it. Likewise, the husband who undertakes a second marriage shall receive nothing from his first wife's estate. And if there are underage children from the first marriage, he must protect their property until they come of age. However, if they are of age, he shall give them the entirety of their mother's property immediately. If he has children with his second wife and then happens to die, the children of both the first and second marriage may inherit from their father; and likewise for the mother.[45]

2.8.2. A woman who marries for a second time, who has children from the first marriage, shall ask for a guardian for her children before contracting the second marriage, and then she may contract the marriage. For if this is not done, her property and that of her second husband shall become liable for the restitution of the property belonging to the father to his children.[46]

2.9.1. The wisdom of God the Maker and Creator of all things teaches that marriage is an indissoluble union of those living together in the Lord. For He who brought mankind from nothingness into being did not form man and woman in the same fashion, although able to, but created her from the man in order that He might wisely ordain the indissolubility of marriage,

44 *Atimia*, the Greek equivalent of *infamia*, apart from its social connotations, brought definite legal penalties. For instance, an infamous person was barred from public office or appearing as an advocate in court. See Berger, s.v. 'Infamia'; Avotins, 'ἀτιμία'.

45 Cf. N.22; Irene Novel II.

46 Cf. N.22.40. The main function of a guardian in Roman law was to protect and administer the property of the minor, and it was only in late antiquity that a widow was permitted to act as her children's guardian. But she was only allowed to remain so while unmarried. The foreseen danger was that if she did retain control over her children's property after remarriage, she might transfer their property to her new family. To protect against any such possibility, the children from the first marriage could claim their paternal inheritance from both their mother's and stepfather's property.

uniting in 'one flesh' two persons.[47] Hence He did not separate them when the woman at the suggestion of the serpent led the man to the bitter taste, nor did He break the marriage when the man worked with the woman to transgress God's commandment, but punished the sin and did not break the union.[48] Moreover, this active law was confirmed anew by the Creator and through the Word, when the Pharisees asked Him, 'may a man divorce his wife for any reason?', and He answered that those who have been joined by God shall in no way be parted by man, 'except for fornication'.[49] And we who follow and obey shall not ordain anything more beyond this. But since the majority of mankind has become naturalised to the state of vice, and hence is not affectionately disposed towards one another, and on many grounds, although they are not such as these [i.e. not the valid grounds given below], cause the dissolution of their life together, we have decided it is necessary to expressly place in the present legislation the grounds by which marriage can be dissolved.

2.9.2. A husband may divorce his wife on the following grounds: if his wife commits fornication; if she plots in any way against his life, or knows another who plots against him and does not inform him; and if she is a leper.[50]

2.9.3. Likewise, a wife may be separated from her husband on these grounds: if within three years of the marriage the husband is unable to have intercourse with his wife; if he plots in any way against her life, or knows another who plots against her and does not inform her; and if he is a leper.[51]

2.9.4. And if it should happen that either of them should after the marriage be possessed by a demon, they shall *not* be separated from one another due to such a cause. Except on these known grounds it is not possible to dissolve a marriage, for as it is written, 'those whom God has joined let no man put asunder'.[52]

47 Genesis 2:24; Matthew 19:5–6; Mark 10:8; I Corinthians 6:16; Ephesians 5:31.

48 Cf. Genesis 2:18–3:24.

49 Matthew 19:3–9; Mark 10:2–12.

50 Cf. N.117.8; E.17.27; AE.5.3.

51 Cf. N.117.9; E.17.27.

52 Matthew 19:6; Mark 10:9.

Title 3: Concerning the contracting but non-payment of a dowry, and concerning dowry law

3.1. Anyone who agrees in writing or orally to receive a dowry and does not receive it may, up to five years only after the marriage, demand the dowry and receive it in its entirety if he is older than twenty-five, assuming that the girl's parents have the means to fulfil the promise. However, if he does not do this and neglects to obtain payment, he is bound to provide his wife's portion, up to the value agreed by him.[53] If he was younger than this [when he married], he can demand the dowry promised to him according to the agreement for a further five years after he has reached the age of twenty-five. After this stipulated time, he may not sue concerning the non-payment of the dowry agreed by him but, as has been said, must provide the wife's portion, which he had agreed upon.[54]

3.2. If a wife brings her husband a dowry and it happens that from some misfortune he suffers losses or falls into debt, either to the Treasury or any other person, and dies, neither the Treasury nor any other person may enter his house and seize anything until his wife has retrieved her dowry. After this is done, the remainder shall be divided proportionally amongst his creditors.[55]

Title 4: Concerning simple gifts, that is ones with immediate transfer of the use and ownership of the property, or only ownership, or anything bequeathed after death, and concerning the grounds by which these gifts may be overturned

4.1. An unwritten simple gift is contracted when anyone who is of age gives anything of his own property before five or three witnesses—before five witnesses in inhabited places where witnesses can be found; three in desolate places where five cannot be found.[56]

53 That is, he had to give his wife the marriage gift he had promised, which was a requirement of E.1.1 and 2.3.

54 Cf. C.5.15; N.100.

55 Cf. C.8.17.12; E.10.3.

56 Cf. I.2.7.2.

4.2.1. A written simple gift is contracted when it is drawn up or signed by someone of age and, as said above, is witnessed in writing and discharged before five or three witnesses summoned for the purpose.

4.2.2. If anyone makes a gift to anyone, with the donated property to be received by them after the death of the donor, and only at that moment is ownership given to them, he must make this written gift before five or three witnesses, as said above.[57]

4.3.1. Gifts made in expectation of death, that is ones that take effect after the death of the donor, shall, as set out above, be completed through the signature of the donor before five or three witnesses.

4.3.2. If the donor himself should ordain in writing that he does not repent of or revoke this gift, then this is valid only if his disposition is clear, in both the text and his signature.[58]

4.4. All gifts shall be revoked on the following grounds: if the recipient of the gift is found to be ungrateful to the giver, if he heaps harsh insults upon him, or strikes him, or causes him serious harm, or plots against his life or does not fulfil the agreements, either written or oral, that were attached to the gift; on one of these grounds, proven in court, the gift, as was said, can be revoked.[59]

Title 5: Concerning persons incapable of making wills, and concerning written and unwritten wills

5.1. The following are prevented from making a will: those mentally deranged due to sickness; the underage, that is men under fifteen and women under thirteen; the utterly insane; prisoners of war; and those under parental power, aside from their own property,[60] and nor may they dispose of those things given to them by their parents as a dowry; the deaf and the dumb from birth, but those who fall to these afflictions from some illness may, if they can write, make a will signed by their own hand.[61]

57 Cf. I.2.7.2.

58 Cf. I.2.7.1; C.8.56.4.

59 Cf. C.8.55.10.

60 Special property could be received that was outside parental power, such as maternal inheritance (E.2.5.2) and property gained through being a soldier (*peculium castrense*) or serving the state (*peculium quasi castrense*) (E.16).

61 Cf. I.2.12.

5.2. A written will is made before seven trustworthy witnesses summoned for that purpose, who at one and the same time shall sign and seal it, and the testator is obliged, either by his own hand or through someone who can write, to note down the name of the heir, and if he wishes he does not have to reveal the content of the will to the witnesses.[62]

5.3. An oral will is contracted when the testator makes his will before seven assembled witnesses.[63]

5.4. But if anyone makes a will, either written or oral, in a place where witnesses cannot be found, then he can make his will before five or three; but if fewer than three, then the testator's will is invalid.[64]

5.5. If parents should make a valid will, according to the above, and in it omit their legitimate children or one of them, then the adjudicating magistrates shall investigate,[65] and if they find that the children have frequently insulted their parents or in any other way injured them, the parents' disposition shall remain unchanged. And if it happens after the making of the will that a child is conceived by them, the manumitted and the legatees shall receive their shares of the will, and the newborn shall be counted among the remaining siblings and inherit with them.[66]

5.6. If parents have a child who causes them injury and is heedless of them in their old age, and then another person provides for them, and since they have been cared for by him they wish to bequeath him their property, their will shall be valid.[67]

5.7. Every heir, whether of a written or an oral will, who delays and postpones for up to a year and does not fulfil the stipulations of the will, shall, if they are a child or grandchild of the deceased, receive the legal share due to them only. The legal share for up to four children is a third of

62 Cf. I.2.10.2–4; C.6.23.21; N.119.9.

63 Cf. I.2.10.14.

64 Cf. C.6.23.31.

65 'Adjudicating magistrates' is the rather cumbersome translation of *akroatai*, which strictly means 'hearers', a term with distinct biblical overtones, and one of three types of judge found in these texts. The others are *archontes* ('magistrates/officials') and *dikastai* ('judges'). What, if any, difference there is between the three is difficult to discern, but I have argued that the *akroatai* were a deliberate rebranding of the *archontes*, that is, they were imperial officials while *dikastai* were delegate judges of those magistrates. See Humphreys, *Law, Power, and Imperial Ideology*, 87–88, 107–13, 218–22.

66 Cf. I.2.13.

67 Cf. N.115.3.12.

the property, and for five or more children is a half. And if he is a different relative he shall lose the entirety of his benefit in the will, and this shall be redistributed among the co-heirs, legatees and other kin. And if the heir is a stranger and he fails to fulfil the terms of the will, the whole inheritance shall go to another.[68]

5.8. If anyone wounded in war or while travelling on the road draws near death and wishes to make a will, and in both cases a notary or anyone else who can write cannot be found, he can make his will before seven or five or three witnesses; if only two can be found, their evidence must be admitted and tried by the adjudicating magistrates.[69]

Title 6: Concerning intestate inheritances and legacies, and concerning those who lose their inheritance due to ingratitude

6.1. If anyone should die intestate and leave behind children or grandchildren, then these are the heirs. And if the deceased has a father or mother, grandfather or grandmother, or further, they shall not inherit if there are surviving children or grandchildren; but if he does not have children or grandchildren, but does have a father or mother, grandfather or grandmother, the nearest kin shall inherit.[70]

6.2. If a son or daughter with living parents should die childless and intestate, but have brothers or sisters of the same father and mother, their inheritance shall go to the parents, and the siblings may not lay claim to it. But if there are no parents, but only a grandfather or grandmother, then they shall inherit equally with siblings from the same father and mother. If the deceased has no grandparents, nor any siblings from the same parents, then the siblings who share one parent shall receive the inheritance. But if, as has been said, he has no siblings, then the nearest kin shall inherit. And if he has no kin, the wife of the deceased shall inherit half of all his property and the other half shall go to the Treasury. And if the deceased has no wife, then as intestate the entirety of his property shall fall to the Treasury.[71]

68 Cf. N.1.1; N.18.1.
69 Cf. C.6.21.15.
70 Cf. N.118.1–2.
71 Cf. N.118.2–3.

6.3. If any testator should bequeath a legacy this shall be given, after of course the payment of due claims, and the heir is not allowed to dispose of the legacy for another purpose, but must hand it over to the legatee.[72]

6.4.1. If an heir has knowledge of what property is bequeathed to him, and also knows that debts are due to it, he must create an inventory of the property before trustworthy witnesses and publicly declare its value. And first the creditors shall be paid, and then the heir shall have the rest.[73]

6.4.2. But if he stubbornly and rashly takes possession of the property, and it turns out that he has paid only part of its debts, he is bound to fulfil the remainder, since he did not declare his possession of the property through a proper inventory.

6.4.3. But if the debts accrued are extreme, and the heir had no knowledge of this, then he shall before witnesses or on oath demonstrate the extent of the property that has come to him, and he shall divide this among the creditors, and nothing more can be demanded of him.

6.5. If it comes to light that any heir or legatee concealed a will left with him, and later it is found on him, then the heir shall lose his inheritance, and the legatee his legacy.[74]

6.6. If someone dies, leaves his property and assigns administration of it to his heir without a written will or without witnesses, and someone else claims that a legacy was given to him by the deceased, but is unable to prove through witnesses or in any other way the truth of his claim, then the word of the heir shall be followed.[75]

6.7. Children shall lose their legal inheritance due to ingratitude: if they hit their parents; if they seriously insult them, bring criminal charges against them or slander them; if they are poisoners or associate with poisoners; if they plot in any way against their life; if a son has carnal intercourse with his stepmother or his father's concubine; if the parents are incarcerated and the male children when asked do not stand surety for them; if a daughter does not legally marry according to her parents' wishes, but prefers to live in shame; and if the parents become insane and the children choose not to help them.[76]

72 Cf. C.6.43.3.2a. A legacy is a deduction from the inheritance given to someone who is not the heir.

73 Cf. C.6.30.22; N.1.2–3.

74 Cf. C.6.37.25.

75 Cf. C.6.42.32.

76 Cf. N.115.3.

Title 7: Concerning orphans and their guardianship

If anyone should leave behind underage orphans and they are granted property, then if the deceased parents appointed a guardian for them, either in writing or orally, [the parent's] will shall be observed. However, if they did not, the holy houses shall have the guardianship—in this God-guarded city, the orphanage and the other holy houses and known churches; in the provinces, the bishoprics, monasteries and churches—until the heirs have reached the age when they can marry and do so. But if they do not wish to marry, then up to the age of twenty the holy houses, monasteries and churches shall guard their property, and then shall return it undiminished to the aforementioned heirs. For it is not pleasing to God, as has been the case up to now, that those appointed guardian of others devour the property of orphans, leaving them to beg. For as the holy houses and churches of God care for others and, in accordance with the commands of the Lord, lodge and show hospitality to strangers, so should they even more guard the property of orphans and in due course restore it to them.[77]

Title 8: Concerning freedom and slavery

8.1.1. Freedom is granted to a slave when publicly announced by his master, either in a church or before five friends summoned for that purpose, or if five cannot be found then before at least three, who must register and record their knowledge [of the emancipation] in a public record; or through a letter of the master signed by five or three witnesses, as said above; or freedom can be given to the slave in a written will.[78]

8.1.2. And also when the slave, by the will of the deceased or the agreement of the heir, wears the cap of liberty on his head when following the funeral procession.[79]

8.1.3. Also if a master marries his slave to a free person.[80]

8.1.4. And finally, if the master of a slave, or his mistress, or their children with the knowledge and permission of the parents, should sponsor the slave

77 Cf. N.131.15. For the provision of orphanages in Constantinople, see D. Constantelos, *Byzantine Philanthropy and Social Welfare* (New Brunswick, 1968), 241–56.

78 Cf. I.1.5.1; C.1.13.1; C.7.6.1c–2.

79 Cf. C.7.6.1.5.

80 Cf. C.7.6.1.9.

in holy and salvation-giving baptism, or if the slave with the knowledge and will of his master becomes a cleric or a monk.[81]

8.1.5. The aforementioned persons shall be given their freedom by their masters immediately or upon condition.[82]

8.1.6. And if anyone who is granted their freedom in these ways falls back into slavery, he shall appeal to the holy church of God and the appropriate magistrates and, having furnished proof of his freedom, shall enjoy the benefit of it.

8.2. Anyone who ransoms a free man captured in war from the enemy, and brings them into their own house, then if [the ransomed] man has the means to pay the price agreed between them, he shall be released as a free man. But if he does not have the means, the ransomer shall keep him as a hired labourer until he has paid what was agreed, with a clearly determined amount owed each year instead of wages to the ransomed to be calculated by the adjudicating magistrates.[83]

8.3. Freedmen, even if servants of the state, can be reduced again to slavery due to ingratitude on the following grounds: if they strike their masters, that is those who freed them, or their children, or insult them, or in their arrogance are haughty towards them, or on any small grounds give offence, cause them damage or plot against them, and one of these is proved before a magistrate or judge.[84]

8.4.1. A slave who is taken by the enemy as a prisoner of war, and there demonstrates some deed for the state against them and then returns, shall immediately be freed. But a slave who is taken as a prisoner of war and then escapes who does not complete any deed for the state against the enemy, but merely returns, shall be enslaved to his master for five years, and then shall be freed.

8.4.2. Anyone who, acting on their own free will, defects to the enemy, and then in regret escapes from them and returns, shall be a slave for the rest of his life, since by running to them he became utterly a deserter.

81 Cf. N.5.2; N.123.17.

82 Cf. D.40.7.1. The manumission of a slave could be delayed until certain conditions were fulfilled.

83 Cf. C.8.50.2, 20; NM.17.

84 Cf. C.6.7.2.

Title 9: Concerning written and unwritten sale and purchase, and deposits

9.1. A written or unwritten sale and purchase of whatever kind of good and business is contracted at an agreed price through the honest agreement of the parties. Therefore, once the price is agreed with the seller and the good is given to the buyer, then neither party can turn back from the sale due to a change of heart; for it is necessary for the buyer before making the contract to make enquiries and investigate thoroughly, and then to enter into the contract. But naturally, if after the sale it is discovered that the person sold is a freeman or mad, then he shall be returned.[85]

9.2. If a deposit is given for whatever kind of business or contract, and the contract is not fulfilled, and it is due to the carelessness of the giver of the deposit, the deposit shall be to the profit of the receiver; but if it is due to the perverseness of the receiver, then he shall give back the deposit and as much again to the giver.[86]

Title 10: Concerning written and unwritten loans, and security given for them

10.1.1. If anyone should borrow cash, money or any other thing on land or at sea, in writing or orally, then the lender shall receive back his property according to the agreement fixed between them, and the borrower may not plead to the lender about hostile incursions, shipwreck or any other excuse for evading or delaying its return. But if the borrower gave a security, he shall receive back his property undiminished after the loan is repaid; and the holder of the security cannot say that they lost it or offer any other excuse, unless of course it is shown that they suffered from the same misfortune and lost their own property along with that of the other; and the adjudicating magistrates shall investigate concerning this.[87]

10.1.2. If anyone lends to another person and the borrower does not repay him at the appointed time, the lender shall formally demand it, and if after

85 Cf. I.3.23.

86 Cf. I.3.23.pr.; NN.3.19; NG.16. Note that here 'deposit' means an *arrabōn* (Latin *arra*), earnest money pledged for completion of a contract, and should not be confused with the case in E.11.

87 Cf. I.3.14.2–4; D.44.7.1.4–5; NN.2.17–19, 3.16–18; NM.11.

two or three behests and pleas the borrower does not promise or make restitution, then the holder of the security may sell it, after making a precise, public appraisal of the security recorded in writing by a *taboularios* or *defensor*, and from the proceeds shall reimburse the sum owed to him, and of course shall hand over any surplus to the debtor.[88] But if the lawful sale of the security does not satisfy the entirety of the debt, then the creditor may demand the rest.[89]

10.2. If a creditor should take and seize as security his debtors' children, or hire them out as servile labour, he shall both forfeit his debt and pay the exact same sum to either the seized children or their parents.[90]

10.3. If a married man should borrow from another and is unable to repay, his wife is not liable to satisfy the debt from her dowry, unless she had freely agreed with her husband to be liable for the debt.[91]

10.4. A partnership is contracted in writing or orally, between two or more persons, whenever each brings their share of the capital, either in equal or lesser portions, or when some provide the capital and another or others provide their labour and work. The resultant profits shall, after deduction of the capital, of course, be distributed according to the agreement struck between them. If it happens that such a partnership suffers a loss to the capital, then each partner shall bear the loss according to his share of the profits.[92]

Title 11: Concerning any kind of deposit

If anyone for any reason or fear entrusts a deposit to another, and it happens that the latter denies that he has received this, and after investigation of

88 A *taboularios* was an official notary charged with the preparation of documents, and was a member of a guild in Constantinople. See *Book of the Eparch*, ed. J. Koder, *Das Eparchenbuch Leons der Weisen* (Vienna, 1991), Chapter 1; A. Kazhdan and A. Cutler, 'Notary', *ODB*, vol. 3, 1495. A *defensor [civitatis]* (Greek *ekdikos*) had been the lowest rank of the late antique judiciary, but the role had declined and here appears to be no more than a notary, though the recording of documents had been a recognised role of *defensores* in late antiquity. See N.15.3. For the late antique institution in general see Jones, *Later Roman Empire*, 479–80.

89 Cf. C.8.33.3.

90 Cf. N.134.7.

91 Cf. N.134.8; E.3.2.

92 Cf. I.3.25.1–2; NN.3.9, 17, 21.

the matter it is shown he is a liar, he shall restore twice the amount to the depositor. But if due to some misfortune, either from fire or theft, that man happened to lose his own property alongside that of the depositor, then the adjudicating magistrates shall investigate and hold them blameless in the safeguarding of the deposit, as its loss was involuntary.[93]

Title 12: Concerning perpetual and limited *emphyteusis*

12.1. Perpetual *emphyteusis*[94] is created on immovable property on agreement of a yearly rent, and the care and improvement of the rented property. And if any *procurators*,[95] *chartoularioi*[96] or other persons involved are found to have caused harm or defrauded the principal owner, they shall lose their position and the lease shall be invalid.[97]

12.2. A tenant by perpetual *emphyteusis* who pays his annual rent without delay and endeavours to maintain and care for the property cannot be removed from his lease, but he has the right to bequeath such *emphyteusis* to his heirs, and to give his *emphyteusis* away, either to give it as a dowry or in any other way to alienate or sell it, though of course the principal owner has a preferential right of purchase before sale to others. But if the owner does not wish to do so, then two months after this offer [for preferential purchase] the tenant may without hindrance sell to persons not forbidden from holding *emphyteutic* contracts and their improvements, and the principal owner is bound to admit in writing the succeeding tenant, so long as he is suitable, into an *emphyteutic* contract. If the tenant does not do these things he shall be discharged from his *emphyteusis*.[98]

12.3. If a tenant by perpetual *emphyteusis* who rents from a religious house is three years in arrears with his annual rent, or lets the leased

93 Cf. D.16.3.1; C.4.34.1.; NN.2.14–15, 3.12–14; NM.12. Note that here 'deposit' refers to *parathēkē* (Latin *depositum*), something entrusted to another for safekeeping. See Berger, s.v. 'Depositum'.

94 *Emphyteusis* was a form of very long-term tenure affording significant rights and privileges to the tenant. See A. Cappel, 'Emphyteusis', *ODB*, vol. 1, 693–94.

95 A *procurator* (Greek *phrontistēs*) was a manager or steward.

96 A *chartoularios* was a generic term for a record-keeper, and also referred to several subaltern positions within various administrative bureaux. See A. Kazhdan, 'Chartoularios', *ODB*, vol. 1, 416.

97 Cf. C.4.66.2; N.120.5.

98 Cf. I.3.24.3; C.4.66.3.

land deteriorate, then the owner may eject him from the property, with, of course, what is owed surrendered. And if an *emphyteusis* contract is made with anyone else, and the tenant does not pay rent for three years or neglects the property, he shall be ejected in a similar manner.[99]

12.4. The most holy church of the Imperial City [i.e. Hagia Sophia] and the most venerable houses in its vicinity, the orphanage, almshouses and hospices, are forbidden to alienate in perpetuity immovable property except ruined places, and may only exchange with the Imperial House. In the provinces, the venerable churches and monasteries, and further the holy monasteries of the Imperial City, may make perpetual *emphyteutic* leases.[100]

12.5. Time-limited *emphyteutic* leases can be made by religious houses, the Imperial House or any other person upon agreement of an annual rent, as stated above, for up to three generations, passed in succession either through will or intestacy, and from the beginning of the contract only a sixth part of the rent may be remitted, and the third and last person may not renew the *emphyteutic* lease, and cannot in this way extend it in a perpetual manner.[101]

12.6. Neither the *procurators* of rented land, whether of the Imperial House or holy houses, nor *chartoularioi*, *dioikētai*,[102] nor their relatives shall receive either perpetual or limited *emphyteusis*, nor through a middleman. Nor can civil or military officials be party to contracts of *emphyteusis* or lease; nor may soldiers enter into contracts for such a purpose, nor be employed on another's private business, nor become guarantors, nor serve or assist in the houses or properties of others, for their sole occupation is to fight for the state against its enemies.[103]

99 Cf. C.4.66.2; N.7.3; N.120.8. In his novels Justinian had granted churches the right to eject non-paying *emphyteutic* tenants after two years, rather than three, thereby giving them an advantage over secular landlords.

100 Cf. N.120.1, 6.

101 Cf. N.7.3; N.120.1.

102 A *dioikētēs* was a tax collector. See Haldon, *Seventh Century*, 196–201.

103 Cf. C.4.65.31; NS.30–1.

Title 13: Concerning leases

Written and oral leases shall be made on agreement of a specified annual rent, and shall not extend beyond twenty-nine years, whether such letting of properties, estates, fields and the rest was received by or made on the part of the Treasury, the Imperial House or a holy place. And in accordance with the agreement of the lessor and the payment of the agreed annual rent by the lessee, neither the lessor nor the lessee may cancel the lease within the first year if the agreement explicitly states this.[104]

Title 14: Concerning trustworthy and inadmissible witnesses

14.1. Witnesses who hold a dignity, serve the state, have an honourable occupation or are wealthy are deemed *a priori* to be trustworthy. If the witnesses are found to be unknown and their testimony is disputed, the judges shall examine and question them under torture in order to ascertain the truth.[105]

14.2.1. Parents and children who speak against each other shall not be admitted.[106]

14.2.2. Nor may a slave or freedman testify for or against their master.[107]

14.3. No one can be compelled to produce witnesses against themselves.[108]

14.4. Witnesses who are called to give their testimony before the judges shall first tell what they know not under oath at two or three preliminary inquiries, and if it is found that they have something to say concerning the investigation, then they shall be put under oath.[109]

14.5. Witnesses in a civil case who live far away shall not be compelled to appear, but shall bear witness as to what they know through representatives sent to them.[110]

104 That is, one could normally cancel within a year. C.4.65.34 states that the norm was that either party could cancel within a year, unless this right was explicitly waived, which is repeated here in a truncated form.

105 Cf. N.90.1.

106 Cf. C.4.20.6.

107 Cf. C.4.20.8, 12.

108 Cf. C.4.20.7.

109 Cf. C.4.20.9.

110 Cf. C.4.20.16.1; N.90.5.

14.6. If anyone should call a witness in their case, and that same witness has already been called by another person in a different case against the same person, that man may not object to this witness being called, unless it is shown that afterwards some enmity has arisen between them, or that a gift or the promise of a gift was given to the witness to corrupt the case.[111]

14.7. If parties agree to appear before ordinary judges[112] and then do not abide by the judgement received, but wish to go to another court, they may call witnesses summoned in the first case, and may not object to this. And if it should happen that a witness dies, then their testimony to the earlier judges may be disclosed through an oath. And if the man who did not abide by the previous decision wins before the final judges, he shall be beyond dispute [i.e. no more appeals]. But if judgement is again given against him, and it seems that his opponent was prosecuted unjustly, then naturally the penalty settled by the previous judges shall be paid to the one who abided by the original decision. But if no penalty had been settled between them, then he shall pay his opponent's expenses or any other penalty which the judges determine.[113]

14.8. Witnesses who offer hearsay evidence that they heard that someone owed this or had discharged that shall not be admitted, even if the witnesses should be *taboularioi*.[114]

14.9. During a deposition the evidence of a *taboularios* shall not be trusted if the borrower, despite knowing how to write and being able to do so, did not sign the contract of debt in his own hand.[115]

14.10. In all criminal proceedings the witnesses must appear before the judge hearing the case.[116]

14.11. Witnesses, whatever their number, shall only be summoned up to four times, each summons only taking one day; and if before the fourth summons the summoner should rest his case and produce their testimony,

111 Cf. C.4.20.17; N.90.7.

112 This is the direct translation of *Koinoi dikastai* and could be the Greek equivalent of *ordinarii iudices*, ordinary judges who heard cases in the first instance. See Haldon, *Seventh Century*, 269. Here though, 'arbiter' may be a better translation, following Burgmann, *Ecloga*, 217.

113 Cf. C.4.20.20; N.82.11.1.

114 Cf. N.90.2. As noted above (60 n. 88), the *taboularioi* constituted a guild of official document writers, hence the special status conferred, if only to be set aside, here.

115 Cf. N.90.3.

116 Cf. N.90.5.1.

then after this he may not call another witness, but must abide by the evidence from witnesses that have already been called.[117]

14.12. Anyone who denies a bond of debt written in their own hand, or acknowledges their handwriting, but disputes the amount of money, and thereby compels proof of the debt to be made, shall be condemned to pay back double the debt after the truth has been shown.[118]

Title 15: Concerning the ratification or revocation of settlements

15.1. A settlement[119] is created in writing through the signatures of three witnesses.[120]

15.2. If a minor should make a settlement with anyone, and due to his lack of years was taken advantage of or harmed on any other grounds, then when he reaches twenty-five and becomes aware of the loss, he may bring his suit before the judges, and if the injustice is proved, his right shall protect him. But if he is unable to prove the wrong, then the settlement shall be confirmed.

15.3. If anyone older than twenty-five is found to have made a settlement through fear of power or some kind of fraud, and this is proved before the adjudicating magistrates, then the settlement shall be revoked and the case investigated from the beginning.[121]

117 Cf. N.90.4.

118 Cf. N.18.8.

119 *Dialusis*, the Greek equivalent of the Latin *transactio*, was a compromise settlement made out of court, cf. D.2.15, C.2.4. See Berger, 'Transactio'.

120 Cf. N.73.1–2.

121 Cf. C.2.4.13.

Title 16: Concerning soldiers' property and the gains subject soldiers receive from their service, and concerning clerics, *chartoularioi* and other state servants

16.1. *Peculium castrense* is property acquired through military service by a soldier subject to the power of his father or grandfather.[122] He may dispose of it by will, even while living in camp, though of course observing the aforementioned rules for composing valid wills.[123] And if through his will this *peculium* should be exhausted, his heirs cannot demand their legal share of it, for it is in his power to give away or bequeath through a will the entirety of the *peculium*.[124] And after the death of his parents, it shall not be collected and distributed as part of the patrimony, but shall be exempted and recognised as belonging solely to the soldier.[125]

16.2.1. If brothers remain after the death of their parents, and one of them is a soldier and the other stays at home, if they have made an agreement between them, that agreement shall hold. But if they have made no agreement, and have lived together for up to ten years from the start of the soldier's service, then all their earnings, whether from his pay[126] or the

122 This title deals with various forms of *peculium*. Under Roman law, the *paterfamilias* officially owed all the property of his (unemancipated) *familia*, that is his household, comprising his descendants and slaves. Given the obvious practical constraints of such an idea, Roman law also included the idea of *peculium*, which was a special class of property granted to those in another's power. In cases of ordinary *peculium*, considered at E.16.5, the son or slave had operational control of the *peculium*, which could be anything from a sum of money to a business. However, the *paterfamilias* remained the ultimate owner of the *peculium*, and as such it could be withdrawn by him and was part of his estate that would be divided among his heirs on his death. The subject of the present chapter, the *peculium castrense*, was a heightened form of *peculium* granted to Roman soldiers by Augustus as a special privilege, whereby they could own outright property acquired through military service independent of their *paterfamilias*. This included the right to alienate and bequeath such property in any way the soldier saw fit. In late antiquity another form, *peculium quasi-castrense* (considered at E.16.4), emerged regarding the property gained through state or ecclesiastical service. See Berger, s.v. 'Peculium', 'Peculium castrense', 'Peculium quasi castrense'.

123 Cf. E.5.

124 That is, they are not bound to respect the share reserved for children proclaimed in E.5.7, unlike the *peculium quasi-castrense* of state servants in E.16.4.

125 Cf. I.2.12.pr.

126 *Roga* was the cash salary paid to both civil officials and soldiers. Probably as a result of the financial crises of the seventh century, when the empire lost its richest provinces, ordinary thematic soldiers were no longer paid annually, but rather were paid their *roga*

joint earnings of the household and the labour of the brother or brothers remaining at home, shall provide for each in equal shares. If after ten years they should live together for another three years, and then it happens that they separate from each other, then the soldier shall only take for his own his horse with its bridle and harness, his arms and, of course, if he has acquired it, his armour, and all the rest shall be divided equally among the brothers. And if they live together more than thirteen years and it is found that after this time the soldier should acquire anything from his pay and save it, then the soldier shall also receive this.

16.2.2. And those things which by the Providence of God the soldier acquired from spoils and gifts, from the first day of his service onwards, and which are saved, then likewise these shall belong to him separately.[127]

16.3. Regarding clerics, *chartoularioi* and others in state service due to their parents' estate: if, on their death, their parents wish to give them this, then let their will be ratified. But if they say nothing about this and then should die, and the co-heirs bring an action against the post-holder for the sum in question, then the income from this service which went to the father shall be calculated, and the difference between that and the amount given for this position shall be brought into the remainder of the property and divided. But, of course, if the given amount is paid in full through this service, then the co-heirs may not make any claim on the money paid for the position, since as was said this had been paid through the service.[128]

---

every four years on a rotational cycle. See M. Hendy, *Studies in the Byzantine Monetary Economy, c.300–1450* (Cambridge, 1985), 645–54; A. Cappel, 'Roga', *ODB*, vol. 3, 1801.

127 The imagined situation is as follows: a soldier has been equipped by a household to serve in the army. To reimburse the household, in particular after the death of the parents, and in order to prevent the civilian brother(s) being disadvantaged by the outlay made to equip his soldier brother, the household is given a claim on the earnings of the soldier, which was previously his own as part of his *peculium castrense*. The household also probably had some form of tax exemption. For up to ten years after the soldier entered military service, and so started receiving *roga*, all household income, whatever the source, is split evenly. If, between ten and 13 years after the soldier entered military service, they decide to separate and create separate households, and so divide the parental inheritance, then the soldier would keep his military gear, but everything else would be divided equally. If, after 13 years, the soldier has anything saved from his pay, he gets to keep this as well. For the significance of this passage see Oikonomidès, 'Middle Byzantine Provincial Recruits: Salary and Armaments', 130–34; Lilie, 'Die zweihundertjährige Reform', 194–97; Haldon, 'Military Service, Military Lands, and the Status of Soldiers', 21–23.

128 Purchase of offices, both secular and ecclesiastical, was widespread in Byzantium, and the cash would often have come from parental estates as envisioned here. Indeed, some

16.4. Regarding the remaining state servants who are allotted imperial pay, rations and customary expenses,[129] that is to say those dignitaries and all others who receive pay from the emperor's hands or rations and gratuities from the Treasury; with the exception of soldiers, when all of these dispose of their *peculium* by will, they must leave their children the legal share, namely a third, of their *peculium* if they have up to four children, but if they have five or more children they must leave half. However, if they do not have children, but still have living parents they shall bequeath the aforementioned third share to the latter; the rest of the *peculium* they can dispose of as seems good to them.[130]

16.5.1. The ordinary *peculium* of those under parental power is that which was given or acquired by them from their parents due to their good behaviour and honour. This shall be considered as parental property, and after the parents' death shall be united with the rest of the parental property and then divided, just as those goods and property acquired by the son from the father shall be considered as the father's property and combined with it.[131]

16.5.2. Regarding the property of the mother that they [subject children] acquired through sweat and labour or by inheritance, this cannot be disposed of by testament by them, but those that have them in their power shall only have the usufruct of it, and shall preserve for them the ownership of this property.[132]

---

officials had the (regulated) right to alienate their posts. See Jones, *Later Roman Empire*, 394–95, 576–77, 909–10; N. Oikonomidès, 'Titles, Purchase of', *ODB*, vol. 3, 2089.

129 Respectively *roga*, *annona* and *solemnion*. As discussed above, *roga* was the cash salary of state servants. However, since the fourth century the major component of remuneration had been reckoned in rations (*annonae*), either in kind or in cash. See Jones, *Later Roman Empire*, 396–401. In Justinianic law, *solemnia* were payments for customary expenditures. See Avotins, s.v. 'σολέμνιος'.

130 Cf. C.6.22.12, 12.30; I.2.11.6; N.18.1; E.5.7.

131 Cf. D.15.

132 Cf. C.6.61.8; E.2.5.2. A usufruct is the right to use and enjoy the produce of a property. See Berger, s.v. 'Ususfructus'.

Title 17: Penalties for criminal cases[133]

17.1. No one shall forcibly remove anyone who has taken refuge in a church, but the charge against the fugitive shall be made known to the priest and he shall receive assurances that the fugitive shall be lawfully tried and the charge against him given. But if anyone ventures to seize the fugitive by force from the church, he shall receive twelve blows and then the charge against the fugitive shall be properly investigated.[134]

17.2. Anyone who holds the holy gospels of God and swears on them during a judicial inquiry, either while bearing witness or bringing a dispute, and afterward is shown to have committed perjury, shall have their tongue cut out.[135]

17.3. Anyone who conspires against the emperor, or plans or plots with others against him or against the Christian state, shall immediately be put to death since he was seeking the dissolution of everything. But in order that nobody should, without trial, kill anyone to whom they are hostile, and later offer the defence that he had spoken against the emperor, it is necessary that the accused shall be placed under strict guard on the spot, and the facts concerning him brought to the emperor; and later he himself shall investigate and determine what is to be done.[136]

17.4. Anyone who lays hands upon a priest, either in a church or in a procession, shall be beaten and exiled.[137]

17.5. Anyone who has a dispute with someone and does not bring it before the authorities, but from arrogance and presumptuousness wilfully lays hands upon and seizes the thing in dispute, then if after inquiries are made it is found that the thing in truth belonged to him, then he shall lose his property and return it. However, if he seized something belonging to another, then he shall be thrashed by the magistrate of the place since he has become ungovernable and lawless, and he shall make restitution of what he robbed.[138]

17.6. Those who are captured by the enemy and renounce our faultless

133 This title of *poinalios* ('penalties') is also used in the second section of the NS and for AE.3: see 83 and 92 respectively.

134 Cf. C.1.12.2–3; NM.46.

135 Cf. NN.3.14; NG.28.

136 Cf. I.4.18.3.

137 Cf. N.123.31.

138 Cf. C.8.4.7; AE.2.9; NG.6, 66, 80.

Christian faith and then return to the empire, shall be given over to the Church.

17.7. If anyone hires a horse to go to a specified place and either takes or sends it beyond this limit, and it happens that the hired horse should be hurt or dies, then, as is fitting, the hirer should make indemnity to the owner of the horse.[139]

17.8. Anyone who shuts up another's animals and they starve to death or are in any other way killed is condemned to restore twice the value.[140]

17.9. If rams or bulls should attack each other, then if the first to attack is killed, the owner of the animal that killed shall not be summoned. However, if the animal that did not attack is killed, then the owner of the killer shall be summoned, and should either hand over the animal that killed to the owner of the dead one, or make indemnity to the man who has suffered damage.[141]

17.10. Anyone who steals either in camp or on the march, if he steals arms, he shall be beaten, if a horse, his hand shall be cut off.[142]

17.11. Anyone who steals in another area of the empire shall, in the first instance, if he is free and has the means, shall hand over twice the value of the stolen thing, besides restitution of the thing stolen; but if he is poor, he shall be beaten and exiled. On the second occasion, his hand shall be cut off.[143]

17.12. If the master of a slave who is a thief desires to keep this same slave, he shall make indemnity to the man who was robbed. However, if he does not desire to keep the slave, he shall give him over in full ownership to the man who suffered the theft.[144]

17.13. Anyone who rustles cattle from another's herd shall be beaten on the first offence; on the second, he shall be sent into exile; on the third, his hand shall be cut off; and of course he is bound to make restitution for his cattle rustling to the rightful owner.[145]

139 Cf. D.13.6.5.7; D.13.6.23; D.47.2.40; NG.36–37.

140 Cf. C.3.35.5; NG.54. *Thremma*, here translated as 'animal', is one of several Greek words used in these texts to denote domesticated animals, and usually refers either to sheep or cattle. The same penalty, but extended to pigs and dogs, is found in NG.54.

141 Cf. D.9.1.11; NG.76–77.

142 Cf. D.49.16.3.14; NS.38.

143 Cf. I.4.1.19; D.48.19.1.3; NS.10, 28; NN.3.1–4, 38; NG.22, 33–35, 61–62, 68–69.

144 Cf. I.4.8.1–3.

145 Cf. D.47.14; NG.41–42, 46–47; NM.15.

17.14. Those who strip the dead in their graves shall have their hand cut off.[146]

17.15. Anyone who enters a sanctuary, by day or night, and steals anything from the priests shall be blinded. Anyone who takes anything from outside of the sanctuary, from the nave, shall be thrashed as impious, have his head shaved and be exiled.[147]

17.16. Anyone who steals and sells a free person shall have his hand cut off.[148]

17.17. Anyone who corruptly procures, hides and makes disappear another's slave shall, besides restitution of the slave, give another slave or the value of one to his master.[149]

17.18. Forgers of money shall have their hand cut off.[150]

17.19. A married man who fornicates shall be beaten with twelve blows as a chastisement,[151] whether he is rich or poor.[152]

146 Cf. D.47.12.

147 Cf. D.48.13.11.

148 Cf. D.48.15; C.9.20; NM.16.

149 Cf. C.6.1.4.

150 Cf. C.9.24.

151 *Sōphronismos*, here translated as 'chastisement', has distinct moral overtones, in particular concerning correction, moderation and self-discipline, especially in regard to sex. For instance, it was used in 2 Timothy 1:7 referring to the self-discipline given by God to Christians. One should also note that this punishment, unlike say E.17.11, is explicitly the same for rich and poor, as part of their moral correction as Christians.

152 What the bounds of *porneia* (fornication or illicit sex and the Greek equivalent of the Latin *stuprum*) were precisely is not here specified, and indeed had rarely been clear-cut and varied over the centuries. Traditionally, Roman law on this matter was concerned with protecting the honour of women, and thereby their suitability as wives, mothers and transmitters of property and status. As such, sex was only illicit if it was extramarital and involved an honourable woman. Only honourable women, that is high-status women, could lose their honour. Men, married or not, could therefore have sex with a prostitute or an actress—essentially the same thing to the Roman mind—and not commit *porneia* as the woman had no honour to besmirch. However, given the moralising, Christian overtones of the present punishment as a form of correction, and the explicit equality of punishment between rich and poor, who were of course equal in the eyes of Christ, it is likely that something broader than the late antique conception is imagined here. Whatever the extent of the definition, the novelty of this provision lies, first, in the equality of corporal chastisement for both rich and poor, and second, in the provision of a definite penalty, something which had previously been left vague in legislation. For more on Roman law, sex and marriage see J. Harries, *Law and Crime in the Roman World* (Cambridge, 2007), 86–105.

17.20. An unmarried man who fornicates shall be beaten with six blows.

17.21. If a married man has sex with his slave, then after the matter has been determined the girl shall be seized by the local magistrate and sold by him beyond the province, the proceeds of which sale shall go to the Treasury.[153]

17.22. Anyone who fornicates with another's slave girl shall pay thirty-six *nomismata* to the slave's master for this sin if he is a man of honour. However, if he is of little worth, he shall be beaten and pay as much of the thirty-six *nomismata* as he can.[154]

17.23. Anyone who fornicates with a nun shall, since they have insulted

153 Cf. AE.4.4. The difference in punishment between husbands and wives (in the AE, when a woman has sex with a slave, she is executed and the slave incinerated) is a striking example of the inbuilt inequality between the sexes in Roman law. Moreover, the present penalty is an innovation. Throughout late antiquity, masters could and did expect slaves to perform sexual duties. The *Ecloga* then makes moves to equalise punishments, adhering to Christian notions of equality, though there are distinct limits to the changes.

154 Cf. D.47.10.25. The gold *nomisma* was the premier coin of the period and lynchpin of the monetary economy; 36 *nomismata* equalled half a pound of gold. This chapter divides offenders into those who were honourable (*entimos*) and those who were of low worth (*eutelēs*), terms that were largely equivalent to the late antique Latin division between the *honestiores* and the *humiliores*, literally the 'more honest' and the 'more lowly'. Although no precise definition of the *honestiores/humiliores* split was ever given in late antiquity, there was a serious legal difference between the two. *Honestiores* were generally accorded a privileged status in Roman law, their testimony being preferred to that of those of low status (see E.14, AE.12). Critically, they were largely exempt from corporal punishment, a privilege repeated here. However, this is the only mention of this social categorisation in the *Ecloga*, though an equivalent division between an *eutelēs* and a *semnoteros* ('one more worthy of respect') is found in AE.5.7, and between an *eutelēs* and a *timios* ('an honourable man') in AE.6.8, both, one should note, translating *honestiores/humiliores* from the same passage of the *Digest*. Moreover, in the present chapter the division is quite clearly defined in monetary terms: you were an *entimos* if you could pay the hefty fine; if not, you were an *eutelēs*. Of course, a large part of what made one elite in late antiquity and Byzantium—and, indeed, in most societies—was wealth. The very terms used, with those of low material worth deemed to be of low spiritual worth and vice versa, are revealing of the marked overlap between status and wealth in the Roman world. However, in the *Ecloga* the functional division of who could pay, also found for example in E.17.11 and 29, is more dominant than the social division of personal status. Indeed, what is perhaps most notable about the *Ecloga*'s criminal penalties is just how many were applied equally to both rich and poor, high and low. In that regard, perhaps the most important word of this chapter is *ptaisma*, literally a 'stumble' but also a common metaphor for sin. Rather than talking about crimes, the text talks about a sin, reminding the reader that the *Ecloga*'s goal was to provide punishments and corrections for such sins, which of course could be committed by both rich and poor. For more on *honestiores* and *humiliores* see P. Garnsey, *Social Status and Legal Privilege in the Roman Empire* (Oxford, 1970).

God's Church, have their nose cut off, for that person has committed adultery and alienated her from the Church; and the nun must guard against the same punishment.[155]

17.24. Anyone who carries off a nun or any secular virgin from whatever place, if he corrupts her, shall have his nose cut off; those who aid in this rape shall be exiled.[156]

17.25. Anyone who intends to take in marriage their godparent in holy and salvation-bringing baptism, or has carnal intercourse with them without marrying, the perpetrators shall be separated from each other and suffer the penalty for adultery, namely both shall have their noses cut off.[157]

17.26. If anyone should be found in such a way to have married their godparent, both shall be severely beaten besides having their noses cut off.

17.27. Any man who commits adultery with a married woman shall have his nose cut off; and likewise the adulteress, who henceforth is divorced and lost to her children, since she has not kept the words of our Lord, who teaches that God had joined them together as 'one flesh'.[158] And after their noses have been cut off, the adulteress shall receive her own property, which she had brought to her husband, and nothing else. But the adulterer shall not be separated from his wife, even though his nose is cut. The case concerning the adultery must be investigated with great care, and the adjudicating magistrates shall interrogate the accusers of such a case; and if the accusers are their husband, father or mother, brother or uncle, then the motive for the suit is more credible. However, if the accusers are strangers, it is necessary for these persons to be assessed as to their character, to confirm this and to demand from them their evidence concerning the case. And if the adultery is proved, both the adulterer and the adulteress shall have their noses cut; however, if it is not proved, but rather the charge is found to be made through malice, then as slanderers the accusers shall suffer the selfsame punishment.[159]

155 Cf. N.123.43.

156 Cf. C.9.13.1; N.123.43.

157 Cf. E.2.2.

158 Genesis 2:24; Matthew 19:5–6; Mark 10.8; I Corinthians 6:16; Ephesians 5:31. Cf. E.2.9.

159 Cf. C.9.9.29; N.134.10; E.17.51; NM.26. In Roman law, adultery meant a married woman having extramarital sex, the marital status of the man being immaterial. As E.17.19 makes clear, a married man who had extramarital sex did not commit adultery (*moicheia*), but *porneia*, illicit sex. See also E.2.9, which lists a wife's fornication, which would

17.28. Anyone who pardons and allows his wife her adultery shall be beaten and exiled; the adulteress and adulterer shall have their noses cut off.[160]

17.29. Anyone who has sex with a virgin girl, with her consent but without the knowledge of her parents, and afterwards they discover this, if he wishes to marry her and her parents are willing, the marriage contract shall happen. However, if one of the parties is not willing, then if the seducer is wealthy he shall give one pound of gold to the corrupted girl; but if he has less means then he shall give her half of his property. But if he is utterly destitute and without means, then he shall be beaten, have his head shaved and then be exiled.[161]

17.30. Anyone who overpowers a girl and corrupts her shall have his nose cut off.[162]

17.31. Anyone who corrupts a girl before puberty, that is before she is thirteen, shall have his nose cut off, and half of his property shall be given to the seduced girl.[163]

17.32. Anyone who corrupts another's fiancée, even if he does so with the girl's consent, shall have his nose cut off.[164]

17.33. Those who commit incest, whether parents with children, children with parents, or brothers with sisters, shall be punished with the sword. Those who corrupt themselves with other kin, that is to say a father with his son's wife or a son with his father's wife (i.e. their stepmother), or a stepfather with his stepdaughter, or a brother with his brother's wife, or an uncle with his niece or a nephew with his aunt, shall have their noses cut off, as shall someone who knowingly has intercourse with two sisters.[165]

17.34. Anyone who knowingly has sexual intercourse with another's mother and her daughter shall have his nose cut off; and they shall be subject to the same penalty if they knowingly sinned with him.

---

include adultery, as a ground for divorce for a husband, but says nothing about a husband's extramarital activities. See also AE.5.2 and 5.

160 Cf. D.9.9.2; NS.52; AE.5.2.

161 Cf. NM.25.1.

162 Cf. NM.25.2.

163 Cf. D.48.19.38.3.

164 Cf. D.48.5.14.3; NM.25.3–4.

165 Cf. N.12.1; NM.30–41.

17.35. Anyone who has two wives shall be beaten, and the second wife banished with the children born to her.[166]

17.36. If a woman has had illicit sex, become pregnant and contrived against her own womb to produce an abortion, she shall be beaten and exiled.[167]

17.37. From this time onwards, cousins who enter into marriage, and also their children, and a father and son with a mother and daughter, or two brothers with two sisters, shall be separated and beaten.[168]

17.38. The wanton [i.e. homosexuals], whether they are active or submissive, shall be punished with the sword. But if the submissive partner is found to be under the age of twelve, he shall be forgiven as due to his age he did not know what he was doing.[169]

17.39. Those who become irrational, that is those who commit bestiality, shall have their penis cut off.[170]

17.40. Anyone who sets fire to another's wood or cuts down trees from it is condemned to pay back twice the value.[171]

17.41. Those who from some feud or for plunder commit arson in a city, shall be given over to the flames; if, outside a city, anyone should deliberately set fire to villages, fields or farmhouses, he shall be punished with the sword. However, if anyone desiring to burn stubble or thorns in his own field sets fire to them, and then the fire spreads further and burns another's fields or vineyard, then the adjudicating magistrate must investigate thoroughly; and if the fire happened due to the inexperience or carelessness of the lighter, then he shall make indemnity to the injured party. For if he lit the fire on a very windy day, or did nothing to prevent the fire from spreading, then he shall be condemned as negligent and careless. But if he did everything to prevent it, but a sudden, violent wind blew and spread the fire further, then he is not condemned. And if it happens that someone's house catches fire and his own property burns, and the fire spreads and sets alight adjacent houses, then he is not liable since the fire was not caused intentionally.[172]

166 Cf. C.5.5.2.

167 Cf. D.48.8.8.

168 Cf. E.2.2.

169 Cf. C.9.9.30; N.77; N.141; NM.43.

170 Cf. NM.29, 42. In Byzantine thought, what set man apart from other creatures was his capacity for rational thought. Therefore, to become irrational was to become beast-like, hence this association with bestiality.

171 Cf. NG.56–57.

172 Cf. D.9.2.30.3; D.47.9.1, 9, 12; D.48.19.28.12; NG.56–58, 63–65; NM.20.

17.42. Anyone, whether free or a slave, found to have given a drink on whatever pretext, whether a wife to her husband, or a husband to his wife, or a female slave to her mistress, and because of this the person taking the drink fell ill and died, he shall be punished with the sword.[173]

17.43. Sorcerers and poisoners who converse with demons for the harm of men shall be punished with the sword.[174]

17.44. Those who make amulets supposedly for the aid of men shall, due to their sordid love of gain, have their property confiscated and be exiled.

17.45. Anyone who intentionally commits murder, whatever his age, shall be punished with the sword.[175]

17.46. Anyone who strikes another with a sword and kills him, he shall be punished with the sword; however, if the struck man does not die, then the striker shall have his hand cut off because he dared to strike with a sword.[176]

17.47. If a fight between anyone occurs and a death ensues, the adjudicating magistrates should examine and investigate the affair as to what caused the death. And if they discover that the death was caused by means of a stick, or a big stone or by kicking, then he who caused the death shall have their hand cut off. But if they find that the death was caused by something lighter, he shall be beaten and exiled.[177]

17.48. Anyone who in a fight hits another with his hands and kills him shall be beaten and exiled, as he did not intend to kill.[178]

17.49. If anyone should beat and kill his own slave with thongs or rods, then the master shall not be deemed a killer. However, if he tortures him excessively, or kills him with poison or burns him to death, then he shall be punished as a murderer.[179]

17.50. Any robber who lies in ambush and commits murder shall be hanged in the place he is seized.[180]

173 Cf. D.48.8.3; AE.5–6.

174 Cf. C.9.18.4, 6; AE.5–6; NM.50. Several MSS add another chapter here, which is numbered E.17.54 in Burgmann's edition. It reads: 'A woman who kills her infant child is subject to the penalty for murder'.

175 Cf. D.48.8.

176 Cf. I.4.18.5; C.9.16.6; NS.45 and 47.

177 Cf. C.9.16.4; NN.3.6–7; NM.46.

178 Cf. NM.45.

179 Cf. C.9.14.1; NM.44.

180 A *lēstēs*, translated throughout as 'robber', was someone who committed armed theft.

17.51. Slanderers, whatever the case they slander in, shall suffer the selfsame punishment [i.e. the penalty for the crime that they maliciously accused someone of committing].[181]

17.52. Manicheans and Montanists shall be punished with the sword.[182]

17.53. Deserters, that is those who run away to the enemy, shall be punished with the sword.[183]

Title 18: Concerning the division of spoils

It is necessary for those who go forth to war against the enemy to guard themselves against all base speech and deeds, and rather keep their thoughts and prayers on God alone, and make war with good counsel; for the 'aid' of God is given 'to the heart of a counsellor',[184] as 'victory in war does not come from might in numbers, but by the power of God'.[185] Therefore, after a victory granted by God, it is fitting that a sixth part of the booty shall be set aside for the Treasury, and all the rest shall be divided among all the men equally, both great and small. For the addition of their salaries is sufficient for the officers. But if any of the officers are found to have distinguished themselves in valour, the general should organise and present them with a fitting reward from the aforementioned sixth share of the Treasury. And the share of those who remained with the baggage train shall, as it is written, be the same as those who took part in the battle.[186]

In this instance, drawn almost verbatim from D.48.19.28.15, it is referring to a highwayman or brigand. However, in multiple instances in the *Rhodian Sea Law* it refers to a pirate (see e.g. NN.3.15). Interestingly, despite multiple chapters dealing with their effects, the NN includes no penalty for pirates, and E.17.50 presumably fills the void.

181 Cf. C.9.46.10; E.17.27.

182 Cf. C.1.5.16; AE.3.

183 Cf. NS.7, 24, 36.

184 Proverbs 24:6.

185 I Maccabees 3:19.

186 Cf. I Samuel 30:24–25.

CONCERNING SOLDIERS WHO ARE SONS-IN-LAW WHO ENTER INTO A HOUSEHOLD AND BRING WITH THEM THEIR SALARY AND THEIR LABOUR[1]

Our pious and justice-loving emperors have decided the following pious law, that whenever [a soldier who is a son-in-law] has brought his goods and property into such a household [i.e. his father-in-law's], the soldier may certainly remove them, whether they are derived from imperial gifts, from his sword or from his salary; clearly the father-in-law should record all his outlay made for him [i.e. the son-in-law], that is for his military equipment,

1 *Krisis peri gambrōn stratiōtōn*, ed. D. Simon, 'Byzantinische Hausgemeinschafts-verträge', in F. Baur, K. Larenz and F. Wieacker (eds), *Beiträge zur europäischen Rechtsgeschichte und zum geltenden Zivilrecht: Festgabe für J. Sontis* (Munich, 1977), 91–128, text at 94. This imperial decision is attributed by its editor to Leo III and Constantine V, and is normally found in MSS appended to the *Ecloga*, frequently as part of a supplementary Title 19. It deals with a similar case to that envisioned in E.16.2. A son-in-law has entered his (potential or actual) father-in-law's household. Evidently the father-in-law has furnished his (potential or actual) son-in-law with his armament, expenses and clothing. In return, the son-in-law has provided his salary and labour. The son-in-law decides to leave, either because the proposed marriage agreement falls through or for some other reason. The soldier is allowed to take all those goods and property that he brought into the household that were derived from his salary, spoils or imperial gifts, that is those goods that were included in his *peculium castrense*, incidentally implying that the soldier was still subject to his own father's power. The father-in-law, though, should record all the martial outlays made by him for his son-in-law, for which, after the son-in-law has left, the father-in-law is no longer being reimbursed through his son-in-law's salary and labour, the implicit idea being that the father-in-law had a claim for the balance against the soldier's *peculium*. Just as in E.16.2, we see the emperors balancing the rights of soldiers, in particular the privilege of *peculium castrense*, against the rights of the households that equipped them, the difference being, of course, that in E.16.2 the soldier also had a claim to the property in question as an heir to his parents. For more on this decision, see Simon, *Byzantinische Hausgemeinschaftverträge*, 95–100; Oikonomidès, 'Middle Byzantine Provincial Recruits', esp. 134; Lilie, 'Die zweihundertjährige Reform', esp. 196–97; Haldon, 'Military Service, Military Lands, and the Status of Soldiers', esp. 21–23; Humphreys, *Law, Power, and Imperial Ideology*, 135–38.

his expenses and his clothing, and in a word anything purchased for him and his outgoings.[2]

2 This is version A in Simon's edition, the version that appears in the MSS with the *Ecloga*, often appended as part of an additional Title 19. Version B is found in the tenth-century compilation the *Ecloga ad Prochiron mutata*, ed. K. Zacharia von Lingenthal, *Jus Graeco-Romanum IV* (Leipzig, 1865), 49–170, and is as follows: 'Our pious and justice-loving emperors have decided the following pious law, that in all cases, when a soldier who is a son-in-law has brought his goods and property into the household of his father-in-law, whether derived from imperial gifts, or his salary or from his sword, he can certainly remove them; clearly the father-in-law should register his outlay made for him, that is for his military equipment, expenses, clothing and, in a word, anything purchased for him and his outgoings'.

THE SOLDIER'S LAW[1]

Concerning penalties for soldiers, taken from Rufus and the Tacticians[2]

1. Whosoever dares to form a conspiracy, sedition or mutiny against their commander for whatever cause shall be subject to capital punishment, especially the ringleaders responsible for the conspiracy or mutiny.[3]

2. If a soldier disobeys and contradicts his *pentarch*, he shall be chastised; likewise, if a *pentarch* disobeys his *dekarch* or a *dekarch* his *hekatontarch*.[4] If anyone in the *tagma* dares to disobey his commanding officer, namely the count or tribune, he shall suffer the ultimate penalty.[5]

1 *Nomos Stratiotikos*, ed. W. Ashburner, 'The Byzantine Mutiny Law', *JHS* 46 (1926), 85–109. A partial English translation based on the Momferratos edition of the *Ecloga* can be found in Freshfield, *Ecloga*, 122–29. As noted in the Introduction, 20, the critical edition produced by Ashburner is ordered oddly, and therefore a different manuscript, Vallicellianus gr. F 47 or V in the critical apparatus of Ashburner's edition, has been proposed as a better exemplar to follow. To ease reference, the footnotes cite chapter numbers from the Ashburner edition.

2 This first section of the NS is taken from the list of martial penalties contained in the late sixth-century military manual the *Strategikon*, to which the title seems to be referring. See the edition of G. Dennis and E. Gamillscheg, *Das Strategikon des Maurikios* (Vienna, 1981). These sections are virtually verbatim repetitions, though with a degree of reordering, and a few chapters of the original are not included presumably because they had become obsolete.

3 Ashburner, 'Byzantine Mutiny Law', 41. Cf. Strat. I.6.5; Leo VI, *Taktika*, ed. G. Dennis, *The Taktika of Leo VI* (Washington D.C., 2010), 8.5.

4 Ashburner, 'Byzantine Mutiny Law', 42. Cf. Strat. I.6.1. These were commanders of five, ten and 100 men respectively.

5 Ashburner, 'Byzantine Mutiny Law', 43. Cf. Strat. I.6.2; *Taktika* 8.2. A *tagma* is the standard military unit of the NS, following the *Strategikon*, and its use here should not be confused with the later *tagmata*, the elite corps founded by Constantine V. See A. Kazhdan, 'Tagma', *ODB*, vol. 3, 2007. When the NS talks about the 'ultimate penalty' it is clearly referring to execution. While this is also nearly always the most likely meaning when the

3. If anyone who has heard the orders of his *dekarch* does not observe them, he shall be chastised. However, if he errs out of ignorance of the orders, the *dekarch* shall be punished for not instructing him beforehand.[6]

4. If a soldier is treated unjustly by anyone, he shall bring a charge before the commander of the *tagma*. However, if he is wronged by that same commander, he should go before a superior officer.[7]

5. If anyone dares to exceed his period of leave, he shall be dismissed from the army, and handed over to the civil authorities as a civilian.[8]

6. If in wartime anyone should dare to let a soldier go on leave, he shall pay a fine of thirty *nomismata*. While in winter quarters, a soldier may go on leave for two or three months. During peacetime the soldier may go on leave within the boundaries of the province.[9]

7. If anyone is convicted of wishing to desert to the enemy, he shall suffer the ultimate penalty, and not only he but anyone who knew about it and kept silent.[10]

8. If anyone causes damage to a soldier or a taxpayer, he shall restore twice the amount of the thing damaged. If any officer or soldier in winter quarters, on the march or encamped should cause damage to a soldier or taxpayer, and does not recompense them as he ought, he shall pay back twice the amount.[11]

9. If anyone who has been entrusted with the defence of a city or fortress betrays it, or withdraws against the wishes of their commander despite being capable of defending it, he shall be condemned to capital punishment unless forced to do so by danger to his life.[12]

term 'capital punishment' is employed, in Roman law capital punishment could also mean loss of liberty or citizenship, perhaps involving exile rather than execution. See Berger, s.v. 'Poena capitalis'.

6 Ashburner, 'Byzantine Mutiny Law', 44. Cf. Strat. I.6.8; *Taktika* 8.8.

7 Ashburner, 'Byzantine Mutiny Law', 45. Cf. Strat. I.6.3; *Taktika* 8.3.

8 Ashburner, 'Byzantine Mutiny Law', 46. Cf. Strat. I.6.4; *Taktika* 8.4.

9 Ashburner, 'Byzantine Mutiny Law', 47. Cf. Strat. I.7.14; *Taktika* 8.15.

10 Ashburner, 'Byzantine Mutiny Law', 48. Cf. Strat. I.6.7; E.17.53; NS.24; *Taktika* 8.7.

11 Ashburner, 'Byzantine Mutiny Law', 49. Cf. Strat. I.6.10 and I.7.13; *Taktika* 8.10, 13–14.

12 Ashburner, 'Byzantine Mutiny Law', 13. Cf. Strat. I.6.6 and I.7.15; *Taktika* 8.6, 16.

10. If anyone finds an animal or anything else small or great and does not report it and hand it over to his commander, he shall be punished as a thief, both he and those who knew about it and kept silent.[13]

11. If a soldier should abandon his post or standard and flee while the lines of battle are being arranged or during combat, or rushes forward beyond his place and plunders the dead, or runs off headlong in pursuit of the enemy, we order that he shall suffer capital punishment and, as is fitting, all his loot shall be confiscated and given to the common fund of his *tagma*, since that man broke ranks and betrayed his comrades.[14]

12. If a rout occurs without reasonable or manifest cause during general marshalling or battle, we order that the soldiers of the *tagma* who fled first and turned back from the line of battle or from their own *meros* shall be decimated and shot down by the other *tagmata*, because they broke the ranks and caused the rout of the whole *meros*.[15] But if it happens that some of them were wounded in the battle itself, they shall naturally be exempt from this penalty.[16]

13. If a standard is seized by the enemy without a good and manifest excuse, we order that those entrusted with the guard of the standard shall be punished and demoted to the lowest rank in the unit or *schola* in which they are registered. But if any of them were wounded in battle, they shall be exempted from this penalty.[17]

14. If a *meros* or formation is routed near camp, and those put to flight do not retire towards the defenders, or seek refuge within the camp itself, but contemptuously run off to a different place, we order that those who dare to do this shall be punished for being guilty of despising the others.[18]

15. If a soldier should throw away his arms during battle, we order him to be punished for disarming himself and arming the enemy.[19]

13 Ashburner, 'Byzantine Mutiny Law', 50. Cf. Strat. I.6.9; E.17.11; NS.28; *Taktika* 8.9.

14 Ashburner, 'Byzantine Mutiny Law', 8. Cf. Strat. 1.8.16; *Taktika* 8.20.

15 Decimation was one of the most extreme forms of Roman military punishment, where a whole disgraced unit had one in ten of its members executed by their fellow soldiers. A *meros* was a division composed of multiple *tagmata*.

16 Ashburner, 'Byzantine Mutiny Law', 9. Cf. Strat. 1.8.17; *Taktika* 8.21–22.

17 Ashburner, 'Byzantine Mutiny Law', 10. Cf. Strat. 1.8.18; *Taktika* 8.23. The *scholae* were special military units that had once formed the imperial guard. See A. Kazhdan, 'Scholae Palatinae', *ODB*, vol. 3, 1851–52.

18 Ashburner, 'Byzantine Mutiny Law', 12. Cf. Strat. I.8.19; *Taktika* 8.24.

19 Ashburner, 'Byzantine Mutiny Law', 11. Cf. Strat. 1.8.20; *Taktika* 8.25.

Martial penalties[20]

16. If officers and those guiding the army in any way whatsoever extort money from the countryside, they are condemned to pay back twice the amount.[21]

17. *From the 19th Title of the 48th Book of the Digest*
The leaders of disorder and disturbers of the people are either beheaded or exiled according to their status.[22]

18. *From the 16th Title of the 49th Book of the Digest*
If anyone should incite disorder amongst the troops as a lone voice, or if many should conspire together to this end, they shall be severely beaten and expelled from the army. If the disorder inflamed and aroused amongst the soldiers is severe, they shall be executed.[23]

19. If a soldier should oppose his commander when the latter intends to strike him, he is to be transferred within the service if he only restrained his staff of office.[24] If, however, he deliberately broke the staff or laid hands on his commander, he shall suffer capital punishment.[25]

20. *From the same*
If soldiers abandon their commander, or leave him and do not protect him despite being able to defend him while withdrawing from the enemy, and it happens that he dies as a result, then they shall suffer capital punishment.[26]

21. *From the same*
Anyone who has been set to guard the palace but abandons his watch and vigil shall suffer the ultimate penalty or, if worthy of humanity, shall be beaten and exiled.[27]

20 Cf. the titles of E.17 and AE.3.

21 Ashburner, 'Byzantine Mutiny Law', 35. Cf. N.130.4, 6; NS.8.

22 Ashburner, 'Byzantine Mutiny Law', 14. Cf. D.48.19.38.2; NS.1, 18.

23 Ashburner, 'Byzantine Mutiny Law', 36. Cf. D.49.16.3.19–21; NS.1, 17.

24 This punishment of *mutatio militiae* meant transfer to a less prestigious and less well-remunerated division. For this and other military punishments and law, see C. Brand, *Roman Military Law* (Austin, 1968).

25 Ashburner, 'Byzantine Mutiny Law', 29. Cf. D.49.16.13.4; NS.44.

26 Ashburner, 'Byzantine Mutiny Law', 17. Cf. D.49.16.3.22, 16.6.8.

27 Ashburner, 'Byzantine Mutiny Law', 37. Cf. D.49.16.10.pr.

22. *From the 40th Title of the 2nd Book of the Codex*
Anyone who goes over to the barbarians, or sells them weapons, finished or unfinished, or any kind of iron while they [the barbarians] are present on the pretence of an embassy, shall suffer the ultimate penalty.[28]

23. *From the 44th Title of the 48th Book of the Digest*
And anyone who incites the enemy to fight or in like manner betrays Romans to the enemy, shall be punished.[29]

24. *From the 8th and 16th Titles of the 48th Book of the Digest*
If anyone plans to desert to the barbarians and is caught, he shall suffer capital punishment.[30] Furthermore, those from Roman territory who desert to the enemy may be killed with impunity as enemies.[31]

25. *From the 16th Title of the 49th Book of the Digest*
If the scouts of the Roman army report the secret plans of the Romans to the enemy, they shall suffer capital punishment.[32] A soldier who disturbs the peace shall suffer capital punishment.[33]

26. If anyone during wartime does something forbidden by the commander, or does not fulfil his commands, he shall suffer capital punishment, even if the action was successful.[34]

27. *From the same*
If someone wounds a fellow soldier with a stone or wounds himself on purpose, to escape bodily suffering, illness or death, he is to be beaten and dismissed from the army.[35]

28. *From the same*
A soldier who steals, wherever or whatever, must pay back double and be demoted.[36] A man sentenced to capital punishment, exile or for some other

28 Ashburner, 'Byzantine Mutiny Law', 51. Cf. C.4.41.2.
29 Ashburner, 'Byzantine Mutiny Law', 38. Cf. D.48.4.3.
30 Ashburner, 'Byzantine Mutiny Law', 6. Cf. D.49.16.3.11.
31 Ashburner, 'Byzantine Mutiny Law', 39. Cf. D.48.8.3.6. E.8.4.2, 17.53; NS.7.
32 Ashburner, 'Byzantine Mutiny Law', 40. Cf. D.49.16.6.4.
33 Ashburner, 'Byzantine Mutiny Law', 28. Cf. D.49.16.16.1; NS.17.
34 Ashburner, 'Byzantine Mutiny Law', 1. Cf. D.49.16.3.15.
35 Ashburner, 'Byzantine Mutiny Law', 52. Cf. D.49.16.6–7.
36 Ashburner, 'Byzantine Mutiny Law', 54. Cf. E.17.10–11; NS.10.

public crime[37] who manages to escape punishment cannot enlist in the army.[38]

29. *From the 35th Title of the 12th Book of the Codex*
Those discharged from the army in infamy through their own fault shall neither hold nor obtain any honour.[39]

Concerning the status of soldiers

30. *From the 64th Title of 4th Book of the Codex*
Soldiers should not be administrators, hirelings or guarantors of other people's properties.[40]

31. *From the 35th Title of the 12th Book of the Codex*
Neither shall soldiers be employed in agriculture or commerce, nor take upon themselves any civil employment, or they shall be dismissed from the army and deprived of the privileges of soldiers.[41]

Further concerning the status of soldiers from the 16th Title of the 49th Book of the Digest

32. If a soldier absents himself in the face of the enemy, or abandons camp,[42] or is the first in the line of battle to flee in sight of [his fellow] soldiers,[43] or throws away his arms or sells them, he shall suffer capital punishment.

37 In Roman law, some crimes were deemed so serious that they offended the whole social order and therefore had to be prosecuted by the state under special statutes, and were therefore called 'public crimes'. See Berger, s.v. 'Crimina publica'. They included such offences as treason, murder and adultery. As the inclusion of the last indicates, what was—and is—considered a grave threat to the social order was—and is—a social construct rather than a fixed category. Indeed, what counts as a 'crime', something punishable by the state, is also a social construct, and the definition altered over the *longue durée* of Roman law. For more see Harries, *Law and Crime*, 1–27.

38 Ashburner, 'Byzantine Mutiny Law', 53.

39 Ashburner, 'Byzantine Mutiny Law', 16. Cf. C.12.35.3.

40 Ashburner, 'Byzantine Mutiny Law', 55. C.4.65.31, 35; E.12.6.

41 Ashburner, 'Byzantine Mutiny Law', 56. Cf. C.12.35.15–16.

42 Cf. D.49.16.3.4.

43 Cf. D.49.16.6.3.

However, if humanity prevails, he shall be beaten and transferred within the service.[44]

33. Whoever feigns illness of the body through fear of the enemy shall suffer capital punishment.[45]

34. If anyone should leave the section of the palisade[46] to which he is posted, he shall suffer capital punishment. If anyone should go beyond his trench,[47] he shall be discharged from the army.[48]

35. A traitor to the emperor shall be killed and his property confiscated. Furthermore, his memory shall be damned after death.[49]

36. If anyone plans to desert to the barbarians and is caught, he suffers capital punishment.[50] A soldier who abandons his station is either whipped or demoted in rank.[51]

37. Anyone who flees to the enemy and returns shall be tortured and either thrown to wild beasts or sentenced to the gallows.[52]

38. A soldier who steals the arms of another shall be reduced in rank.[53]

39. If anyone inflames or rouses soldiers to severe disorder, he shall suffer capital punishment. But if the martial disorder produced was limited to a lone voice, merely exciting some complaints among others or indiscipline, then he is reduced in rank. And when many soldiers conspire together for some absurd thing or their legion revolts, it is customary to discharge them.[54]

44 Ashburner, 'Byzantine Mutiny Law', 2. Cf. D.49.16.3.13.

45 Ashburner, 'Byzantine Mutiny Law', 3. Cf. D.49.16.5.5.

46 The *charakōma*, or *vallum* in Latin, was the wooden palisade that ran about a Byzantine camp.

47 The *phōssa*, or *fossa* in Latin, was the trench around the outside of a Byzantine camp, the spoil from which was used to create an internal rampart often topped with a palisade. For more on Byzantine camps see E. McGeer, 'Camp', *ODB*, vol. 1, 369.

48 Ashburner, 'Byzantine Mutiny Law', 4. Cf. D.49.16.3.17–18.

49 Ashburner, 'Byzantine Mutiny Law', 5. Cf. C.9.8.6.2; E.17.1. Strictly speaking, the translation should be 'those who sin against the emperor', which is reflective of both the emperor's quasi-sacral status and the vow sworn by soldiers, which the traitors were breaking. *Damnatio memoriae* was the ultimate form of infamy under Roman law, whereby the offender's very memory was to be obliterated, their name chiselled from monuments and expunged from documents, all their acts rendered legally invalid. See Berger, s.v. 'Damnatio memoriae'.

50 Ashburner, 'Byzantine Mutiny Law', 6. Cf. D.49.16.3.11; E.17.53; NS.7, 24.

51 Ashburner, 'Byzantine Mutiny Law', 7. Cf. D.49.16.3.5.

52 Ashburner, 'Byzantine Mutiny Law', 15. Cf. D.49.16.3.10.

53 Ashburner, 'Byzantine Mutiny Law', 18. Cf. D.49.16.3.14; E.17.10.

54 Ashburner, 'Byzantine Mutiny Law', 19. Cf. D.49.16.3.19–21; NS.1, 17–18.

40. Anyone who has been deported, escapes from the punishment and afterwards endeavours to enlist in the army, having concealed his deportation, or allows himself to be enlisted, shall suffer capital punishment. Anyone who has been temporarily exiled and voluntarily enlists shall be deported to an island, but if he dissembles and allows himself to be enlisted, he shall be exiled permanently. And if anyone who has been exiled temporarily escapes the punishment, and enlists after the completion of his time of exile, the reasons as to why he was sentenced to exile shall be enquired into, and if they confer permanent infamy then the same penalty shall be observed.[55]

41. Those condemned for adultery or another public crime are not to be accepted should they wish to enlist.[56]

42. Whoever flees from military service is subject to martial punishment. For it is a grave sin to avoid the duties of military service if enlisted. For those who are called up for military service and flee shall be enslaved as betrayers of their own liberty.[57]

43. If anyone takes his son away from the army during wartime, he shall be exiled and part of his property confiscated. If anyone disables his son during wartime so that he is found unfit for the army, he shall be exiled.[58]

44. If any soldier should lay hands on his officer, he shall suffer capital punishment.[59]

45. If anyone wounds a fellow soldier with a stone, he is dismissed from the service; if he does so with a sword, he shall suffer capital punishment.[60]

46. If a soldier wounds himself or attempts suicide in some other way due to bodily pain or being weary of life, or due to insanity or being ashamed he preferred to die, he should not suffer capital punishment but shall be

55 Ashburner, 'Byzantine Mutiny Law', 20. Cf. D.49.16.4.2–4. This chapter highlights some of the different degrees of exile envisioned under Roman law. The severest form was deportation (*deportatio* in Latin), whereby the deportee lost his property and citizenship, and was confined to a particular place, usually an island. Other, milder forms could be limited to mere banishment from a particular place, and the penalty could also be time limited. See Berger, s.v. 'Deportatio'; 'Exilium'. For the Roman concept of infamy see 50 n. 44.

56 Ashburner, 'Byzantine Mutiny Law', 21. Cf. D.49.16.4.7; E.17.27. For the concept of a public crime see 85 n. 37.

57 Ashburner, 'Byzantine Mutiny Law', 22. Cf. D.49.16.4.9–10.

58 Ashburner, 'Byzantine Mutiny Law', 23. Cf. D.49.16.4.11–12.

59 Ashburner, 'Byzantine Mutiny Law', 24. Cf. D.49.16.6.1; NS.19.

60 Ashburner, 'Byzantine Mutiny Law', 25. Cf. D.49.16.6.6; E.17.46.

dishonourably discharged from the army. However, if none of these are offered as an excuse for the attempted suicide, he shall suffer capital punishment.[61]

47. The first man who flees from the line of battle in sight of [his fellow] soldiers shall suffer capital punishment. And if the scouts of the Roman army reveal the secret plans of the Romans they shall suffer capital punishment. And a soldier who wounds a fellow soldier with a sword shall be beheaded.[62]

48. A soldier who breaks out of prison and escapes shall suffer capital punishment.[63]

49. Those who through wine, strong drink or some other wantonness cause soldiers to slip and harm themselves are forgiven capital punishment. Instead they bring upon themselves a transfer within the service.[64]

50. A man who falls out of line during battle is either beaten with cudgels or is transferred within the service.[65]

51. If those guarding people should lose them through negligence, they are either beaten or demoted in the service, according to the degree of their fault. However, if the prisoners were released through pity, they are transferred to another branch of the service. But if they did this because of some villainy, they either suffer capital punishment or are demoted to the lowest rank of the service.[66]

52. If a soldier comes to an agreement with his wife's lover he is dismissed from the service.[67]

53. If anyone does something forbidden by the commander or does not fulfil his commands during wartime, he shall suffer capital punishment, even if the action was successful. If a soldier absents himself in the face of the enemy, or abandons camp, or is the first in the line of battle to flee in sight of [his fellow] soldiers, or throws away his arms or sells them, he shall suffer capital punishment. However, if humanity prevails he is beaten and transferred within the service.[68]

61 Ashburner, 'Byzantine Mutiny Law', 26. Cf. D.49.16.7.

62 Ashburner, 'Byzantine Mutiny Law', 27. Cf. D.49.16.3–4, 6; E.17.46; NS.25, 32, 45, 53.

63 Ashburner, 'Byzantine Mutiny Law', 30. Cf. D.49.16.13.5.

64 Ashburner, 'Byzantine Mutiny Law', 31. Cf. D.49.16.6.7.

65 Ashburner, 'Byzantine Mutiny Law', 32. Cf. D.49.16.3.16.

66 Ashburner, 'Byzantine Mutiny Law', 33. Cf. D.48.3.14.2.

67 Ashburner, 'Byzantine Mutiny Law', 34. Cf. D.48.5.12; E.17.28.

68 Ashburner, 'Byzantine Mutiny Law', 1–2. Cf. D.49.16.3.4, 13, 15, 6.3; NS.26, 32, 47.

THE APPENDIX ECLOGAE[1]

Title 1: Concerning guarantees and sureties

1. *From the 5th Title of the 13th Book of the Paratitla*
Anyone who gives a guarantee or stands surety on behalf of another becomes liable [to pay the debt] himself, but the original person is not released [from the debt].[2]

2. *From the 6th and 8th Titles of the 2nd Book of the Digest*
All relatives and kin are acceptable [as sureties], even if they are poor; and if anyone should accept guarantees from poor people, he shall not demand other [guarantors] unless the guarantor dies or by chance utterly loses his property.[3]

3. *From the 103rd New Constitution*
Anyone who stands surety and says, 'I will make satisfaction [for the debt]' is liable. If he says, 'I *and* so-and-so and so-and-so [will make satisfaction]', he is bound, while not prejudicing the others. If he says, 'I *or* so-and-so [will make satisfaction]', he is liable for the whole; but if he says, 'You will be satisfied [for the debt]', this shall not be effective.[4]

4. *From the 40th Title of the 8th Book of the Codex*
If anyone gives a guarantee to produce someone [in court] within a stated time, or stands surety to pay a stipulated sum [instead], payment shall not be demanded immediately after this time has expired; and if the appointed

1 *Appendix Eclogae*, ed. L. Burgmann and S. Troianos, 'Appendix Eclogae', *FM* III (Frankfurt, 1979), 24–125. A partial English translation of AE.1–9, 11, based on the Momferratos edition of the *Ecloga*, can be found in Freshfield, *Ecloga*, 120–21, 129–41.

2 Cf. D.13.5.28. *Paratitla* were summaries of Justinianic law made by the *Antecessores*, legal specialists in the sixth century. See Introduction, 4.

3 Cf. D.2.6.1–3, 2.8.2 and 10.

4 Cf. N.115.6.

time [within which to bring the party to court] is six months or more, then he shall have a further six months [to pay or produce the person]. But at the completion of the second term the man who gave the guarantee may delay no longer, and must pay the penalty.[5]

5. *From the 4th New Constitution*
Anyone who is owed something in any way shall first bring an action against the principal party. If that man is insolvent or absent, he shall sue the guarantor. And if the debt is not thereby fulfilled, then he shall bring an action against those who possess the property of the principal, and then against those who possess the property of the guarantor or his debtors.[6]

Title 2: Concerning boundary stones and the borders of fields[7]

1. *From the 47th Book of the Digest, Title 11*
Anyone who removes ancient boundary stones or plants boundary stones on another's field by force shall suffer capital punishment.[8]

2. *From the same, Title 21*
If a male or female slave deceitfully removes another's boundary stones without the knowledge of their master, he or she shall suffer capital punishment.[9]

3. *From the same book and title*
Those who overturn field boundaries, if they are of high rank and dare to do this for their own profit, shall be beaten and exiled in perpetuity.[10]

4. *From the Codex Book 9 Title 2*
Those who remove field boundaries shall be punished at the discretion of the judge.[11]

5 Cf. C.8.40.26. This compressed version of a Justinian law is saying that someone who stood surety for another to appear in court did not have to pay the penalty for the non-appearance of the party immediately. Instead, they had a sixth-month grace period to either pay or produce the party in court, but after that six-month period elapsed they had to pay the penalty.

6 Cf. N.4.1–2.

7 Cf. NG.7 and Irene Novel I.

8 Cf. D.47.11.9.

9 Cf. D.47.21.3.1.

10 Cf. D.47.21.1–2.

11 Cf. C.9.2.1.

5. *Book 11 Title 26*
No one shall destroy ancient boundary markers, [a crime] which is subject to confiscation of [the perpetrator's] property and exile.

Concerning those who build, sow or plant on another's land or ground

6. *From the Institutes Book 2 Title 1*
If anyone should build a house with his own materials on another's land, the owner of the land will be the owner of the house, according to the rule that says, 'that which is above yields to that which is underneath'.[12] Therefore, the landowner shall enjoy perpetual ownership of the house along with the building materials, and [the builder] may not bring an action for the value of the materials.[13]

7. *From the Codex Book 3 Title 33*
Anyone who builds, sows or does anything else on another's land shall lose his ownership, and shall not recover his costs.[14]

8. *From the same, Book 9, Title 12*
If someone forcibly enters another's fields and one of his party is killed, or one of the opposite party, then as one convicted of homicide his head shall be cut off.[15]

9. *From the same*
Anyone who considers that a field or other property possessed by another belongs to him must go to the magistrate. And if after accusing him of force [in acquiring the property] he cannot prove his case, let him suffer the same penalty [as a person who had acquired another's property by force]. But if, despising the court, he should bring force against him [the possessor], let him firstly lose his possession, and then he shall be condemned for force and exiled, losing even his own property.[16]

12 A translation of the Latin *superficies cedit solo*. For the law concerning *superficies*, anything connected to the ground, whether built on it or coming out of it, see Berger, s.v. 'Superficies'.

13 Cf. I.2.1.30; NG.21, 66, 80–81.

14 Cf. C.3.32.11; NG.1–2, 20.

15 Cf. C.9.12.6.

16 Cf. C.9.12.7; E.17.5; NG.6, 66, 80.

10. *Constitution 121, Chapter 14*
All civil and military officials shall themselves investigate the perpetrators of violence, rape[17] or other offences in the provinces, and punish them according to the law.[18]

Title 3: Penalties against heretics, Manicheans and the remaining heresies, and against enchanters and poisoners[19]

1. *From the Beginning, Title 5 of the Constitutions*
Heretics shall neither teach, nor declare their unbelief nor be made clerics. A heretic, who is subject to the laws against heretics, is someone who deviates however little from the orthodox faith.[20]

2. *Another from the same*
The Orthodox Church punishes meetings of heretics, even if held in private houses. They shall not hold services, by night or by day; if anything of the kind should happen, whether in public or a private house, then the officials of the *Eparch*[21] who acquiesced in it shall pay a penalty of one hundred pounds [of gold], while [officials of magistrates] in the provinces shall pay fifty pounds [of gold].[22]

3. It is a public crime to be a Manichean or a Donatist, and it is an insult to God. They do not hold anything in common with the customs or the

17 This could be rape of property or women, as is explicitly stated in N.128.21.

18 Cf. N.128.21.

19 Cf. the titles of E.17 and the second section of the NS.

20 Cf. C.1.5.2; *Collectio Tripartita*, ed. N. Van der Wal and B. Stolte, *Collectio Tripartita: Justinian on Religious and Ecclesiastical Affairs* (Groningen, 1994), 1.5.2. The *Collectio Tripartita* is a sixth-century text that excerpted and reordered various pieces of Justinianic legislation on religious matters. As such, it provided the compilers of the AE with a useful collection of law already translated into Greek and thematically organised, and it is therefore unsurprising that it forms the basis of several of the titles of the AE.

21 The *Eparch* or Prefect of Constantinople was one of the most senior officials in the Roman Empire, responsible for multiple aspects of life in the capital. See A. Kazhdan, 'Eparch of the City', *ODB* vol. 1, 705.

22 Cf. C.1.5.3; *Coll. Trip.* 1.5.3. While *hoi epichōrioi* would translate as 'those in the region' more naturally than '[officials of magistrates] in the provinces', the original Latin of C.1.5.3 makes clear that it is the officials of the prefect of Constantinople and the staff of provincial magistrates who are penalised. Moreover, in Justinian's *Edict* 13.18 one can find 'a provincial magistrate' (*ho epichōrios archon*), along with his staff. Finally, it simply makes more sense for the staff of magistrates to be penalised than all the inhabitants of a region.

laws. Their property shall be confiscated, they shall be deprived of all gifts and inheritances, and they can neither sell nor buy. Those knowingly concealing them shall be punished.[23]

4. *Another from the same*
Heretics shall not possess the privileges granted by reason of religion, but shall be liable to public obligations.[24]

5. *Another from the same*
Jews shall neither possess any dignities, nor acquire any office, nor hold state posts, but are subject to the status of the *cohortales* and hence their burdens.[25] Anyone who audaciously acquires one of the aforementioned [dignities, offices or posts] shall lose it and be fined thirty pounds of gold. Should one of the parents desire their child to become a Christian, their opinion shall prevail. And the father must support the child and cover the costs of necessities, and provide a dowry for a daughter.[26]

6. *Another from the same*
Heretics may not hold meetings, religious assemblies, synods, ordinations or baptisms, or have leaders, or be entrusted with or have care for the offices of father or defender [of the city],[27] or manage estates, either themselves or through fictitious persons, or do anything that is forbidden. Anyone who transgresses runs the ultimate risk.[28]

7. *Another from the same*
Anyone who has become orthodox after being a Manichean, if he is found to be going astray, or merely lives or consorts with Manicheans and does not immediately hand them over to a lawful judge, shall suffer the ultimate punishment. And persons in positions of rank and state service shall carefully seek for men such as these among them, and shall hand them over; and if after the Manichean's arrest it appears that he was known to

23 Cf. C.1.5.4; *Coll. Trip.* 1.5.4. For 'public crime' see 85 n. 37.

24 Cf. C.1.5.1; *Coll. Trip.* 1.5.1.

25 *Cohortales* was the name given to provincial officials, that is, the most junior rung of state service. Their privileges were few and their burdens, normally associated with tax collection, heavy. See Jones, *Later Roman Empire*, 363, 594–95.

26 Cf. C.1.5.12; *Coll. Trip.* 1.9 Parat.1.

27 The 'father of the city' (*pater civitatis*) was a late antique official in charge of city finances, while the 'defender of the city' (*defensor civitatis*), oversaw municipal justice. Together they were the most important civic officials in late antiquity. See Jones, *Later Roman Empire*, 726–27.

28 Cf. C.1.5.14; *Coll. Trip.* 1.5.14.

them they shall be fittingly punished as committing the same sin, even if they are not such a person [i.e. a Manichean]. For those who know the sinner and do not declare him shall seem guilty of the same sin. Anyone who has Manichean books and does not produce them to be burned shall be punished.[29]

8. *From the same*
The temples shall be closed and no one shall sacrifice. If anyone should so sin, he shall be beheaded and his property confiscated; the magistrate would likewise be punished if he did not prosecute him.[30]

9. *Another from the same*
The synagogues of the Samaritans shall be demolished, and if they attempt to build others they shall be punished.[31]

10. *Another from the same*
Heretics who gather together, hold meetings or perform baptisms shall be punished as transgressors of the law.[32]

11. *Another from the same*
The Arians, the Macedonians who war against the Holy Spirit, the Apollinarians, the Novatians or Sabbatians, Eunomians, Tetraditai or Tessareskaidekatitai, the Valentinians, Papianistai, the Montantists or Priscillianists, or Phrygians or Pepuzitai, the Marcianists, Borborians, Messalians, Eutychians or Enthusiasts, the Donatists, Audians, Hydroparastatai, Taskodrougoi, Bathrakitai, Hermitai, Paulians, Marcellians, Ophites, Encratites, Apotactites, Saccophori and, the worst of all, the Manicheans, shall not be allowed to meet or pray. Also, the Manicheans shall be expelled from the cities and suffer the ultimate punishment. And all the laws enacted against heretics shall remain in force.[33]

29 Cf. C.1.5.16; *Coll. Trip.* 1.5.16.

30 Cf. C.1.11.1; *Coll. Trip.* 1.11.1.

31 Cf. C.1.5.17; *Coll. Trip.* 1.5.17.

32 Cf. C.1.5.20; *Coll. Trip.* 1.5.20.

33 Cf. C.1.5.5; *Coll. Trip.* 1.5.5. When there is a term for one of these heresies in widespread use I have used it, but otherwise I have kept to the Greek spellings. To explain what each of these heresies believed, or more accurately what their opponents said they believed, would require a truly gargantuan footnote, especially as several of them are exceedingly obscure. However, one should note that this list was one of the products of late antique heresiology, the classification and cataloguing of heresies, which helped to establish what orthodoxy was through defining and condemning what it was not. Emperors seeking to please God and

12. *Another concerning apostates*
A Christian who becomes a Jew shall have his property confiscated.[34]

13. *Another from the same*
Any orthodox cleric or monk who worships according to the practices of the Eutychians or Apollinarians shall be subject to the laws against heretics and expelled from the Roman Empire in accordance with the legislation concerning Manicheans.[35]

14. *Another from the same*
Anyone who re-baptises an orthodox person shall suffer the ultimate punishment, along with the person baptised—if, that is, he was of an age capable of crime.[36]

15. *Another from the Canons*
A bishop who baptises the same person twice shall be dethroned.[37]

16. *Book 1 of the Codex, Constitution 7*
Let apostates and those who make sacrifices and erect temples be accused by all men; and if they were pagans before they became Christians and were baptised, then they shall be subject to the ultimate penalty.[38]

17. *Another from the same*
Those who persist in the deceits of the pagans after holy baptism shall suffer the ultimate punishment. And let those who are not yet baptised be brought to the holy churches along with their children, wives and their entire household. And their young children shall be baptised without delay, while those of age shall first be taught the Scriptures in accordance with the canons. But those who pretend to be baptised for the sake of obtaining or retaining imperial service, rank or property, and leave their children,

---

burnish their orthodox credentials became bound up in this process, and so the cataloguing and punishing of heresy became part of the legal apparatus. For more see R. Flower, 'The Insanity of Heretics Must Be Restrained: Heresiology in the *Theodosian Code*', in C. Kelly (ed.), *Theodosius II: Rethinking the Roman Empire in Late Antiquity* (Cambridge, 2013), 172–94. Of course, the repetition of the list here was due to similar reasons, viz. the desire to please God and broadcast imperial piety and orthodoxy through denouncing and punishing heretics, something that the Isaurian emperors—if they were behind the creation of the AE—had every reason to do considering the aspersions cast on their own orthodoxy.

34 Cf. C.1.7.1; *Coll. Trip.* 1.7.1.

35 Cf. C.1.7.6; *Coll. Trip.* 1.7.6.

36 Cf. C.1.6.2; *Coll. Trip.* 1.6.2.

37 Cf. C.1.6.1; *Coll. Trip.* 1.6.1.

38 Cf. C.1.7.4, 1.11.10.

wives, households and those related to them in the error of paganism, shall have their property confiscated, be suitably punished and shall not enjoy their civil rights. Those who will not be baptised shall not enjoy anything from their citizenship, nor be allowed to be owners of movable or immovable property, but these shall be forfeited to the Treasury and they shall be suitably punished and exiled. And if anyone should be found sacrificing or worshipping idols they shall suffer the ultimate punishment like the Manicheans.[39]

18. *Another from the same*
A Samaritan or Jew who tries to make anyone apostatise from the Christian faith shall be subject to confiscation of their property and beheaded.[40]

19. *Another from the same*
The worshippers of the heavens are subject to the laws against heretics, and the Church shall seize their meeting places. For what differs from the Christian faith is contrary to it.[41]

20. *From the Council of Nicaea*
Manicheans shall be baptised, Phrygians shall be baptised, Eunomians shall be anointed, Arians shall be anointed, Paulicans baptised, Photians baptised, Novatians anointed and Apollinarians shall profess the faith set down at Nicaea.[42]

Title 4

1. *From the 5th Book of the Codex, Title 6. Concerning the fact that notable men should not have worthless wives*
Senators may not marry degraded women, such as a slave or her daughter, or likewise a freedwoman or her daughter, or an actress or shopkeeper or their daughter, or the daughter of a brothel-keeper or a charioteer.[43]

2. No one shall marry his brother's wife, even if she is still a virgin. For marriage is not based on consummation but is contracted by agreement.

39 Cf. C.1.11.10; *Coll. Trip.* 1.11.10.

40 Cf. C.1.9.18; *Coll. Trip.* 1.7 Parat.

41 Cf. C.1.9.12; *Coll. Trip.* 1.9.12.

42 *Pace* the rubric, in actuality, the closest canon is Canon 7 of the Second Ecumenical Council of 381.

43 Cf. C.5.5.7; E.2.2; Irene Novel II.

Nor may the children born of such people marry, with the exception of those Egyptians who have already done so.[44]

3. No one may through an imperial beneficence contract an unlawful marriage, such as with the daughter of a sister or the wife of a brother, and marriages so made shall be overturned.[45]

4. *Book 9 of the Codex, Title 11*
If a woman through lust has intercourse with her own slave, she shall be decapitated and the slave burnt; let such goings on and arrangements be denounced, and the slave [who denounces it] shall be honoured with freedom. Furthermore, their children shall have neither rank nor any other honour, for it is enough for them to be free.[46] They shall have nothing from their mother, either through intestacy or by will; but if she has surviving legitimate children or relatives these shall be her heirs, and they shall receive the property bequeathed either to her lover or to his children.[47]

Title 5

1. *From the 48th Book of the Digest, Chapter 8, Constitution 3. Concerning murderers and sorcerers*
Included among murderers and sorcerers is someone who makes, possesses or sells drugs intended to kill men, and someone who publicly sells baneful poisons or possesses them for the purpose of killing men. But there are good drugs. For the term 'drug' is neutral, and encompasses both drugs prepared for healing and for destruction; and it also covers aphrodisiacs, which are called love philtres and are included in the law on the possession

44 Cf. C.5.5.8. The reason for the mention of Egyptians here is that the original law of Zeno in 475, here summarised, was addressed specifically to Egyptians who, following local customs, married their deceased brother's wife on the grounds of the marriage not being consummated, which was not a requirement of Roman law, which based marriage on mutual agreement rather than consummation.

45 Cf. C.5.8.1–2; E.2.2. The 'imperial beneficence' referred to was a rescript from the emperor to a petition requesting authorisation of a marriage whose illegality had been hidden from the emperor. This law is declaring that even if someone managed to get such a rescript the marriage was still invalid.

46 Someone born of a free mother inherited her free status. See D.1.5.5; AE.11.1.

47 Cf. C.9.11.1; E.17.21; Irene Novel II. For discussion of this law and general issue see J. Evans Grubbs, '"Marriage More Shameful than Adultery": Slave-Mistress Relationships, "Mixed Marriages", and Late Roman Law', *Phoenix* 47 (1993), 125–54.

of drugs intended to kill men. However, it has been ordered by degree of the Senate that a woman who did not mean to do ill, but who through application of a drug causes harm shall be exiled.[48]

2. *Another from the same*
An adulterer and the go-betweens and helpers of such an impious act shall be subject to capital punishment.[49]

3. *Athanasius Scholasticus, from the Digest and the 9th Book of the Codex*
If in any way a woman plots against the life of her husband, or knowing about such a plot does not inform her husband, or against her husband's will drinks or bathes with strange men, or against her husband's wishes sleeps outside his house, except at her parents' house, she shall be separated from him.[50]

4. *From the Penalties of John Kobidas the Antecessor*
Those who summon demons to harm men shall be thrown to the wild beasts.[51]

5. Anyone who commits adultery with someone who has debauched herself for profit with many men shall not be condemned for the crime of adultery, since you cannot commit adultery with someone who works in a brothel.[52]

6. *Another from the same, the 48th Book of the Digest, Constitution 8, Title 19*
If a woman takes money from the substituted heirs to abort her pregnancy, [the aborted child] being her established heir, and through some drug produces a miscarriage, she shall suffer capital punishment.[53]

48 Cf. D.48.8.3; E.17.42.

49 Cf. N.134.10.pr.; E.17.27–28; NM.26.

50 Cf. E.2.9. Athanasius Scholasticus, like John Kobidas and Stephen mentioned below, was an *Antecessor*, a legal expert who in the sixth century created commentaries and summaries in Greek of Justinian's law. As the latter was often in Latin, the works of *Antecessores* rather than the Justinianic original often became the more immediate source for much of Roman law. For more see Introduction, 4.

51 Cf. C.9.18.6.

52 Cf. C.9.9.22; E.17.27. In Roman law, adultery concerned the besmirching of the honour of married women. By (Roman) definition, a prostitute had no honour to besmirch, and therefore one could not commit adultery with a prostitute.

53 Cf. D.48.19.39. In Roman law one could nominate 'substitute heirs' who would take the place of the main heir(s) if he/she/they were unable or unwilling to inherit. See Berger, s.v. 'Substitutio'. In this instance the woman has taken money from these 'substitute heirs'

7. *Another from the same, Book of the Digest, Title 19, Chapter 38*
Those who supply draughts for abortions or aphrodisiacs, even if they do so without any guilty intention, because they set the worst example, those who are of little worth shall be handed over to the mines, while the more honourable shall be exiled to an island and part of their property confiscated. But if for this reason [i.e. supplying the drug] a man or woman should die, then they shall suffer the ultimate penalty.[54]

Title 6

1. *Book 9 of the Codex Digest 7; a Decision*[55]
Anyone who gives poison to a slave instead of medicine shall be liable for the result, since he brought the cause of death. And the person who rashly gave the poison, [brought the cause of death] in the same way as [someone who gives a sword to] a madman.[56]

---

in order to abort her pregnancy, thus allowing them to take up the inheritance that would otherwise go to the unborn child.

54 Cf. D.48.19.38.5; E.17.42; AE.6.8.

55 Burgmann and Troianos suggested that the word 'decision' (*diakrisis*), repeated at AE.6.2–3, 5 and 9, is probably a corruption of the name Ulpian, the prominent third-century jurist whose works form a substantial part of the *Digest*. See 'Appendix Eclogae', 54. It is clear that AE.6 is a virtually verbatim copy of a whole section of the *Collectio Tripartita* (*Coll. Trip.* 2.87–96) the only difference being that anything that remained in Latin in the *Collectio*, such as the names of the jurists, was translated into Greek in the AE. How precisely Ulpian became *diakrisis* is unclear, but a more obvious transformation occurred for another jurist, Modestinus, for which see 101 n. 63.

56 Cf. D.9.2.7.6; *Coll. Trip.* 2.87. As mentioned in the note above, all the chapters of AE.6 are taken verbatim from *Coll. Trip* 2.87–96, which consists of Greek translations of several sections of the *Digest*. Those translations of the *Coll. Trip.* can be so concise that their meaning is rendered unclear, especially once removed from their original context, as is the case here. An added problem has been created by the compilers of AE.6, for they decided to render the legal term *in factum*, left in Latin in the *Coll. Trip.*, as *to ergon*, which in its most natural reading would be read as 'the result', the reading I give above. However, it is referring to the legal term *actio in factum*, a supplementary action appended to the *Lex Aquilia*—on which see 100 n. 58—under which the person who gave the poison to the slave could be sued. How such an action differed in practice from an *actio legis Aquiliae* is unclear in the *Digest*, and was probably even more unclear to the compilers of AE.6, especially considering that the *Coll. Trip.* had removed the clause from the wider context of D.9.2.7.6 that established a difference between an *actio in factum* and an action under the *Lex Aquilia*. Whether the compilers understood the concept of *actio in factum* or not, the overall gist of the chapter is clear: if one negligently poisoned a slave, having meant to give them medicine, then one was liable to provide restitution to the slave's master.

2. *Constitution 8 and 9; a Decision*
If a midwife gives a drug to a slave woman, and the slave dies, she is liable for the result.[57] But if the midwife administers the drug with her own hands, then the *Lex Aquilia* shall apply,[58] just as when someone anoints someone with a drug, or by force or persuasion injects it either through the mouth or through a syringe.[59]

3. *Another from the same Codex, Book 10, Title 2, Constitution 3; a Decision*
Poisons, books on magic and the like found in an inheritance shall not be divided amongst the heirs, but shall be destroyed by the authority of the judge.[60]

4. *Another from Book 18, Title 1, Constitution 35; from Gaius*
Harmful poisons cannot be sold. However, they may be sold if they can act as an antidote when mixed with something else.[61]

5. *Another from Book 48, Title 8, Constitution 2; a Decision*
Anyone who makes, sells or possesses a drug intended to kill men shall be seized and beheaded. But there are drugs that restore health, and others called love philtres. If anyone without evil intent gives a drug designed to promote conception to a woman who then dies, he shall be exiled, as

57 As in the footnote above, *to ergon* has been employed to render the Latin *in factum*, so the midwife is liable to an *actio in factum* for causing the death of the slave.

58 The *Lex Aquilia*, originally passed in the third century BC, regulated issues of damage to other people's property, including damage done to another's slave. In essence, the wrongdoer had to restore the damaged property and, depending on their liability, could be forced to pay some additional multiple of the damaged property as a punishment. To be liable, the damage done had to be the result of a wrongful act, but Roman jurists recognised that in the messy realities of property disputes there existed a huge range of cases, complicating factors and potential liabilities beyond the original confines of the *Lex Aquilia*. Thus arose the theoretical difference between an *actio legis Aquiliae*, an action that was laid down in the original statute, and an *actio in factum*, an action that followed the model of the *Lex Aquilia*. The present chapter ordains that a midwife who supplied but did not directly administer a drug that caused the death of a slave was liable to *actio in factum*, while if a midwife directly administered the drug she could be sued directly under the *Lex Aquilia*. What the practical difference was between the two, such as a difference in penalty, is unknown. Moreover, as stated above, whether there was any practical difference in Justinian's day is unclear, as is whether the compilers of AE.6 had any conceptual grasp of the difference. However, as in AE.6.1, the overall gist is clear: a midwife who caused the death of a slave through provision of a drug was liable to provide restitution to the slave's master. For more on the *Lex Aquilia*, see Berger, s.v. 'Lex Aquilia'; Harries, *Law and Crime*, 46–49.

59 Cf. D.9.2.9.pr.–1; *Coll. Trip.* 2.88.

60 Cf. D.10.2.4.1; *Coll. Trip.* 2.89.

61 Cf. D.18.1.35.2; *Coll. Trip.* 2.90.

will any apothecary who recklessly gives anyone hemlock, salamander, aconite, pinecones, venomous beetles, mandrake or Spanish fly, as is laid down in the third Constitution [D.48.8.3]; also consult the first constitution of the same title [D.48.8.1].[62]

6. *From the same Title, Constitution 13; in the same manner again*[63]
Anyone who makes or holds forbidden sacrifices shall be subject to beheading.[64]

7. *Title 9, Constitution 30; in the same manner*
Anyone who does anything to pervert the more simple-minded from the worship of God shall be exiled.[65]

8. *Constitution 35; Paul again*
Anyone who gives a draught as an aphrodisiac or to produce an abortion, even if done without malice, shall be condemned to the mines if he is of little worth, but if he is honourable he shall be exiled and have part of his property confiscated; but if anyone should die from this, he shall bring upon himself the ultimate penalty.[66]

9. *Book 47, Title 10, Constitution 15; a Decision*
Anyone who drives someone insane with a drug is liable to infamy and guilty of insult.[67]

62 Cf. D.48.8.1, 3; *Coll. Trip.* 2.91.

63 According to Burgmann and Troianos, *tropos palin*, '[in the same] manner again', with *tropos* repeated on its own at AE.6.7, is a corruption of Modestinus, the third-century Roman jurist. See 'Appendix Eclogae', 54. Their argument is that in the original, *Coll. Trip.* 2.92–93, Modestinus is rendered in Latin characters as 'Mod.', with the addition of *idem*, 'again', in the first instance. Rather than recognising the name of the jurist, the compilers of AE.6 took 'Mod.' to mean *modus*, and translated it into Greek as *tropos*. See also Van der Waal and Stolte, *Collectio Tripartita*, xxxi.

64 Cf. D.48.8.13; *Coll. Trip.* 2.92.

65 Cf. D.48.19.30; *Coll. Trip.* 2.93.

66 Cf. D.48.19.38.5; *Coll. Trip.* 2.94. This chapter covers exactly the same portion of the *Digest* as AE.5.7, though the latter is distinctly closer to the Latin original than this summary taken from the *Collectio Tripartita*. That this obvious overlap was retained is further evidence of the extremely limited editing undertaken by the compilers of AE.6.

67 Cf. D.47.10.15.pr.; *Coll. Trip.* 2.95. Interestingly, the compilers of AE.6 decided to render *iniuria*, the wide-ranging delict of injury or insult, as *atimia* ('infamy'), which strictly was the result of being condemned for *iniuria*. They then added a clause that made clear that the condemned were guilty of *iniuria* and, more precisely, its subcategory of *contumelia*, insult or *hubris* in Greek. For *iniuria* and *contumelia*, see I.4.4.pr; Berger, s.v. 'Contumelia' and 'Iniuria'; Harries, *Law and Crime*, 49–50.

10. *A Constitution from the same*
If an astrologer or other practitioner of forbidden divination should, on being consulted, say that someone is a thief when he is not, he shall not be liable to infamy, but subject to the imperial constitutions [i.e. those against astrologers and diviners].[68]

Title 7

1. *From the Paratitla of the Codex, Title 18, Constitution 3*
Anyone who divines through sacrifices or is a priest of the pagans and enters another's house shall be burned alive, while the one who summoned him shall have his property confiscated and be deported.[69]

2. *Another, Constitution 4*
A magician, even if he is not practising, shall be punished for his knowledge.[70]

3. *Another, Constitution 6*
Magicians shall be thrown to the wild beasts.[71]

4. *Another, Constitution 7*
Those in Constantinople who practise divination, even if they are of high rank, shall be hung on a piece of wood and scourged.[72]

5. *Another, Constitution 9*
A charioteer or other such person who consults with a sorcerer shall suffer the ultimate punishment.[73]

68 Cf. D.47.10.15.13; *Coll. Trip.* 2.96. Once again the compilers of AE.6 have rendered *iniuria* as *atimia* rather than the more accurate *hubris*.

69 Cf. C.9.18.3.

70 Cf. C.9.18.4.

71 Cf. C.9.18.6.

72 Cf. C.9.18.7.

73 Cf. C.9.18.9.

Title 8: Concerning that no heretic, Jew or pagan may have, possess or circumcise a Christian slave

1. *Book 1 of the Codex, Title 10*
A Jew may not by any means whatsoever possess a Christian slave or another of any heresy or ethnicity. And if he has a slave and circumcises him, then the slave shall be freed, while he shall suffer capital punishment.[74]

2. *Another from the same*
A pagan, Jew, Samaritan and whoever is not orthodox shall not be able to possess a Christian slave, and therefore he shall be freed and his owner shall pay thirty pounds of gold to the *Res Privata*.[75]

3. *Another from the Paratitla of the same Book, Title 3, Constitution 54*
No Jew, pagan or heretic may possess a Christian slave; and if anyone is found doing so the slave shall immediately be carried away to freedom.[76]

4. *Another from the same Book, Title 7, Constitution 5*
Anyone who forces or persuades a slave to depart from Christianity and go over to an unlawful heresy, shall have his property confiscated and be beheaded.[77]

5. *Another from the same Book, Title 9, Constitution 16*
We impose confiscation of property and perpetual exile on Jews proven to have circumcised a Christian or to have commanded another to do this.[78]

6. *Another from the same Book of the Paratitla, Title 3, Constitution 54*
If a slave who serves a pagan, Jew, Samaritan or heretic is not a Christian but now desires to become one, he shall at the same time as being baptised be carried away to freedom, and his master cannot return him to slavery, even if he himself becomes a Christian.[79]

74 Cf. C.1.10.1; *Coll. Trip.* 1.10.1.

75 Cf. C.1.10.2; *Coll. Trip.* 1.10.2. The *Res Privata* was one of the great finance departments of late antiquity, whose primary responsibility was management of the emperor's property. See Jones, *Later Roman Empire*, 412–27.

76 Cf. C.1.3.54.8; *Coll. Trip.* 1.10. Parat. 1; AE.8.6.

77 Cf. C.1.7.5; *Coll. Trip.* 1.10. Parat. 2.

78 Cf. C.1.9.16; *Coll. Trip.* 1.10. Parat. 3.

79 Cf. C.1.3.54.9–10; *Coll. Trip.* 1.13. Parat. 1; AE.8.3.

Title 9: Concerning the degrees of kinship[80]

From the 3rd Book of the Institutes
Kinship is a generic term. It is divided into three orders: into ascendants, that is those who made us; into descendants, that is those born of us; and across, i.e. collaterals, that is to say the siblings of our father and mother, both uncles and aunts and their offspring in succession.

1. Of the first degree are ascending father and mother, descending son and daughter.

2. Of the second degree are ascending grandfather and grandmother, descending grandson and granddaughter, and collaterally brother and sister born of both our father and mother.

3. Of the third degree are ascending great-grandfather and great-grandmother, descending great-grandson and great-granddaughter, and collaterally son and daughter of brother and sister, and paternal and maternal aunt and uncle.

4. Of the fourth degree are ascending great-great-grandparents, descending great-great-grandchildren, and collaterally the grandchildren of a brother and sister, and correspondingly great uncles and great aunts, either paternal or maternal, that is the brother and sister of a grandfather or grandmother, and cousins, male or female, who are the offspring of two siblings.

5. Of the fifth degree are ascending great-great-great-grandparents, descending great-great-great-grandchildren, and collaterally great-grandchildren of a brother or sister, and correspondingly great-great uncle and aunt on either side, that is the brother or sister of a great-grandfather or great-grandmother, and the brother and sister of an uncle or aunt on either side, that is the son and daughter of a great aunt or uncle, and the grandchildren of a paternal and maternal aunt or uncle.

6. Of the sixth degree are ascending great-great-great-great-grandparents, descending great-great-great-great-grandchildren, and collaterally great-great-grandchildren of a brother or sister, and correspondingly great-great-great uncles and aunts, that is brothers or sisters of great-great-grandparents, are of the same degree, as are the offspring of two cousins, that is those who are son or daughter of a great-great uncle or aunt, the

80 Cf. I.3.6.pr.–6, 9; E.2.2.

grandchildren of a great aunt or uncle, and the great-grandchildren of an aunt or uncle, either maternal or paternal.

7. But since seeing is more precise than hearing, we have attached to this present book along with the narration of the degrees a diagram of them, so that the readers might learn by hearing and seeing the entirety of the system.[81]

8. This is a diagram of degrees; there are three orders of kinship: ascendants, descendants and across, i.e. collaterals. Higher kin are parents, lower are children, and collaterals are siblings, their descendants, and correspondingly uncles and aunts, either paternal or maternal, and their offspring according to the present form of this diagram.

Title 10: Concerning natural children, legitimate and illegitimate

1. *From the 115th New Constitution*
Children born from different marriages, even if one of the marriages was without a dowry, shall be equal successors of their father. And after a divorce the children shall be their parents' heirs, and they shall stay with and be supported by their father if he did not give the grounds for divorce. But if he did give the grounds for divorce, then they shall live with their mother so long as she does not remarry, and be maintained by their father. But if the father is poor they shall be supported by and live with their mother.[82]

2. *From the 18th New Constitution*
Anyone who has children with a freedwoman and then makes a dowry contract, makes the children legitimate, even those who were born before. And anyone who has children with a slave woman, and later makes her, and simultaneously their children, free and then makes a dowry contract with the woman, then the marriage shall be lawful and the children legitimate.[83]

3. *From the 87th New Constitution*
Anyone who, dying, has a concubine and illegitimate children, if he has legitimate children and is without a wife, he can only leave [his concubine

81 In some MSS, though not all, a consanguinity table showing the different degrees of kinship is appended.

82 Cf. N.117.3–7; E.2.9.

83 Cf. N.18.11.

and illegitimate children] at most one twelfth [of his estate]; and if he only has a concubine then he can give her one twenty-fourth; and if he should give more, then his legitimate children can claim this. If he has no legitimate children or ascendants, then if he wishes he can give everything to them [his concubine and illegitimate children]; but if he is survived by ascendants, they shall receive their legal share, and the rest shall be divided as he wishes. If a man dies intestate and has illegitimate children, and also a wife and/or legitimate children, then the illegitimate shall receive nothing, but shall be supported by the heirs; but if he does not have legitimate heirs, the illegitimate children shall receive one sixth only, either with their mother or, she being dead, they alone; and the remainder shall go to the next of kin or, if there is no next of kin, to the Treasury. Anyone who has a wife cannot have a concubine. Neither can the children from different concubines be the heirs of their father, for they are neither illegitimate children of an unlawful marriage, nor legitimate heirs of their father, nor supported by him.[84]

4. *From the 5th Title of the 1st Book of the Digest*
Those children born from fornication and of unknown birth are called bastards. These follow their mother, while legitimate children follow their father.[85]

Title 11

1. *From the 1st Book of the Digest Title 5*
All law that is administered by us refers to persons, things or actions. Since therefore all law has been established for the sake of mankind, we shall speak first about men. All men are either free or slaves. Freedom is the ability to do as one pleases, save for what is prevented by law or force. Slavery is an institution of the Law of Nations, through which someone is subject to a master. Slavery is undifferentiated; but of the free, some are born free, while others are emancipated. The freeborn are those born of a free woman, whether she was free at the time of conception, or at the time of the birth, or anytime in between, and whether she conceived in lawful wedlock or illicit sex. Freedmen are those who have been manumitted from slavery.[86]

84 Cf. N.89.12.

85 Cf. D.1.5.23–24.

86 Cf. D.1.5. Most MSS do not include this chapter.

2. Concerning justice and law
From the 1st and 2nd Titles of the 1st Book of the Institutes
Justice is a constant and perpetual desire to apportion to each their rights. Learning in the law entails the knowledge of things divine and human, and of what is just and unjust. The commandments of the law are to live honourably and harm nobody.[87]

3. Concerning divine and human law
From the 8th Title of the 1st Book of the Digest
All things are either of divine law or human. And those things which are subject to divine law belong to no one, while those of man are someone's property. Further, some things are corporeal, which can be touched, while others are incorporeal, such as inheritance, usufruct, obligation, servitudes.[88] And some things belong to all men through natural law, some to the community, some to no one and some to individuals. By natural law the air, flowing water, the sea and the seashore belong to all. Rivers and harbours are public property. Theatres, stadia and the like belong to the community. The walls are sanctified, that is holy, and anything that violates them is forbidden. Sacred places are those consecrated in public, either in the city or the countryside.[89]

4. *From the Digest, Book 1, Title 1*
Nearly all rivers and harbours are not common to all men, but are owned by the state. However, the use of the rivers and their banks is naturally common to all. Wherefore everyone is allowed to anchor their boat to a bank, and tie their ship's cable to a tree rooted in the bank, and to dry their nets and place cargo on a bank. But the ownership of all riverbanks belongs to those whose fields join it, and the trees growing on the bank also belong to them. Those who fish in the sea may have a hut on the shore.[90]

5. Concerning natural law, the law of peoples and civil law
From the 1st Title of the 1st Book of the Digest
The law is divided into public and private. Public law is that directed towards the constitution of the state, and concerns holy things, the

87 Cf. I.1.1.pr.–1, 3.

88 Usufruct, *chrēsis* in Greek, was a right to use another's property and enjoy its produce without impairing its substance. An obligation, in Greek *enochē*, was a legal tie to do or give something. A servitude was a right to make a certain use of another's property. See Berger, s.v. 'Obligatio', 'Servitus (servitutes)' and 'Ususfructus'; Avotins, 'χρῆσις' and 'ἐνοχή'.

89 Cf. D.1.8.1–2, 4, 6.1, 8.2–9.pr.

90 Cf. D.1.8.4–5. This chapter only appears in the same MSS that include AE.11.1.

priesthood and public officials. Private law is divided into natural law, the law of peoples and civil law. Natural law is that which is common to all animals, such as union, procreation, rearing of children and the like. The law of peoples is that which is common to all men, such as natural reason, the worship of God, obedience to parents and fatherland, slavery, all transactions and the right to avoid violence or injustice, for it is allowed for everyone to do something for the safety of their own body. The same law concerns manumission, after the introduction of slavery; thus there came to be three classes of men: free men, slaves and freedmen. From this law came wars, separate nations, kingdoms, property, boundaries of farms, lawful sale, purchase and all obligations, with the exception of those introduced through civil law. Civil law is specific to each polity, and is divided into written and unwritten, and consists of the law of all the people, statutes and edicts, and also the decrees of the emperor, whether given in a judgement or prescribed through an edict. It is altered either by disuse or the giving of other laws. And all people are subject either to the law of peoples or civil law.

All law refers to either persons, things or actions. All men are either free or slaves, and people become slaves either by the law of peoples or civil law; by the law of peoples as prisoners of war, and by civil law as someone who is sold. Therefore slaves have a single condition, while the free are divided into those who were born free and freedmen.[91]

Title 12

From the ancient law; Concerning witnesses; from the Codex, Title 20, Constitution 9

Witnesses must be put on oath before they give their testimony, and the testimony of the more honourable shall be more favourably received; but the testimony of only one [witness] shall be rejected, even if the witness happens to be a curial.[92]

91 Cf. D.1.1.2–7, 9; D.1.5.1, 3, 5.pr.–1.

92 Cf. C.4.20.9; E.14; NM.48–49. A *curial*, or *bouleutēs* in Greek, was a member of a municipal council. The institution largely died out in the sixth century, though the status lingered on for some time. It is unlikely that it had any sense in the eighth century. See Jones, *Later Roman Empire*, 737–57.

Title 13

1. *From the Book of the Codex of Justinian by Stephen the Antecessor; Concerning the appointment of heirs, and those who can and cannot be appointed; Chapter 5*
A wife is not invalid as an heir of her husband because in the will she is not called wife but a relative or fiancée.[93]

2. *From the same Book of the Codex; Concerning legacies*
Even if a husband has only been married to his wife for two months, or even less time, he is not invalid as a testamentary heir, or to receive legacies and gifts.[94]

3. *From the same, Title 38, Chapter 4*
If someone should say, 'Let so-and-so or so-and-so be my heir, let this or that person be given a legacy, let so-and-so or so-and-so be free or be a guardian', then let each one be named as heir, legatee, free or guardian. But if one person only is mentioned, but two properties, this or that, then the ancient rules shall apply without innovation. And this shall also apply to contracts.[95]

4. *From the 7th Book; Concerning all pleas to a judge; Chapter 9*
The magistrate shall not give a decision concerning something that has already been brought before him and decided according to law; but neither can a sentence concerning possession prejudge one concerning ownership, nor can an interlocutory decision generally destroy a cause of action.[96]

5. *From the 8th Book; Concerning pledges; Chapter 27*
A [hypothecated] field which fulfils the debt through payment of its produce shall be released from the *hypothec*, and because of this the field cannot be alienated by the creditor.[97]

93 Cf. C.6.24.5.

94 Cf. C.6.37.19.

95 Cf. C.6.38.4.

96 Cf. C.7.45.9. What this law is saying is that, in general, a magistrate cannot give a second ruling on the same dispute, but if he gives a ruling on possession, this does not automatically preclude a ruling on ownership. Moreover, an interlocutory statement, that is a provisional decree given during the course of a trial, did not quash further legal actions.

97 Cf. C.8.27.1; NG.67. A *hypothec* was a form of security against a debt. Originally it referred to a pledge that physically remained in the hands of the debtor, but which he could not alienate. However, Justinian's reforms turned it into an ordinary pledge or *pignus*,

6. *From the 8th Book of the Codex, abridged by Stephen the Antecessor, Chapter 11*
Anyone who without force has occupied the vacant possessions of an absent person can in general only keep possession when the plea of thirty years of possession has been completed.[98]

7. *From the same 8th Book of the Codex, by Stephen the Antecessor, Concerning when the property of absent people is plundered by force or other means; Title 5, Chapter 1*
Whatever relative, friend, tenant or slave possesses an absent person's property on his behalf for whatever cause, the magistrate must maintain the possession unchanged, with that person restoring it to the absentee; nor shall [the magistrate] reject [hearing] the person ejected from possession desiring to bring a case, even if he has no mandate to bring the suit, nor even if the time determined for bringing a suit concerning restoration has passed. And if the aforementioned persons [i.e. those entrusted with possession who have been ejected from the property] should be neglectful [in bringing an action to restore possession], the completion of time for restitution shall not be held against the owner, but the possession shall be restored, while maintaining the action concerning ownership.[99]

8. *From the 7th Book of the abridged Codex of Justinian; Concerning freed slaves and creditors discovered after the manumission and the death of the testator; Chapter 15*
If anyone should die, either testate or intestate, and make bequests of freedom, but on account of the poverty of the estate no one wants to succeed to the inheritance, it is allowed for one of those manumitted or

---

whereby the pledged thing was handed over to the creditor. What this law is saying is that if the income from the farm pays the debt for which the farm was pledged as security, the creditor has no right to alienate it. See Berger, 'Hypotheca', 'Pignus'.

98 Cf. C.8.4.11.

99 Cf. C.8.5.1. This law concerns the property of absentee landowners, which they have entrusted to another, and has then been occupied by a third party. Magistrates were instructed to hear cases brought for restitution of property either by those who had been entrusted with the property or, should the former fail to do so, by the owner. Moreover, the usual time limitations on bringing a case concerning restitution of possession of property were waived when absent persons were concerned, who, thanks to their absence, were unable to personally uphold their possession in court. The resolution of correct possession did not necessarily resolve questions of rightful ownership, however, and so the action to restore correct ownership was still open.

any free outsider to accept the inheritance, provided that he gives security regarding the payment of creditors and gives freedom to those slaves granted it. But if it happened that the inherited estate was sold to multiple purchasers, it is still possible for the aforementioned [i.e. the manumitted or a free outsider], upon giving securities concerning the debts and the manumissions, to receive the bought property within a year [of the death]. But if he promises to pay the creditors only a part of what was promised and they agree to this, this shall be acceptable. And if any of those granted their freedom decline it, only those who desire it shall be freed. But if the property is insufficient to grant freedom to all, it is acceptable for the claimant to promise freedom to some of them. If many simultaneously claim the inheritance and undertake to furnish security for all the debts, they shall receive it; but if they come forward at different times, then the first to do so shall be preferred, unless he cannot give the security, when the next one who can shall have it. This shall be done within a year. And if one of them promises to free some of the slaves, while a second promises to give all of them freedom and fulfil the debts the latter shall be preferred. It is allowed for an inherited slave to do this, even if he has not been granted his freedom. In which case, if the first claimant has already received the property and given some of the slaves freedom, and a second promises to do more, then the property shall be taken away from the first, but definitely not his freedom; again, this shall be done within a year of the first claimant. Take note that no one may decline Roman citizenship beyond the present case.[100]

9. *From the same 7th Book; Concerning those who write they are a slave, Chapter 6*
Even if anyone should freely write that they are a slave this would not invalidate their status, and even more so if this was done under compulsion.[101]

100 Cf. C.7.2.15.
101 Cf. C.7.16.6.

Title 14

From the 7th Book of the Code of Justinian; Concerning freedmen
Imperial slaves, that is the *coloni* and their offspring, who have fled and entered state service or obtained a dignity through deceit, shall have the girdle of office removed and be returned to the patrimony.[102]

102 Cf. C.7.38.1. The 'girdle of office' (Greek *zōnē*, Latin *cingulum*) was originally a legionary's sword belt, but from the reign of Diocletian onwards became a central part of the official insignia of all Roman officials, both civil and military. See Jones, *Later Roman Empire*, 566. *Coloni* were peasants tied to cultivation of a particular piece of land. See Jones, *Later Roman Empire*, 795–803.

THE RHODIAN SEA LAW[1]

Part II[2]
The chapters of the Rhodian law

1. A captain's pay is two shares.[3]
2. A steersman's pay is a share and a half.
3. A commander of the bow's pay is a share and a half.
4. A ship carpenter's pay is a share and a half.
5. A boatswain's pay is a share and a half.
6. A sailor's pay is one share.
7. A cook's pay is half a share.[4]
8. A merchant may have on board two boys, but he must pay their fare.
9. A passenger's space is three cubits in length, one cubit in width.[5]

1 *Nomos Rhodion Nautikos*, ed. W. Ashburner, *The Rhodian Sea-Law* (Oxford, 1909), with an English translation and commentary. See also the new edition of the *Rhodian Sea Law* as it was incorporated into the *Basilica*: G. Rodolakes, *Apo to Nomo Rodiōn sto 53o Biblio tōn Basilikōn: sumbolē stē meletē tou Buzantinou nautikou dikaiou* (Athens, 2007). This latter version is almost identical to Ashburner's text.

2 Note that Part 1, the legendary and almost certainly later account of the *Rhodian Sea Law*'s creation, is not included here.

3 The *nauklēros*, the Greek equivalent of the Latin *navicularius*, was in late antiquity a shipper, and either a member of the guild that supplied Rome and Constantinople, or the owner of the ship. See Jones, *Later Roman Empire*, 827–30, 866–72. However, throughout most of the *Rhodian Sea Law* he is clearly a captain who may or may not own the ship. See NN.3.8 for an example where the captain is not the owner of the ship.

4 Ashburner speculates that the Greek term *parascharitēs* actually refers to a deckhand, rather than a ship's cook, whom one would expect to be paid more than half a share. Although plausible, this cannot be proved. See *Rhodian Sea-Law*, 58–59.

5 A cubit (*pēchus*) was the length of a forearm, and was given different lengths in different circumstances, with variants from one-and-a-third to two Roman feet, or 46.8 cm to 62.5 cm. See E. Schilbach, *Byzantinische Metrologie* (Munich, 1970), 43–55.

10. A passenger may not fry fish on board; the captain must not allow him.

11. A passenger may not split wood on board; the captain must not allow him.

12. A passenger on board shall receive water by measure.

13. Women on board shall have a space of one cubit; a grown-up child half a cubit.

14. If a passenger comes aboard a ship and has gold, he shall deposit it with the captain. But if he does not deposit it and says that he has lost his gold or silver, then his words shall have no effect since he did not deposit it with the captain.

15. The captain, passengers and sailors who sail together shall give an oath on the gospels.[6]

16. A ship with all its equipment shall be valued at fifty gold pieces for every thousand *modii* [of capacity] and shall come into the contribution; but when the ship is old it shall be valued at thirty gold pieces [per thousand *modii* of capacity]. And in the valuation a third shall be deducted, and as such the ship shall come into the contribution.[7]

17. The law orders: one shall not write out land loans, free from risk, on the sea, and if they are written they shall be invalid according to the Rhodian law. But land loans, free from risk, may be written on fields or mountains according to the Rhodian law.[8]

18. If anyone should borrow at interest, and for eight years pays the legal interest, and then it happens after eight years that there is destruction, fire or plundering by barbarians, then the payment of interest shall end according to the Rhodian law. If he does not pay the legal interest, then the

6 NN.2.14–15. Cf. NN.3.13; E.11.

7 A *modius* was a standard measure of capacity, and equalled 40 pounds of grain or 17.084 litres. See Schilbach, *Metrologie*, 56–59, 95–108. The phrase 'come into the contribution' (*eis sumbolēn*), repeated throughout the *Rhodian Sea Law*, refers to the principle that losses caused by the perils of the sea, along with any resultant salvage, should be shared proportionally between parties on a sea venture. It is with fixing the liabilities of various parties in widely differing scenarios that the bulk of the *Rhodian Sea Law* is concerned.

8 For NN.2.17–19 cf. D.22.2; I.3.14; E.10; NN.3.16–18. Roman law distinguished between ordinary, or 'land', loans and more risky maritime loans. In the former the lender had the right of a return of the capital, while in the latter he shared in the risk. To compensate for this, maritime loans commanded a higher rate of interest.

written agreement shall prevail according to the former agreement, just as the document says.[9]

19. Captains who own the ship, who contribute no less than three quarters of the value of the ship, wherever they are dispatched, may borrow money as is necessary and dispatch it by ship for a summer or a voyage, and what they have contracted shall prevail. The lender shall send a man to administer the loan.

Part III
Chapters selected from the Rhodian law concerning sailors

1. Concerning anchors stolen from a ship.
2. Concerning anchors and other stolen equipment.
3. Concerning a sailor who commits a theft.
4. Concerning a ship plundered by thieves or pirates.
5. Concerning sailors who cause injuries in a fight.
6. Concerning sailors who commit homicide in a fight.
7. Concerning sailors who maim an eye or cause a genital hernia in a fight.
8. Concerning a captain and sailors who take someone else's cargo and run away with the ship.
9. Concerning a captain and passengers deliberating about jettison.
10. Concerning a ship that is damaged or wrecked.
11. Concerning merchants hiring ships.
12. Concerning all deposits given on a ship or in a house.
13. Concerning a disputed deposit of gold.
14. Concerning a depositary who denies receipt of the deposit.
15. Concerning a merchant, passenger or slave who has been deposited, left on the shore by a ship fleeing from pillage or attack by robbers.

9 This rather cumbersomely written chapter seems to be saying that if someone has not paid eight years of interest the terms of the contract still apply, and that none of the disasters listed relieved the debtor of his debt.

16. Concerning transmarine loans that have been lent out.[10]

17. Concerning gold and silver lent against a share of profits.

18. Concerning borrowing money for a fixed time and going abroad.

19. Concerning hiring a ship and giving a deposit.

20. Concerning hiring a ship and agreeing either in writing or coming to terms orally.

21. Concerning disputes of two captains in partnership.

22. Concerning a merchant who hires the whole cargo hold of the ship.

23. Concerning a captain and a merchant who make an agreement about cargo.

24. Concerning a change of mind after a captain and a merchant have made an agreement, and the half-freight charge is paid.

25. Concerning a merchant who goes beyond the time fixed by the contract.

26. Concerning a ship wrecked while the sailors are asleep.

27. Concerning a ship wrecked while en route to be loaded by a merchant or partner.

28. Concerning a ship wrecked due to the fault of a merchant or partner.

29. Concerning a ship wrecked either before or after the time agreed in the contract.

30. Concerning a ship loaded with cargo that is lost while the merchant, who is carrying gold, is saved.

31. Concerning a ship that suffers harm and a portion of the cargo is saved.

32. Concerning a ship hired or sailing in partnership that is wrecked en route to be loaded.

33. Concerning a ship wrecked after unloading.

34. Concerning a ship carrying silk and the cargo is damaged by a storm or bilge water.

10 *Chrymata epipontia*, here translated as 'transmarine loan', is the Greek equivalent of *pecunia traiecticia*, money that was lent as part of a *fenus nauticum* loan, a loan connected with the transportation of merchandise by vessel. See Berger, s.v. 'Fenus nauticum'; Ashburbner, *Rhodian Sea-Law*, 74.

35. Concerning a ship that jettisons its mast.

36. Concerning a ship which hits another ship while sailing.

37. Concerning a ship wrecked while the merchants' and passengers' goods are saved.

38. Concerning a ship loaded with grain that is caught in a storm.

39. Concerning a loaded ship that sinks while the cargo is saved.

40. Concerning a ship that is wrecked and a portion of the ship and the cargo are saved.

41. Concerning a ship that is destroyed, and the goods of the merchants are either saved or lost.

42. Concerning a ship that springs a leak while carrying cargo.

43. Concerning a ship that jettisons cargo and equipment.

44. Concerning a ship that jettisons its mast or its tillers in a storm.

45. Concerning anyone who brings to safety something from the open sea to the land from a wrecked ship.

46. Concerning anyone who saves a boat that has broken off from a ship.

47. Concerning anyone who brings to safety something from the depths from a wrecked ship.

The beginning of the law

1. If a ship moored in harbour or on the coast is robbed of its anchors, and the caught thief confesses, then the law orders that he be tortured and shall make good the damage caused twice over.[11]

2. If the crew, following the wishes of their captain, rob the anchors of another ship which is lying in harbour or on the coast, and in consequence of the theft of the anchors it happens that the ship is lost, and this is conclusively proved, then the captain who ordered the theft shall make good all the damage caused both to the ship and what was on it. If anyone should steal the equipment of the ship or anything used aboard ship (i.e. ropes, hemp, sails, skins, boats and the rest), the thief shall pay back twice the value.

3. If a sailor robs a merchant or passenger on the orders of the captain, and is caught red-handed, the captain shall restore twice the value of the thing stolen, and the sailor shall receive a hundred blows. If the sailor stole on his own volition and is either caught or proved guilty through witnesses, then he shall be severely tortured, especially so if the thing stolen was gold, and he shall make restitution to the person robbed.

4. If a ship puts into a place infested with thieves and robbers, after the passengers have testified to the captain about the reputation of the place, and a robbery occurs, then the captain shall make good the loss to those robbed. However, if the passengers should bring in the ship despite the captain's protests and something happens, then the passengers shall bear the loss.

5. If sailors fight, then let them do it with words and let no one strike another. However, if someone should strike another on the head and opens it or injures him in any other way then he shall pay the doctor's fees and expenses to the person he has injured, and his wages for all the time he is away from work recovering.[12]

11 For NN.3.1–4 cf. E.17.11. All the cases here involve some form of aggravated or complex theft not adequately covered by the basic injunction of E.17.11. At the same time, the *Rhodian Sea Law* has no general rule concerning theft, presumably because it was considered superfluous, either because the general Roman principles were well known or because the *Ecloga*, drawing on those principles, had provided the rule.

12 Cf. NM.45.

6. If sailors fight and someone strikes with a stone or piece of wood, and having been struck the other hits back at the first striker, having been compelled to do so, then if the struck man should die and it is proved that he struck first with either a stone, or a piece of wood or iron, then the person who struck back shall be guiltless of murder; for he [who died] suffered what he wished to do.[13]

7. If one of the officers,[14] merchants or sailors should strike another with his fist and should blind him, or giving him a kick should cause a hernia, then the assailant must pay for a doctor, and for an eye twelve gold pieces, and for a hernia ten. If the kicked man should die, then the assailant shall be liable to trial for homicide.

8. If a captain who has been entrusted with a ship sets sail and runs away to another country with gold and with the consent of the crew, then all their property—movable, immovable and self-moving[15]—as much as they own, shall be seized. And unless the value of the things seized and sold is equal to the value of the ship and the profits of the time,[16] then the crew together with the one acting for the shipowner[17] shall be let out for hire and so make up the loss.

9. If the captain is deliberating about jettison he must inquire of the passengers who have goods on board, and they shall vote on what should be done. The goods shall be brought into the contribution; bedding, clothes and utensils shall all be valued, and if there is a jettison, [the share of] the captain and [each of] the passengers [that is jettisoned] shall not exceed the value of one pound, [the share of] of a steersman and a commander of the bow no more than half a pound, [and the share of] a

13 NN.3.6–7, cf. E.17.45–48; NM. 46.

14 'Officers' seems the most natural translation of *nauklēroi*, which would normally be translated as 'captains'. Certainly the Latin plural in the central Middle Ages could be used to mean the whole mass of officers on a ship. See Ashburner, *Rhodian Sea-Law*, cxxxvii.

15 Roman law divided property into three categories: movable (*res mobiles*; *pragmata kinēta*), immovable (*res immobiles*; *pragmata akinēta*) and self-moving (*res se moventes*; *pragmata autokinēta*). See e.g. C.1.3.43.4. Self-moving property included such things as slaves and animals.

16 The rubric tells us that the ship was carrying *enthēkē*, capital or cargo, and it is for the lost profit on this that the miscreants could be charged.

17 The *pronauklēros*. This was the same *nauklēros*, 'captain', who was entrusted with the ship, and this chapter is one of the few in the *Rhodian Sea Law* that reveal that the captain and shipowner were not necessarily one and the same.

sailor no more than three *grammata*.[18] Boys and anyone else on board who are not being carried for sale shall be valued; if anyone is being carried to be sold they shall be valued at two *minas*.[19] Similarly, if goods have been taken away by enemies, robbers or by those on state service, these shall be brought into the calculation, together with the belongings of the sailors, and shall come into the contribution on the same principle. If there is an agreement to share profit in common, then after everything on board the ship and the ship itself have been brought to contribution, then each man shall bear the loss that has occurred in proportion to his share of the profit.[20]

10. If the captain, together with the crew, is negligent and some damage or shipwreck occurs, the captain and the crew are liable to make restitution to the merchant for the loss. However, if it is through the negligence of the merchant that the ship and cargo are lost, then the merchant is liable for the loss of the ship and the wreck. But if there is no negligence by the captain or the crew or the merchant and a wreck happens, then the salvage from the ship and cargo shall come into the contribution.

11. Merchants and passengers shall not load heavy or valuable goods onto an old ship. If they do, and the ship is damaged or destroyed while sailing, then the person who loaded their cargo onto the old ship has ruined himself on the land.[21] Whenever merchants hire a ship they must strictly enquire from other merchants who have sailed on that ship before, and before putting aboard their cargo, [enquire] whether the ship is completely prepared, with a strong mast and yard,[22] sails, skins, anchors, hemp ropes of high quality, completely furnished boats with suitable tillers and sailors sufficient for sailing who are vigorous and watchful, and that the ship's

18 3 *grammata* = 1/8 of an ounce, or 1/96 of a pound, or 9 *miliaresia*. See Schilbach, *Metrologie*, 184. This seems distinctly small and could be a scribal error for an ounce, which would mean that a sailor's share would be capped at 1/4 of a pound, which would accord with the general pattern. One MS has it as 3 *nomismata* or 1/24 of a pound, which would also make more sense than 3 *grammata*. See Ashburner, *Rhodian Sea-Law*, 88–90.

19 A *mina* was a classicising way of saying *litra* or pound. See Schilbach, *Metrologie*, 171–76.

20 Cf. E.10.4.

21 Presumably an idiom meaning that they have only themselves to blame. See Ashburner, *Rhodian Sea-Law*, 92.

22 For *histokeraia* as mast and yard rather than sail-yard, see M. McCormick, *Origins of the European Economy: Communications and Commerce, AD 300–900* (Cambridge, 2001), 410 n. 97.

sides are not loose. In a word, the merchants shall enquire into everything and then embark.

12. If anyone makes a deposit on a ship or in a house, then he shall deposit with a man known to him and trustworthy and before three witnesses. If the deposit is large, then he shall make a written document when handing over the deposit. If the man who accepted to keep the deposit should say that it is lost, he must show where the opening was forced through or how the theft took place, and swear that he has not undertaken a fraud. If he does not demonstrate this, then he shall restore the goods just as he received them.[23]

13. If a passenger comes on board a ship and has gold or something else, then he must deposit it with the captain. But if he does not deposit it and says that he has lost his gold or silver, then his words shall have no effect. But the captain and the crew and all those on board shall together give an oath.[24]

14. If a man who has received a deposit denies it, and testimony is taken on the matter and in due course it is found on him after he has sworn an oath or denied his liability in writing, then he shall restore twice the amount and suffer the penalty for perjury.[25]

15. If a ship carries passengers, merchants or slaves who have been received as a deposit by the captain,[26] and the captain goes to some city, harbour or shore, and while some of them are disembarked from the ship it happens that robbers give chase or pirates attack,[27] and the captain, having given the order [to sail], escapes and the ship is saved along with the property of the passengers and merchants being carried, then each shall take back his own goods, and those who left the ship shall also receive their goods and chattels. But if anyone wishes to make a claim against the captain, that he left him on shore in a place infested with robbers, his words shall have no effect, since the captain and crew fled while being pursued. But if any of the merchants or passengers who have received another's slave as a deposit should leave [the slave] behind in any place whatsoever, then he shall make good the loss to his master.

23 NN.3.12–14 cf. E.11.

24 Cf. NN.2.14–15.

25 Cf. 17.2.

26 Slaves, as property, were described as being deposited when entrusted to someone's safekeeping.

27 For the punishment of robbers and pirates see E.17.50.

16. Captains and merchants who borrow whatever sum of money upon a ship shall not make a land loan, nor for a freight charge or cargo, with the ship and the money having been kept safe, lest the money fall prey to the hazards of the sea or the plots of pirates. Let them pay back a land loan with maritime interest.[28]

17. If anyone gives gold or silver for the business of a partnership, and this for the purpose of a sea voyage, and he writes down, as it pleases him, up to when the partnership should last, and then the man who took the gold or the silver does not hand it over to its owner after the time is fulfilled, and it happens that misfortune befalls through fire or robbers or shipwreck, then the owner of the money shall remain non-liable and shall receive back his own. However, if the duration of the agreement is not completed and a loss happens due to the dangers of the sea, then it seems good that the loss should be borne just as the share of the profit is divided according to the contract.[29]

18. If anyone who has borrowed money goes abroad, and the agreed upon time [for repayment] expires, then the money may be recovered from his landed property according to the law. If the debt cannot be recovered, the principal shall be considered a land loan, but the interest shall be maritime for all the time he is abroad.[30]

19. If anyone hires a ship and gives a deposit and afterwards says, 'I have no need of it', then he shall lose his deposit. But if the captain does something other than is agreed, he shall pay the merchant double his deposit.[31]

20. Whoever hires a ship, the agreement must be written and sealed[32] to be effective; if this is not done then it is not valid; they can also include penalties, if they wish. If they do not include any penalties and either the captain or the hirer should break their word: if the hirer provides the goods, that is the cargo, then he shall pay half the freight charge to the

28 For NN.3.16–18, cf. D.22.2; I.3.14; E.10; NN.2.17–19. This rather obscure passage is essentially saying that one cannot make a land loan for hiring ships, transporting goods or buying goods on board. It does not matter whether the ship and the money safely make port, maritime interest shall be levied as there was always the extra risk. As such, any loan will turn into a transmarine loan, the *fenus nauticum*, which is referred to in the chapter heading, see 116 n. 10.

29 Cf. E.10.4.

30 This meant that the principal could be recovered whatever happened to the borrower, but the interest, charged at the higher maritime rate, was subject to risk.

31 Cf. E.9.2.

32 Or subscribed. See Ashburner, *Rhodian Sea-Law*, 98–99.

captain. If the captain should break his word, then he shall pay half the freight charge to the merchant. If the merchant wishes to take off the cargo, he shall pay the whole freight charge to the captain. The document of these penalties shall be followed just as when anyone brings a claim against another.

21. If two people form an unwritten partnership and both the parties attest that 'we formed an unwritten partnership on another occasion and kept faith with each other, and always paid the taxes as one capital', and then the ship is damaged, either while being loaded with ballast or with cargo, then a fourth share of what is saved shall go to the sufferer, since they did not bring forward a written document but agreed a partnership by word of mouth only. Written documents that are sealed[33] shall be secure and strong and what is salvaged shall be shared among the losers.[34]

22. The captain shall not bring on board anything save water, supplies and ropes for the use of the ship, if the merchant has loaded the entire cargo hold according to the written contract. And if the captain wishes to put in other cargo after this, then if there is space on the ship he can load; if there is no space then the merchant must make an objection to the captain and the crew before three witnesses, and if any jettison occurs then it shall fall to the captain. But if the merchant does not hinder this then he shall come into the contribution.

23. If the captain and the merchant make a written agreement, it shall be valid; but if the merchant does not provide the cargo in full, then he must pay the freight charge for the remainder, just as they agreed in writing.

24. If the captain takes the half-freight charge and sails, and the merchant wishes to renege from the written and sealed[35] agreement, then the merchant shall lose his half-freight charge for his obstruction. But if the captain should do something other than the contract, then he shall pay back twice the half-freight charge.

25. If the fixed number of days for the contract passes, then the merchant must provide the crew's provisions for up to ten days. If the second limit passes, then before all else the merchant shall pay all the freight charge and depart. If the merchant wishes to add anything to the freight charge, let him pay it and sail as he pleases.

33 Or subscribed.

34 Cf. E.10.4.

35 Or subscribed.

26. If any of the sailors or the officers[36] sleep off the ship and it happens that the ship is lost, at night or day, all the losses shall be borne by the sailors and officers who slept off the ship, while those who remained on board shall not be liable. Those who are negligent must make good to the owner of the ship the damage caused by their negligence.

27. If a ship sets sail for loading by a merchant or a partnership and it happens that the ship is damaged or lost due to the negligence of the sailors or the captain, then the cargo in storage is not in danger [of a claim]. If testimony is given that the ship was lost in a storm then the salvage from the ship along with the cargo shall come into the contribution, and the captain shall keep the half-freight charge. If anyone denies the partnership and is convicted by three witnesses, then he shall pay his share of the partnership, and suffer the penalty for his denial.

28. If a ship is hindered while loading by the merchant or the partner and the time fixed for loading passes, and it happens the ship is lost due to piracy, fire or shipwreck, the one who caused the delay shall bear the loss.

29. If the merchant does not provide the cargo at the place agreed, and the agreed time passes, and it happens that the ship is lost to piracy, fire or shipwreck, then the merchant shall bear all the losses of the ship. If the days set have not passed and one of these said things happens, then they shall all come into the contribution.

30. If the merchant, having loaded the ship, has gold with him and it happens that the ship suffers one of the dangers of the sea and the cargo is lost and the ship destroyed, then the salvage from the ship and the cargo shall come into the contribution, but the merchant shall take his gold with him. He shall pay a tenth [of the gold] if he survived without holding fast to the tackle of the ship—he shall also pay the half-freight charge in accordance with the contract—but if he survived by holding on to the tackle of the ship, he shall pay one fifth [of the gold].[37]

31. If the merchant has loaded the ship, and something happens to the ship, all the salvage shall come into the contribution from both sides. But if the silver is saved, he [the merchant] shall pay a fifth of it. The captain and the crew shall help in the salvage.

36 See 119 n. 14.

37 Here I follow the corrections of I. Spatharakis, 'The Text of Chapter 30 of the Lex Rhodia Nautica', *Hellenika* 26 (1973), 207–15.

32. If a ship is on its way to be loaded, either hired by a merchant or a partnership, and one of the risks of the sea befalls it, the merchant cannot demand back the half-freight charge, and what remains of the ship and the cargo shall come into the contribution. If the merchant or the partner gave an advance, then what they agreed is valid.

33. If the captain places the cargo in the place agreed and the ship suffers some harm, then the captain shall receive the entirety of the freight charge from the merchant, but the goods that have been unloaded into storehouses shall not be at risk from those who are on the ship with the ship, but those goods found on the ship along with the ship shall come into the contribution.

34. If a ship is carrying fine linen or silk garments the captain must supply good skins so that the cargo is not damaged during storm by the flooding of the waves.[38] If the ship is waterlogged, the captain shall say so immediately to those who have cargo on the ship so that the cargo can be hauled up. But if the passengers make it known to the captain then the captain and the crew shall be liable for the damage to the cargo. If the captain and the crew declare beforehand that the ship is waterlogged and the goods must be hauled up, but those who have cargo loaded fail to haul it up, then neither the captain nor the crew shall be liable.

35. If a ship jettisons its mast, whether it breaks on its own or is cut down, then all the crew and the merchants and the cargo and the ship, whatever is saved, shall come into the contribution.

36. If a ship is sailing and hits another ship which is lying at anchor or has slackened its sails and it is daytime, then all the damage and the losses shall be borne by the captain and those on board. The cargo shall also come into the contribution. But if this happens at night, the man who slackens his sails must light a fire. If he does not have a fire, he must give a shout. If he neglects to do this and a loss occurs, then he has ruined himself, if testimony is given to this effect. However, if the one sailing was negligent and the watchman fell asleep, with the result that the ship sailing is lost on the shallows, then the struck ship shall not be liable.

37. If the ship should suffer something and the property of the merchants or the passengers is saved while the ship is wrecked, then the saved

38 *Othonē* (linen) and *bestē* (finished silk) were both important enough trades to be regulated by the *Eparch* of Constantinople. See *Book of the Eparch*, chapters 9 and 4.

instruments of debt[39] must pay a fifteenth [of their value], but the merchant and the passengers shall not give the ship to the captain.[40]

38. If a ship carrying grain is caught in a storm, the captain shall provide skins and the crew shall bail out the bilge water. If they are negligent and the cargo has become wet from the bilge water, the crew shall make good the loss. But if the cargo is damaged by the storm, then the captain and the crew together with the merchant shall bear the loss, and the captain together with the ship and the crew shall receive six hundredths of what is salvaged. If jettison into the sea occurs, the merchant shall be the first to throw and then the crew shall set to work. After this none of the crew shall steal. If anyone does so, the thief shall pay back double and lose all of his gain [from the salvage].[41]

39. If a ship laden with grain, wine or olive oil is sailing, and on the wishes of the captain and the crew the sails have been slackened, and the ship goes into a place or onto a shore against the will of the merchant, and the ship is lost but the cargo or the freight is saved, then the merchant shall not be liable for the loss of the ship, since he did not wish to go into that place. But if while the ship is sailing the merchant says to the captain, 'I want to go to this place', and the place is not included in the written contract, and the ship is lost but the cargo is saved, then the ship shall be restored safe and sound to the captain by the merchant. If the ship is lost due to the wishes of both parties, then everything shall come into the contribution.

40. If a ship is wrecked and part of the cargo and the ship is saved, then if the passengers carried with them gold, silver, whole silks or pearls, then the saved gold shall pay a tenth, the silver shall contribute a fifth; the whole silks, if they are saved without getting wet, shall contribute a tenth as equal to gold, but if they get wet, then an allowance shall be made for the abrasion and the wetting and as such be brought into the contribution. The pearls shall, according to their value, contribute to the lost cargo just like gold [i.e. they shall pay a tenth].[42]

39 A *grammation* was an instrument whereby A acknowledged his indebtedness to B, giving details of the debt, such as any security held against it or interest due. Holding the *grammation* signified the debt, which could be transferred by the creditor by transferring the document. Destruction of the document was presumed to mean that the debt was extinguished. Such an important document was therefore a valuable item, and its salvage paid a higher rate than normal goods. See Ashburner, *Rhodian Sea-Law*, 111–12.

40 Cf. NN.3.30–31, 40.

41 Cf. E.17.11; NN.3.1–3.

42 Cf. NN. 30–31, 37.

41. If there are passengers on board and the ship is damaged or lost, but the goods of the passengers are saved, then the passengers shall contribute to the loss of the ship. If two or three passengers lose their gold or goods, then they shall receive [compensation] for their loss from all according to their capacity [to pay], along with the contribution of the ship.

42. If a ship springs a leak while it is carrying goods, and the goods are taken out, then it is up to the captain if he wishes to carry the goods to the trading place agreed upon, if the ship is repaired. If the ship is not repaired, and the captain carries the goods in another ship to the agreed trading place, he shall pay the entire freight charge.[43]

43. If a ship is caught in a storm and jettison of goods happens and its sailyards, mast, tillers, anchors and rudders[44] break, then all these shall come into the contribution along with the value of the ship and the salvaged cargo.

44. If a ship carries cargo and in a storm the mast is jettisoned, or the tillers broken or one of the rudders[45] lost, then if it happens that the cargo gets wet from the storm, then it is necessary that all these shall come into the contribution. But if the cargo is damaged more by the bilge water than the storm, then the captain shall receive the freight charge and shall hand over the goods dry and in the same quantity as he received them.

45. If a ship in open sea is capsized or destroyed, then anyone who brings to safety anything from it to land shall receive as a reward a fifth portion of what they saved.

46. If a boat breaks away from the ropes of its ship and is lost with all her crew, then if those on board are lost or die, the captain shall pay their annual wages for a whole year to their heirs. Anyone who brings the boat to safety along with its rudders[46] shall return everything just as he found it, and he shall receive a fifth part of what he saves.

47. If gold or silver or anything else is lifted up from a depth of eight fathoms, then the salvager shall receive a third share. If from fifteen fathoms, the

43 That is, the captain can choose either to repair his own ship or charter another, and if the latter he must pay for it.

44 McCormick suggests that *epholkia* refers not to rudders but to the ship's boats. See *Origins*, 409 n. 87.

45 Ibid.

46 McCormick suggests that the Greek term used here, *epholkia*, might mean the cargo aboard the towed boat or perhaps the general fittings of the boat. See *Origins*, 409 n. 87.

salvager shall receive half due to the danger of the depth. When things are cast from sea onto land and are found there or are carried as far as one cubit, then the salvager shall receive a tenth part of the salvage.

THE FARMER'S LAW[1]

Chapters of the Farmer's Law selected from the book(s) of Justinian[2]

1. It is necessary for the farmer working his own field to be just and not encroach on his neighbour's furrow. If anyone persistently encroaches on and curtails a neighbouring plot during ploughing time he shall lose his ploughing, but if he makes this encroachment during sowing time, then the encroaching farmer shall lose the seed, his tillage and the produce.

2. If a farmer enters land and ploughs or sows it without the knowledge of its master, he shall not receive either wages for his work or the produce from his sowing, nor even the seed he has sown.[3]

3. If two farmers agree to exchange lands before two or three witnesses, and they agree to do so in perpetuity, then their agreement shall stand valid, secure and irrevocable.

4. If two farmers agree to exchange lands for the sowing season and one of the parties reneges, then if the seed has been sown they may not renege; but if it has not been sown they may renege. However, if the one who reneges did not plough while the other did, then he shall plough and then may renege.

1 *Nomos Georgikos*, ed. I. Medvedev et al., *Vizantiĭskiĭ zemledel'cheskiĭ zakon* (Leningrad, 1984), with a parallel Russian translation. For the older but still highly serviceable edition see W. Ashburner, 'The Farmer's Law I', *JHS* 30 (1910), 85–108. Ashburner also wrote a commentary and English translation: 'The Farmer's Law II', *JHS* 32 (1912), 68–95.

2 The manuscripts vary over whether it is one or many books, or indeed whether there is a book at all. See Medvedev et al., *Vizantiĭskiĭ zemledel'cheskiĭ zakon*, 96.

3 Cf. AE.2.7. Throughout *kyrios* has been translated as 'master' rather than 'owner'. This is because although it most certainly could mean owner, and probably did mean this for the all or most of the chapters of the *Farmer's Law*, it could also mean someone who possessed the usufruct of the land. See P. Sarris, 'Economics, Trade, and "Feudalism"', in L. James (ed.), *A Companion to Byzantium* (Chichester, 2010), 25–42, esp. 28–29.

5. If two farmers exchange lands either for a season or in perpetuity, and one plot is found to be undersized in comparison to the other, and this was not in the agreement, then the one who has more shall give an equivalent amount to the one who has less. But if it was in the agreement, he shall give nothing in return.

6. If a farmer who has a claim on a field enters it against the will of the sower and reaps without authority, he shall get nothing from it. But if the claim he pleads is baseless, he shall hand over twice the amount of the crops that were reaped.[4]

7. If two districts dispute a boundary or a field, the adjudicating magistrates shall investigate[5] and render judgement in favour of the district that held possession the longer; but if there is an ancient boundary stone the ancient possession shall be irrevocable.[6]

8. If a division [of land] harmed anyone in either lots or lands, they have permission to undo the division.

9. If a farmer on shares [i.e. a farmer whose rent was a share of the crop] reaps without the consent of the grantor of the land and carries off his sheaves, then he is a thief and shall lose the entirety of his crop.[7]

10. The [farmer] on shares' portion is nine bundles, and the grantor's share is one bundle; anyone who divides outside these limits is accursed of God.

11. If anyone should receive land from a farmer without the means to sow, and he agrees to plough only and divide [the crop], their agreement shall prevail; and if they agree on sowing also, this shall prevail according to their agreement.

12. If a farmer receives land to sow on a half-share and during the required season does not plough, but throws the seed on the surface, he shall receive none of the crop because he cheated and deceived the master of the land.

13. If a farmer should receive from any farmer without means a vineyard to work on a half-share, and he does not prune it as is fitting, or dig it,

4 Cf. E.17.5; AE.2.9; NG.66, 80.

5 This phrase, *tēreitōsan hoi akroatai*, 'the adjudicating magistrates shall investigate', is repeated in E.5.5, 10.1.1, 11, NG.37 and 67, and slightly altered in E.17.27 and 17.47. For the *akroatai* see Humphreys, *Law, Power, and Imperial Ideology*, 87–88, 107–13, 218–22.

6 Cf. AE.2, Irene Novel I.

7 NG.9–17 cf. E.12–13. For the law on tenure in the *Ecloga* and the *Farmer's Law* see Humphreys, *Law, Power, and Imperial Ideology*, 212–13.

or prop up the vines or dig it over, he shall receive nothing from the produce.[8]

14. If someone takes a half-share of a field from a farmer without means who has gone abroad then, changing his mind, does not work the field, he shall give [the farmer] twice the amount of produce.

15. If someone takes a half-share and, changing his mind before the time for working, informs the master of the field that he has not the strength, and the master of the field neglects this, then the man who took the half-share shall not be liable.

16. If a farmer takes over cultivation of a vineyard or a piece of land on agreement with the master of it, and receiving a deposit begins [to cultivate], but then reneging gives it up, he shall give the monetary value of the field, and its master shall have possession of the field.[9]

17. If a farmer enters into and works another farmer's woodland, he shall receive the profits for himself for three years, and then return it to its master.[10]

18. If a farmer without the means to work his own field runs away and lives abroad, then those who have demands laid upon them by the public treasury shall work it, and the farmer on his return may not fine them for this.[11]

19. If a farmer who has run away from his field pays every year the extraordinary [taxes] of the public treasury, then those who gather in [the crop] and occupy his field shall be fined twice the amount.[12]

8 On the importance of pruning, digging and propping up vines see M. Decker, *Tilling the Hateful Earth: Agricultural Production in the Late Antique East* (Oxford, 2009), 125–29.

9 Cf. E.9.2.

10 That is, he has permission to improve the land in return for three years' profit.

11 A few MSS have a vineyard instead of a field, and many refer to wine rather than a general fine. See Medvedev et al., *Vizantiĭskiĭ zemledel'cheskiĭ zakon*, 103.

12 By the seventh century 'extraordinary' had ironically become the ordinary form of taxation. See Haldon, *Seventh Century*, 147–48. Together, NG.18–19 reveal something important about the attitude of the imperial government. What mattered to it above all was that it received its taxes, and if the absentee landowner paid them then his neighbours could not invade his property. If he did not, then the rights of private property could be suspended to meet a communal tax demand. This reflected the important principle in Roman taxation that communities were jointly liable for a stated amount, a principle that helped ensure that the imperial government received the amount it was expecting.

20. Anyone who cuts down another's wood without its master's knowledge, and works and sows it, shall have none of the crop.[13]

21. If a farmer builds a house or plants a vineyard on another's unproductive land, and afterwards the masters of the place arrive, they may not pull the house down or uproot the vineyard, but may take an equivalent in land. But if the person who built or planted on another's land absolutely refuses to give an equivalent amount of land, then the master of the place has permission to uproot the vineyard and pull down the house.[14]

22. If a farmer steals a spade or fork at the time for digging and is afterwards discovered, he shall pay the daily hire for it of twelve *folles*; likewise someone who steals a pruning knife at the time for pruning, or a scythe at the time for reaping, or an axe at the time for cutting wood.[15]

23. If a herdsman of oxen receives an ox from a farmer in the morning and mixes it in with the herd, and it happens that the ox is taken by a wolf, then he shall show the corpse to its master and shall be guiltless.[16]

24. If a herdsman who has received an ox loses it and does not inform its master on the same day that, 'I saw the ox until this or that point, but I do not know what happened after', then he shall not be guiltless; but if he does inform him, then he shall be guiltless.

25. If a herdsman receives an ox from a farmer in the morning and he goes away, and the ox, becoming separated from the majority of the oxen, wanders off and enters fields or vineyards and causes damage, he shall not be deprived of his wages, but he shall pay for the damage.[17]

26. If a herdsman receives an ox from a farmer and the ox then disappears, he shall swear in the name of the Lord that he himself has not acted maliciously, and that he had nothing to do with the loss of the ox and shall not be liable.[18]

13 Cf. AE.2.7.

14 Cf. AE.2.6; NG.66, 81–82.

15 Cf. E.17.10–11; NG.33–35, 61–62, 68–69. A *follis* was a bronze coin and the standard unit of small change for the period; 12 *folles* = 1/24 *nomisma* = 1/2 *miliaresion* = 1 carat. For theft in the *Ecloga* and the *Farmer's Law*, see Humphreys, *Law, Power, and Imperial Ideology*, 217–18.

16 Cf. NM.13. Before this chapter the subtitle *Concerning herdsmen* appears in many MSS.

17 Cf. NM.18. This chapter also uses the same word for 'damage' (*praida*, from the Latin *praeda* for spoils or booty), that NM.18 employs in its rubric.

18 Cf. NM.13. The difference with NG.24 is that there the loss is distinctly linked with

27. If a herdsman receives from a farmer an ox which is not weak but healthy in the morning, and it happens that it is wounded or blinded, the herdsman shall swear that he himself has not acted maliciously, and shall not be liable.[19]

28. If, on the loss of an ox, or its wounding or blinding, a herdsman swears an oath and it is later proved by two or three trustworthy witnesses that he swore falsely, then after his tongue has been cut out he shall make indemnity to the master of the ox.[20]

29. If a herdsman with a staff in his hand kills, wounds or blinds an ox, then he is not guiltless and shall pay the penalty; but if he did this with a stone he is guiltless.

30. If anyone cuts a bell from an ox or a sheep and is discovered, he shall be whipped as a thief; and if the animal should disappear, the man who stole the bell shall make good the loss.

31. If a tree stands in a plot of a field and the neighbouring plot is a garden, and this is overshadowed by the tree, then its [the garden's] master may trim its branches; but if there is not a garden, the branches shall not be trimmed.[21]

32. If a tree is cultivated by someone in an undivided place, and then after a division takes place it is allocated to another's portion, then none shall have ownership of the tree except for the person who cultivated it. But if the master of the place complains that, 'I am injured by the tree', then in place of the tree he shall give another tree to the man who cultivated it, and he shall possess it [i.e. the original tree].

33. If the guardian of the fruit is found stealing from the place he guards, he shall be deprived of his wages and violently beaten.

34. If a hired shepherd is found milking the flock unbeknownst to its master, and selling the milk, then he shall be beaten and deprived of his wages.

35. If anyone is found stealing another's straw, he shall pay back double the amount.

---

destruction, that is, the ox is dead and presumably there were some corporeal remains to show, while in NG.26 the ox has mysteriously disappeared, that is, there is nothing to show that the herdsman had not stolen it.

19 Cf. NM.13.

20 Cf. E.17.2.

21 Cf. D.43.27.

36. If anyone takes an ox, an ass or any such beast without its master's knowledge and departs on business, he shall give twice the value of its hire; and if it should die on the journey he shall give two for one, of whatever kind it may be.[22]

37. If anyone receives an ox for work and it dies, the adjudicating magistrates shall investigate, and if it died in the work it was sought for, he shall not be liable. However, if it died doing other work, he shall give a whole ox.

38. If anyone finds an ox causing damage in a vineyard, field or other place and does not give it back to its master with the intention of demanding restitution for all the damage to his produce, but instead kills or wounds it, then he shall give an ox for an ox, an ass for an ass, a sheep for a sheep.

39. If anyone is cutting wood in a copse and is not attentive, and a tree falls down and kills an ox, an ass or anything else, he shall give a life for a life.

40. If anyone is cutting a tree and in ignorance throws downs the axe from above and kills another's beast, he shall give the same [i.e. give a beast in return].

41. If anyone steals an ox or an ass and this is proved, then after being whipped he shall give twice the number and all its work.

42. If anyone attempts to steal an ox from a herd, and puts the herd to flight and it is then eaten by wild beasts, he shall be blinded.[23]

43. If anyone goes out to bring in his own ox or ass and while chasing his own animal chases away another with it, and does not bring it in with his own but it is lost or eaten by wolves, he shall give an equivalent to the master of the ox or ass. But if he fully discloses this and indicates the place, and defends himself by showing he was not able to get hold of it, then he shall not be liable.

44. If anyone finds an ox in a wood and slaughters it and takes the carcass, he shall have his hand cut off.

45. If any slave slaughters an ox, a ram or a pig in a wood, his master shall make restitution for it.

46. If any slave, while trying to steal at night, drives the animals from the fold and they are lost or eaten by wild beasts, he shall be hanged as a killer.

22 NG.36–37. Cf. E.17.7.

23 For NG.41–42, cf. E.17.13, NG.46–47.

47. If someone's slave often steals animals at night and frequently rustles from the flock, his master shall make good the loss as he knew he was responsible for the slave, while the slave himself shall hang.[24]

48. If a man finds an ox causing damage and the finder does not give it back to its master, but cuts its ear, or blinds it, or cuts its tail, then its master shall not take it but shall receive another in its place.[25]

49. If anyone finds a pig causing damage, or a sheep or a dog, on the first instance he should hand it over; on the second instance, on handing it over he should inform its master; on the third occasion, he may cut its tail, or cut its ear or shoot it with impunity.[26]

50. If an ox, in trying to enter a vineyard or garden, falls into the ditch of the vineyard or garden and dies, the master of the garden or vineyard shall not be liable.

51. If an ox or an ass, in trying to enter a vineyard or a garden, impales itself on the stakes of the fence, the master of the vineyard or garden shall not be liable.

52. If anyone sets up a snare during harvest time and a dog or pig falls into it and dies, the master of the snare shall not be liable.

53. If anyone, after the first or second payment for damages, kills the animal [that caused the damage] rather than handing it over to its master in order to receive compensation for the damage, he shall give the same as he killed.

54. If anyone confines another's pig or dog and destroys it, then he shall repay him twice the amount.[27]

55. If anyone kills a sheepdog and does not confess it and an attack of wild beasts on the fold occurs, and afterwards the killing of the dog is discovered, then he shall pay for the entire loss of the flock along with the value of the dog.[28]

56. If anyone lights a fire in his own wood and it happens that the fire spreads and burns houses and fruitful fields, he shall not be condemned so long as he did not do so in a strong wind.[29]

24 For NG.46–47, cf. E.17.13; NG.41–42. For the *Ecloga* and the *Farmer's Law* on various forms of animal theft see Humphreys, *Law, Power, and Imperial Ideology*, 209–10.

25 Cf. NM.18.

26 Cf. NM.18.

27 Cf. E.17.8.

28 Cf. NG.75.

29 Cf. E.17.41; NM.20.

57. Anyone who sets fire to another's hillside or cuts another's trees is condemned to pay double.[30]

58. Anyone who burns the fence of a vineyard shall be beaten, have his hand branded and be fined for twice the damage.

59. Anyone who cuts another's fruitful vines or pulls them up shall have his hand cut off and be fined.

60. Those who enter another's furrows and steal bundles or ears of grain or pulses during harvest shall be stripped of their shirts and whipped.

61. Those who enter another's vines or figs for the sake of eating shall go unharmed, but if they came to steal they shall be beaten and stripped of their shirts.[31]

62. Those who steal a plough, ploughshare, yoke or yoke-straps shall pay a fine according to the number of days from when the theft occurred, twelve *folles* for each day.[32]

63. Those who burn or steal another's wagon shall pay back twice the amount.

64. Those who avenge themselves on an enemy by setting fire to a threshing floor or heaps of grain, shall be burned alive.[33]

65. Those who set fire to a storage house for hay or chaff shall have their hand cut off.

66. Those who without authority pull down another's house or render useless another's fence, on the grounds that the fence or building was erected on their land, shall have their hand cut off.[34]

67. If people receive fields on account of interest, and are shown to have enjoyed the fruits of the field for more than seven years, then the adjudicating magistrate shall take account after seven years, and he shall credit against the principal of the debt the whole of the revenue after the seven years, and half the revenue before.[35]

30 Cf. E.17.40; NM.20. For the relationship between the *Ecloga* and the *Farmer's Law* on arson see Humphreys, *Law, Power, and Imperial Ideology*, 215–17.

31 Cf. Leviticus 19:9–10, 23:22; Deuteronomy 24:19–21.

32 Cf. E.17.11, NG.65.

33 Cf. E.17.41; NM.20, which also uses the same rare term, *halōn*, for threshing floor.

34 Cf. E.17.5; AE.2.6 and 9; NG.21, 80.

35 Cf. Deuteronomy 15:1–2; AE.13.5. This chapter concerns someone who has taken land as security for a loan. For the first seven years half the income from the land must go to

68. Anyone who is discovered in a granary stealing grain shall on the first occasion be beaten with a hundred lashes, and shall make indemnity to the person he stole from. If this should happen a second time, after being beaten he shall be fined for twice the amount of the theft; on a third occasion, he shall be blinded.[36]

69. Anyone who steals wine from a jar or vat at night shall suffer the same penalty as above.[37]

70. Those who have a short measure of grain or wine and do not follow the ancient practices of their fathers in measurement, but through sordid love of gain have unjust measures contrary to the agreed ones, shall be beaten as impious.[38]

71. If anyone who hands over animals for pasture to a slave without his master's knowledge, and the slave sells them or in any other way renders them useless, then the slave and his master shall not be liable.

72. If a slave with his master's knowledge receives animals of any sort whatsoever and eats them or in any other way destroys them, the master of the slave shall make indemnity to the master of the animals.

73. If anyone is passing along the road and finds a wounded or slain animal and having pity reports this, but the master of the animal has a suspicion that the informer acted maliciously, then he shall swear an oath concerning the wounding, but no one shall be examined concerning the loss.

74. Anyone who destroys another's animal from any motive shall, after judgement, make indemnity to its master.

75. Anyone who destroys a sheepdog through use of a drug shall receive one hundred lashes and give twice the value of the dog to its master. But if the flock also is lost, then the killer shall pay for the entire loss as he was the cause of the watchdog's destruction. Testimony shall be given about the dog, and if it was a fighter of beasts, then it shall be as said above; but

---

paying off the principal of the loan; after seven years all the income must be set against the principal. This would limit the extent of interest payable, thereby protecting the debtor landowner from his creditor. For this reading see, A. Laiou, 'A Note on the Farmer's Law, Chapter 67', *Byzantion* 41 (1971), 197–204. The present ruling complements AE13.5, which stated that if the produce of the field fulfilled the entire debt it could not be alienated by the creditor, and implicitly that the field should return to the debtor.

36 Cf. E.17.11.

37 Cf. E.17.11.

38 Cf. NM.9.

if it was an ordinary dog, then after a beating he shall give the value of the dog only.[39]

76. If two dogs are fighting and the master of one of them gives the other dog [a blow] with a sword, a staff or a stone, and from the blow that dog is blinded, killed or suffers some other critical injury, then the slayer shall make indemnity to its master.[40]

77. If anyone has a powerful dog that is arrogant towards its fellows, and he inflames the powerful dog against the weaker ones, and it happens that one of them is maimed or killed, then he shall make indemnity to its master and receive twelve lashes.

78. If anyone reaps his plot before his neighbours have reaped theirs, and brings in his animals and causes harm to his neighbours, he shall be beaten with thirty lashes and shall make indemnity to those he has harmed.[41]

79. If anyone gathers in the fruits of his vineyard while most other plots remain ungathered, and brings in his animals, he shall be beaten with thirty lashes and shall make indemnity to those he has harmed.

80. If anyone who has a suit against another, and without authority cuts his vines or any other kind of tree, he shall have his hand cut off.[42]

81. If anyone living in a district discerns that a common place is suitable for the building of a mill and takes possession of it, and then after completion of the building the community of the district complains that the master of the building has taken possession of common land, then they shall give him all the costs due to him for the construction of the building and they shall become joint owners with its builder.[43]

82. If after a division of the land of the district someone finds that in his own plot there is a place suitable for the building of a mill and he attends to this, then the farmers of the other plots may not say anything concerning the mill.

83. If the water that goes to the mill leaves the fields or vineyards dry, then he shall make good the damage; if he does not, the mill shall be left idle.

39 Cf. NG.55.
40 NG.76–77 cf. E.17.9.
41 NG.78–79 cf. NM.18.
42 Cf. E.17.5; AE.2.9; NG.21, 66.
43 Cf. AE.2.6.

84. If the owners of the cultivated fields are not willing for the water to go through their fields, they may prevent it.

85. If a farmer finds another's ox causing damage in another's vineyard and does not inform its master but, having decided to chase it, kills it or impales it on a stake, he shall be fined for all the damage.

THE MOSAIC LAW[1]

Chapters selected from the Commandments of Moses[2]

1. Concerning judgement and justice.
2. Concerning the Ten Commandments written on stone tablets.
3. Concerning blasphemers.
4. Concerning the honouring of old men and elders.
5. Concerning parents not being condemned for their children or children for their parents.
6. Concerning those who strike their fathers.
7. Concerning not depriving a poor man or any labourer of his wage.
8. Concerning not maltreating widows and orphans.
9. Concerning just weights and measures.
10. Concerning heirs.

1 *Nomos Mosaikos*, ed. L. Burgmann and S. Troianos, 'Nomos Mosaikos', *FM* III (Frankfurt, 1979), 126–67. A partial English translation of the headings, based on the Momferratos edition of the *Ecloga*, can be found in Freshfield, *Ecloga*, 142–44. As noted in the Introduction, 30, the main content of the NM comprises excerpts taken from the *Septuagint*, though in places there are divergences. Therefore, I have based my translation of the biblical excerpts on L. Brenton, *The Septuagint with Apocrypha: Greek and English* (London, 1851). I have, however, modernised the language and of course altered those sections where the NM deviates from the *Septuagint*. Moreover, to ease general reference, I have not given the Old Testament references according to the *Septuagint*, but according to the mainstream practice of modern, English translations of the Bible.

2 Cf. the title of the contents list of the *Ecloga* and *Rhodian Sea Law*, and the title of the *Farmer's Law*, see respectively 38, 115, 129. As noted on 38 n. 22, in one manuscript where the NM precedes the *Ecloga* this title is given as 'Concerning the chapters of the old legislation', in direct contrast to the 'new legislation' of the *Ecloga*.

11. Concerning loans, interest and security.

12. Concerning any kind of deposit, partnership, robbery or injustice.

13. Concerning those who take any animal for safekeeping and it is stolen or taken by wild beasts.

14. Concerning those who borrow an animal from their neighbour and it is injured or dies.

15. Concerning thieves.

16. Concerning the seizing of free persons and selling them.

17. Concerning those who purchase a free person.

18. Concerning those who cause damage.

19. Concerning those who open a pit and do not cover it.

20. Concerning those who cause fires.

21. Concerning a bull that gores a man or ox.

22. Concerning a mistress.

23. Concerning someone who rejects and defames his wife.

24. Concerning a wife who lays hold of her opponent's genitals in a fight.

25. Concerning corrupters.

26. Concerning adulterers.

27. Concerning a woman caused to miscarry by people fighting.

28. Concerning the daughter of a priest who prostitutes herself.

29. Concerning a woman who becomes irrational.

30. Concerning incest with one's mother.

31. Concerning the same with one's stepmother.

32. Concerning the same with one's sister.

33. Concerning the same with one's granddaughter.

34. Concerning the same with one's aunt.

35. Concerning the same with one's daughter-in-law, that is the wife of one's son.

36. Concerning the same with a brother's wife.

37. Concerning the same with a woman and her daughter.

38. Concerning the same with the daughter of one's stepmother.

39. Concerning the same with two sisters.
40. Concerning the same with an uncle's wife.
41. Concerning the remaining relatives.
42. Concerning those who commit bestiality.
43. Concerning the wanton [i.e. homosexuals].
44. Concerning those who kill or maim a limb of their household slave.
45. Concerning anyone who strikes his neighbour in a fight.
46. Concerning those who kill intentionally and unintentionally.
47. Concerning the killing of man and beast.
48. Concerning witnesses and disregarding them.
49. Concerning witnesses and false witnesses.
50. Concerning poisoners, diviners and enchanters.

A selection from the Law given by God through Moses to the Israelites[3]

Title 1: Concerning judgement and justice[4]

1.1. *From Exodus, Chapter 69*
Do not accept an idle report. Do not agree with the unjust to become an unjust witness. Do not follow the multitude in evil. Do not side with the many to pervert judgement. And do not have pity on the poor man in judgement.[5] Do not distort judgement in the suit of the poor. Keep away from all unjust speech. Do not kill the innocent and just, nor justify the impious. And do not take gifts, for gifts blind the eyes of the seeing and corrupt just words.[6]

1.2. *From Leviticus, Chapter 93*
Do not act unjustly in judgement. Do not receive the person of the poor, nor admire the person of the mighty. With justice judge your neighbour. Do not walk deceitfully among your people. Do not rise up against the blood of your neighbour. I am the Lord your God.[7]

Title 2: Concerning the Ten Commandments written on stone tablets

From Exodus Chapter 63 and Deuteronomy Chapter 7
1. I am the Lord your God, who brought you out of the land of Egypt, out of the house of slavery; you shall have no other gods besides me.

2. You shall not make for yourself an idol, nor the likeness of anything that is in the heaven above, or the earth below, or the waters beneath the earth; you shall not bow down to them, nor worship them.[8]

3. You shall not take the name of the Lord your God in vain; for the Lord shall not acquit one who takes His name in vain.

3 Cf. the title of the *Ecloga*, 34.
4 Cf. E.pr., 36; AE.XI.
5 Exodus 23:1–3.
6 Exodus 23:6–8.
7 Leviticus 19:15–16.
8 NM.2.1–2 = Exodus 20:2–5; Deuteronomy 5:6–9.

4. Remember the Sabbath day by keeping it holy. For six days you shall labour and do all your work; but the seventh day is the Sabbath of the Lord your God. On it you shall not do any work, neither you, nor your son or daughter, nor your manservant or maidservant, nor your ox or ass, nor any stranger that dwells with you.[9]

5. Honour your father and your mother, so that things may be well with you and that you may live for a long time on the earth.[10]

6. Do not commit adultery.[11]

7. Do not murder.[12]

8. Do not steal.

9. Do not give false witness against your neighbour.

10. Do not covet your neighbour's wife, nor his fields, nor his manservant, nor his maidservant, nor his ox, nor his ass, nor any beast of his, nor anything that is your neighbour's.[13]

Title 3: Concerning blasphemers

From Leviticus Chapter 110
The Lord spoke to Moses, saying,[14] 'Speak to the sons of Israel and say to them "Whosoever shall curse God shall suffer for his sin. And he who names the name of the Lord shall surely be put to death; let the assembly stone him with stones; whether he is a stranger or a native, let him die for naming the name of the Lord"'.[15]

9 NM.2.3–4 = Exodus 20:7–10; Deuteronomy 5:11–14.
10 Exodus 20:12; Deuteronomy 5:16. Cf. E.2.5.
11 Exodus 20:14; Deuteronomy 5:18.
12 Exodus 20:13; Deuteronomy 5:17.
13 NM.2.8–10 = Exodus 20:15–17; Deuteronomy 5:19–21.
14 Leviticus 24:13.
15 Leviticus 24:15–16.

Title 4: Concerning the honouring of old men and elders

From Leviticus Chapter 93
Stand up in the presence of the grey-haired, honour the face of the elderly and fear the Lord your God; I am the Lord your God.[16]

Title 5: Concerning parents not being condemned for their children or children for their parents

From Deuteronomy Chapter 87
Fathers shall not be put to death for their children, and sons shall not be put to death for their fathers; each shall die for their own sin.[17]

Title 6: Concerning those who strike their fathers

6.1 From Leviticus Chapter 94
If a man speaks evil of his father or his mother, he shall surely be put to death; he is guilty.[18]

6.2 *From Exodus Chapter 67*
Whoever strikes his father or mother shall surely die.[19]

6.3 *From Deuteronomy 59*
If anyone has a disobedient and rebellious son who does not hearken to his father's voice, and does not listen to him when he corrects him, then his father and mother shall seize him and bring him to the elders of their city at the gate of that place, and they shall say to the men of their city, 'This son of ours is disobedient and rebellious, he does not listen to our voice, he is a glutton and a drunkard'. And the men of the city shall stone him with stones and he shall die.[20]

16 Leviticus 19:32.
17 Deuteronomy 24:16.
18 Leviticus 20:9.
19 Exodus 21:15.
20 Deuteronomy 21:18–21.

Title 7: Concerning not depriving a poor man or any labourer of his wage

7.1 *From Leviticus Chapter 93*
Do not hold back the wages of the hired worker until the morning.[21]

7.2 *From Deuteronomy Chapter 86*
Do not rob the wages of the poor and needy of your brothers, or from the strangers in your cities. Pay him his wages on the same day; the sun shall not go down upon it, for he is poor and anxious for it. Otherwise he may cry to the Lord against you, and you will be guilty of sin.[22]

Title 8.1: Concerning a man's or woman's vow, oath or pledge to God, and concerning not maltreating widows or orphans.[23]

From Numbers Chapter 120
Moses spoke to the heads of the tribes of the Children of Israel, saying, 'This is what the Lord has commanded: any man who vows a vow to the Lord, or swears an oath, or binds himself with a pledge upon his soul, shall not break his word; he shall do everything that came out of his mouth. And if a woman in her youth and still living in her father's house should vow a vow to the Lord, or bind herself with a pledge, and her father, hearing her vow and her pledge by which she bound her soul, keeps silent, then all her vows shall stand, and all the pledges by which she bound her soul shall remain. But if her father strictly forbids her on the day he hears it, all the vows and pledges by which she bound her soul shall not stand, and the Lord will release her since her father forbade her. And if she is married and makes a vow or by an utterance of her lips she binds her soul, and hearing this her husband keeps silent, then the vows by which she bound herself shall stand. But if her husband strictly forbids her on the day he hears it, then all her vows and the pledges by which she bound her soul shall not remain, since her husband forbade her, and the Lord shall release her. And any vow made by a widow or divorced woman by which she vowed upon her soul shall stand'.[24]

21 Leviticus 19:13.
22 Deuteronomy 24:14–15.
23 This chapter is only found in a (probably later) version of the NM.
24 Numbers 30:2–10.

Title 8.2: Concerning not maltreating widows and orphans

From Exodus Chapter 68
Do not maltreat any widow or orphan; if you do afflict them with any maltreatment and they should cry aloud to me, I will surely hear their cry, and my wrath shall be provoked and I shall slay you with the sword, and your wives shall become your widows, and your children orphans.[25]

Title 9: Concerning just weights and measures

From Leviticus 93
Do not act unjustly in judgement, in measures, weights and scales. You shall have just scales, just measures and just measurements.[26]

Title 10: Concerning heirs[27]

From Numbers Chapter 109
The Lord said to Moses,[28] 'You will speak to the Children of Israel, saying, "If a man should die and have no son, you shall bestow his inheritance on his daughter. If he has no daughter, you shall give his inheritance to his brother. If he has no brothers, you shall give the inheritance to his father's brothers. If there are no brothers of his father, you shall give the inheritance to his nearest relative in his clan, that he may inherit it"'.[29]

Title 11: Concerning loans, interest and security[30]

11.1 *From Exodus Chapter 68*
If you should lend money to your poor brother who is beside you, do not press him and do not charge him interest. If you take your neighbour's cloak as security, return it by sunset. For this cloak is the only covering he

25 Exodus 22:22–24.
26 Leviticus 19:35–36. Cf. NG.70.
27 Cf. E.6.
28 Numbers 27:6.
29 Numbers 27:8–11. Cf. E.5–6.
30 Cf. E.10.

has for his nakedness; what else can he sleep in? If then he cries out to me, I shall listen, for I am merciful.[31]

11.2 *From Leviticus Chapter 119*
If your brother who is with you should become poor and is unable to support himself among you, you should help him as you would a foreigner and a stranger, and your brother shall live with you. Do not take interest from him; do not lend him money at interest or sell him food for a profit.[32]

11.3 *From Deuteronomy Chapter 36*
If anyone among your brothers is poor, do not harden your heart nor close your hand against your brother who is in need. Rather, open your hands to him and lend him as much as he wants according to his needs. Do not let your eye be an evil to your brother and not give him anything, for he shall cry to the Lord against you, and your sin shall be great. Rather give generously to him and lend him as much as he wants.[33]

11.4 *From the same, Chapter 78*
Do not charge your brother interest, whether on money, on food or on anything else you may lend. You may charge a foreigner interest, but not your brother, so that the Lord God may bless all your works in the land.[34]

11.5 *From the same, Chapter 85*
If your neighbour owes you a debt, any debt whatsoever, do not go into his house to take his pledge; stand outside, and the man to whom you made the loan shall bring the pledge out to you. And if the man is poor, do not go to sleep with his pledge, but you shall surely return his pledge to him before sunset, and he shall bless you.[35]

31 Exodus 22:25–27.
32 Leviticus 25:35–37.
33 Deuteronomy 15:7–10.
34 Deuteronomy 23:19–20.
35 Deuteronomy 24:10–13.

Title 12: Concerning any kind of deposit, partnership, robbery or injustice[36]

12.1 *From Exodus 68*
If anyone gives to his neighbour money or goods to keep, and they are stolen from the man's house, then if the thief is found he shall repay double. But if the thief is not found, the master of the house shall come forward before God and swear that he has not done evil in regard to any part of his neighbour's deposit. In all cases of alleged wrongdoing concerning a calf, an ass, a sheep, a garment and all other disputed property, whatever it should be, the judgement of both parties shall be brought before God,[37] and the one shall swear that he was not an accomplice in the matter of the neighbour's deposit, and the other shall accept this and will not receive repayment.[38]

12.2 *From Leviticus Chapter 22*
And the Lord spoke to Moses, saying, 'A soul that sins and deliberately disregards the Lord's commandments, and deceives his neighbour regarding his deposit, or their partnership, or robs him, or does any injustice to their neighbour, or has found something that was lost and lied about it, and has sworn unjustly about any one of these things, has thereby sinned. And it shall come to pass that whenever he sins and errs, he shall restore what he stole, or redress the wrong he committed, or restore the deposit that was entrusted to him or the lost property he found and about which he swore unjustly, and he shall make restitution in full and an additional fifth, on the day he is convicted'.[39]

Title 13: Concerning those who take any animal for safekeeping and it is stolen or taken by wild beasts

From Exodus Chapter 68
If anyone gives an ass, a calf, a sheep or any animal to his neighbour for safekeeping, and it is injured, or dies or is taken, and nobody knows what happened, then the issue between them shall be settled by a neighbour

36 Cf. E.11.
37 Exodus 22:7–9.
38 Exodus, 22:11.
39 Leviticus 6:1–4.

taking an oath before the Lord that he has done no evil regarding his neighbour's deposit. And the owner shall accept this, and there shall be no restitution. But if it was stolen from him, restitution must be made to the owner. And if the animal was taken by wild beasts, the neighbour shall bring the remains as evidence and shall not have to make restitution.[40]

Title 14: Concerning those who borrow an animal from their neighbour and it is injured or dies

From Exodus Chapter 68
If anyone borrows an animal from a neighbour and it is injured, or it dies or is taken while the owner is not present, he shall make restitution. But if the owner is with the animal, then he shall not make restitution. If the animal was hired out, only the hiring fee is due.[41]

Title 15: Concerning thieves[42]

From Exodus Chapter 68
If anyone should steal a calf or a sheep, slaughter it and sell it, he shall pay back five calves for a calf, and four sheep for a sheep. If the thief is caught breaking in at night, and is struck and dies, the defender is not guilty of homicide; but if it happens after sunrise, the defender is guilty of homicide. If the thief has nothing, let him be sold in compensation for the theft. If the stolen animal is found alive in his possession, whether calf, ass or sheep, he shall pay back double.[43]

40 Exodus 22:10–13. Cf. NG.26–28.
41 Exodus 22:14–15. Cf. E.17.7.
42 Cf. E.17.10–13.
43 Exodus 22:1–4.

Title 16: Concerning the seizing of free persons and selling them[44]

16.1 From Exodus 67
Anyone who seizes one of the Children of Israel and having got control of him sells him, or is found with him, shall certainly be put to death.[45]

16.2 *From Deuteronomy Chapter 83*
If someone is caught kidnapping one of his brothers and, having overcome him, sells him, that thief shall die. You must purge the evil from among you![46]

Title 17: Concerning those who purchase a free person[47]

From Leviticus Chapter 120
If your brother should be humbled and sold to you, he shall not serve you as a slave. Rather treat him as a hired worker or stranger. He shall work for you until the year of release. Then he and his children shall be released, and shall go back to his family and return to possess their patrimony. He shall not be sold as a slave. Do not oppress him with work, and fear your God.[48]

Title 18: Concerning those who cause damage

From Exodus Chapter 68
If anyone should graze their flocks in a field or vineyard and send his animals to graze on another's field, he must make restitution from his own field according to its produce. But if the entire field was grazed, then he must make restitution from the best of his field and the best of his vineyard.[49]

44 Cf. E.17.16.
45 Exodus 21:17.
46 Deuteronomy 24:7.
47 Cf. E.8.2.
48 Leviticus 25:39–43.
49 Exodus 22:5. Cf. NG.25, 48–49, 78–79.

Title 19: Concerning those who open a pit and do not cover it

From Exodus Chapter 68
If anyone should open a pit or dig one and does not cover it, and a calf or ass falls into it, the owner of the pit shall make restitution; he shall pay money to the owner and shall keep the dead animal.[50]

Title 20: Concerning those who cause fires

From Exodus Chapter 68
If a fire breaks out and spreads to thorns and sets fire to threshing floors or ears of grain, the person who lit the fire must make restitution.[51]

Title 21: Concerning a bull that gores a man or ox

From Exodus Chapter 68
If a bull should gore a man or woman and they die, then the bull shall be stoned with stones and its flesh shall not be eaten, and the owner of the bull shall not be held responsible. However, if the bull has been in the habit of goring and the owner has been warned, but does not remove it, and it kills a man or woman, the bull shall be stoned and the owner shall also be put to death. However, if atonement money is demanded of him, he shall pay whatever ransom is demanded of him for his life. If the bull gored a son or a daughter, he shall be treated according to this ordinance. However, if the bull gored a male or female slave then he shall pay thirty silver *didrachm*s to their owner, and the bull shall be stoned.[52] And if anyone's bull should gore his neighbour's bull and it dies, they shall sell the living bull and divide the money, and they shall divide the dead bull. But if it was known that the bull was in the habit of goring, and the owner had been told and yet did not remove it, then he shall repay bull for bull, but shall have the dead animal.[53]

50 Exodus 21:33–34.
51 Exodus 22:6. Cf. E.17.40–41; NG.64.
52 Exodus 21:28–32.
53 Exodus 21:35–36.

Title 22: Concerning a mistress

From Deuteronomy Chapter 57
If you go to war against your enemies and the Lord your God delivers them into your hands, and you take plunder, and amongst the plunder you notice a beautiful woman and you desire her, you may take her as your wife,[54] and you shall go to her and be her husband, and she shall be your wife. If you are not pleased with her, send her forth free and do not sell her for money. You shall not treat her contemptuously, since you have dishonoured her.[55]

Title 23: Concerning someone who rejects and defames his wife

From Deuteronomy Chapter 64
If anyone takes a wife, lives with her, and dislikes her, and attaches to her reproachful words and gives her a bad name, saying, 'I took this woman to wife, but when I approached her I did not find proof of her virginity', then the young woman's mother and father shall bring proof to the city elders at the gate that she was a virgin. And the father of the girl shall say to the elders, 'I gave my daughter to this man as a wife, but he dislikes her and attaches to her reproachful words, saying, "I did not find your daughter to be a virgin". These are the proofs of my daughter's virginity'. Then the parents shall unfold the cloth before the elders of the city, and the elders shall take the man and punish him. They shall fine him one hundred shekels and give them to the girl's father, because he gave an Israelite virgin a bad name, and she shall be his wife. He shall never be able to divorce her. But if the report is true and no proof of the girl's virginity is found, then they shall bring the girl out to the door of her father's house, and the men of the city shall stone her with stones and she shall die, for she has wrought folly among the sons of Israel by committing fornication in her father's house.[56]

54 Deuteronomy 21:10–11.
55 Deuteronomy 21:13–14.
56 Deuteronomy 22:13–21.

Tile 24: Concerning a wife who lays hold of her opponent's genitals in a fight

From Deuteronomy Chapter 93
If men are fighting each other, a man with his brother, and the wife of one of them rushes forward to rescue her husband from the hand that hits him, and she stretches out her hand and seizes his genitals, you shall cut off her hand; your eye shall not spare her.[57]

Title 25: Concerning corrupters[58]

25.1. *From Exodus Chapter 68*
If anyone deceives a virgin who is not engaged and sleeps with her, he must give her a dowry and she shall be his wife. However, if her father absolutely refuses and will not consent to give her to him as a wife, then the man must pay to him as much money as the dowry for virgins.[59]

25.2. *From Deuteronomy Chapter 68*
If anyone should find a young virgin who is not engaged and forcibly sleeps with her and is discovered, then the man who slept with her shall give to the young girl's father fifty silver *didrachms* and she shall be his wife, for he has violated her. He shall never be able to divorce her.[60]

25.3. If a young virgin who is engaged is found to have to slept with a man inside the city, both shall be taken out to the gate of the city, and they shall be stoned with stones and shall die, because the young girl did not cry out in the city, and the man violated his neighbour's wife. You must purge the evil from among you![61]

25.4. If a man finds an engaged girl in the fields and forcibly sleeps with her, you shall only kill the man and do nothing to the girl. For the girl has committed no sin deserving death, since this is like the case when a man attacks and murders his neighbour, for the man found her in the fields, and though the betrothed girl cried out there was no one to hear her.[62]

57 Deuteronomy 25:11–12.
58 Cf. E.17.29–32.
59 Exodus 22:16–17.
60 Deuteronomy 22:28–29.
61 Deuteronomy 22:23–24.
62 Deuteronomy 22:25–27.

Title 26: Concerning adulterers[63]

26.1. *From Leviticus Chapter 94*
Any man who commits adultery with another man's wife or the wife of a neighbour, both the adulterer and adulteress shall surely die.[64]

26.2. *From Deuteronomy Chapter 65*
If a man is found sleeping with another man's wife, both shall be killed, the man who slept with the woman and the woman herself.[65]

Title 27: Concerning a woman caused to miscarry by people fighting

From Exodus Chapter 67
If two men are fighting and hit a pregnant woman, and the child arrives not fully formed, he shall be punished with a fine; as much as the woman's husband lays upon him, he shall pay with a valuation. But if the child was fully formed, then he shall give a life for a life.[66]

Title 28: Concerning the daughter of a priest who prostitutes herself

From Leviticus Chapter 95
If a daughter of a priest pollutes herself by becoming a prostitute, she pollutes the name of her father; she must be burned in the fire.[67]

63 Cf. E.17.27–28; AE.5.2.
64 Leviticus 20:10.
65 Deuteronomy 22:22.
66 Exodus 21:22–23.
67 Leviticus 21:9.

Title 29: Concerning a woman who becomes irrational[68]

From Leviticus Chapter 94
If a woman approaches any animal to have sex with it, she and the animal shall be killed.[69]

Title 30: Concerning incest with one's mother[70]

From Leviticus Chapter 90
No one shall approach any close relative to uncover their nakedness. I am the Lord. You shall not uncover the nakedness of your father or the nakedness of your mother; for she is your mother.[71]

Title 31: Concerning the same with one's stepmother

From the same, Chapter 94
If anyone should sleep with his father's wife, he has uncovered his father's nakedness and they shall both surely die, for they are guilty.[72]

Title 32: Concerning the same with one's sister

From the same, Chapter 94
Whosoever should take his sister by his father or by his mother and sees her nakedness and she sees his nakedness, it is a disgrace. They shall be destroyed utterly before the children of their family.[73]

68 Cf. E.17.39; NM.42.
69 Leviticus 20:16.
70 NM.30–41. On incest cf. E.17.33.
71 Leviticus 18:6–7.
72 Leviticus 20:11.
73 Leviticus 20:17.

Title 33: Concerning the same with one's granddaughter

From the same, Chapter 90
The nakedness of your son's daughter or your daughter's daughter, their nakedness you shall not uncover.[74]

Title 34: Concerning the same with one's aunt

From the same, Chapter 94
You shall not uncover the nakedness of your father's sister or your mother's sister, for that would uncover his near of kin. They shall bear their guilt.[75]

Title 35: Concerning the same with one's daughter-in-law, that is the wife of one's son

From the same, Chapter 94
If anyone should sleep with their daughter-in-law, they shall both surely die. They have committed sacrilege, they are guilty.[76]

Title 36: Concerning the same with a brother's wife

From the same, Chapter 94
Whatever man should take his brother's wife, it is an unclean thing. He has uncovered his brother's nakedness, and they shall die childless.[77]

74 Leviticus 18:10.
75 Leviticus 20:19.
76 Leviticus 20:12.
77 Leviticus 20:21.

Title 37: Concerning the same with a woman and her daughter

From the same, Chapter 94
Whosoever should take a woman and her mother, it is a transgression of the Law. They shall be burned with fire, both he and they, so that there might be no lawlessness among you.[78]

Title 38: Concerning the same with the daughter of one's stepmother

From the same, Chapter 90
You shall not uncover the nakedness of the daughter of your father's wife; for she is your sister from the same father.[79]

Title 39: Concerning the same with two sisters

From the same, Chapter 90
You shall not take your wife's sister as a rival to your wife and uncover her nakedness, while your wife is still living.[80]

Title 40: Concerning the same with an uncle's wife

From the same, Chapter 90
You shall not uncover the nakedness of your father's brother, and you shall not go into his wife, for she is your relation.[81]

78 Leviticus 20:14. Cf. E.17.34.
79 Leviticus 18:11.
80 Leviticus 18:18.
81 Leviticus 18:14.

Title 41: Concerning the remaining relatives

From the same, Chapter 94
Whosoever shall sleep with his relative, he has uncovered his relative's nakedness. They shall bear their sin; they shall die childless.[82]

Title 42: Concerning those who commit bestiality[83]

42.1 *From Exodus Chapter 68*
Everyone who sleeps with a beast shall surely be put to death.[84]

42.2 *From Leviticus Chapter 94*
And whosoever shall lie with an animal shall surely die, and the beast shall be killed.[85]

Title 43: Concerning the wanton

From the same, chapter 94

Whosoever shall sleep with a man as with a woman, they have wrought an abomination. They shall both be put to death.[86]

Title 44: Concerning those who kill or maim a limb of their household slave[87]

From Exodus Chapter 66
If anyone beats their man servant or maid servant with a rod, and they should die by his hand, he shall be rightly punished. But if the servant continues to live for a day or two, he shall not be punished, for he is his money.[88] And if anyone smites the eye of his man servant, or the eye of his

82 Leviticus 20:20.
83 Cf. E.17.39.
84 Exodus 22:19.
85 Leviticus 20:15.
86 Leviticus 20:13. Cf. E.17.38.
87 Cf. E.17.49.
88 Exodus 21:20–21.

maid servant, and strikes it out, he shall let them go free for their eye's sake. And if he should knock out their tooth, he shall do likewise.[89]

Title 45: Concerning anyone who hits his neighbour in a fight

From Exodus Chapter 66
If two men abuse each other, and one hits his neighbour with a stone or his fist, and he does not die but is laid upon his bed, if the man should arise and walk on his staff, then he that hit him shall be guiltless; he shall only pay for his loss of wages and healing.[90]

Title 46: Concerning those who kill intentionally and unintentionally[91]

46.1 *From Exodus Chapter 66*
If a man strikes another and he should die, he shall certainly be put to death. But if he did not do it deliberately, but God delivered him into his hands, I will give you a place to which the killer can flee. And if any one lies in wait to kill his neighbour by craft and then flees to the refuge, you shall take him from my altar and put him to death.[92]

46.2 *From Numbers Chapter 136*
If anyone should strike his neighbour with an iron object, and he dies, then he is a murderer; the murderer shall surely be put to death. Or if anyone strikes someone with a stone in hand which could cause death, and he dies, then he is a murderer; the murderer shall surely be put to death. Or if anyone should strike someone with a wooden object that could cause death, and he dies, then he is a murderer; the murderer shall surely be put to death.[93] If someone in hatred pushes another or someone lying in wait hurls any object at them, and he dies, or in enmity strikes someone, and he dies, then the striker shall surely be put to death. But if anyone should suddenly push another without hatred, or hurls any object at someone without lying

89 Exodus 21:26–27.
90 Exodus 21:18–19. Cf. E.17.48; NN.3.5 and 7.
91 Cf. E.17.1, 45–48; NN.3.6–7.
92 Exodus 21:12–14.
93 Numbers 35:16–18.

in wait, or holding any stone that could cause death unintentionally drops it on another, and he dies, though he was not his enemy, and did not seek to harm him, then the assembly shall judge between the striker and the avenger of blood in accordance with these ordinances, and the assembly shall rescue the killer from the avenger of blood, and the assembly shall send him back to the city of refuge.[94]

46.3 *From Deuteronomy Chapter 50*
And there shall be a place of refuge for any killer; and this shall be the ordinance for the killer, who might flee there and live: whosoever should unintentionally strike his neighbour, when there had been no enmity before, and whosoever should go into the forest with his neighbour to gather wood, and as he swings the axe to cut down the tree, the head of the axe slips from the handle and strikes his neighbour, who dies, the killer shall flee to one of these cities, and live. Lest the avenger of blood, following the killer because his heart is hot, should overtake him because the way is too long, and kill him, even though he did not deserve the death sentence because there was no previous enmity between them, for this reason I command this [i.e. that a place of refuge should be established.][95]

Title 47: Concerning the killing of man and beast

From Leviticus Chapter 111
Anyone who takes the life of a man shall surely be put to death. And anyone who takes the life of a beast shall make restitution, a life for a life. And if anyone injures their neighbour they shall be injured in the same manner.[96]

94 Numbers 35:20–25.

95 Deuteronomy 19:37. Interestingly, this misses out the original instruction that three cities should be established as places as refuge. This perhaps reflects the fact that all churches were now classed as places of refuge. See E.17.1.

96 Leviticus 24:17–19. Cf. NG.39–40.

Title 48: Concerning witnesses and disregarding them[97]

From Numbers 137
Anyone who takes a life, shall be killed on the testimony of witnesses, but no one shall be put to death on the evidence of one witness. And you shall not accept ransom for life from the murderer, who is worthy of death, for he shall surely be put to death. You shall not accept a ransom from someone who has fled to a city of refuge so that he can live in the land again.[98]

Title 49: Concerning witnesses and false witnesses[99]

49.1 *From Deuteronomy Chapter 44*
On the evidence of two or three witnesses shall a murderer be killed; he shall not be killed on the evidence of only one witness. The hands of the witnesses shall be the first raised against the person to be put to death, and then the hands of all the people. You must purge the evil from among you![100]

49.2 *From the same, Chapter 52*
One witness shall not stand to testify against a man for any crime or wrongdoing or sin which he may commit. Only from the mouths of two or three witnesses shall any charge stand. If a malicious witness alleges any iniquity against a man, then both parties to the dispute shall appear before the Lord, and before the priests and judges, and the judges shall make a thorough inquiry. If the malicious witness has given false testimony against his brother, then you shall do to him what he meant to do against his brother. You shall purge the evil from among you! And the rest shall be afraid.[101]

97 NM.48–49. Cf. E.14; AE.12.
98 Numbers 35:30–32. Cf. E.17.45.
99 Cf. E.14; AE.12.
100 Deuteronomy 17:6–7.
101 Deuteronomy 19:15–20.

Title 50: Concerning poisoners, diviners and enchanters

50.1 *From Exodus Chapter 78*
Do not allow poisoners to live.[102]

50.2 *From Leviticus Chapter 53*
Do not follow diviners or seek out enchanters, and so be defiled by them. I am the Lord your God.[103]

50.3 *From the same, Chapter 54*
A soul who follows diviners or enchanters, thereby prostituting himself to them, I will set my face against that soul and cut it off utterly from the people.[104] And a man or a woman who becomes a diviner or enchanter shall surely be put to death; they shall be stoned to death, for they are guilty.[105]

102 Exodus 22:18. Cf. E.17.43; AE.5.1, 6.5.

103 Leviticus 19:31.

104 Leviticus 20:6.

105 Leviticus 20:27. Cf. AE.7.

THE NOVELS OF IRENE[1]

Novel I

In the name of the Father, and of the Son and of the Holy Ghost

Irene, Pious Emperor

Knowing that God is the Bestower, Giver, Maker and Master of all good things, and trusting in the fulfilment of His holy commandments for the progress of our empire and the advancement in goodness of the Christian people entrusted to us, and calling upon Him to be a helper and assistant to us in all the affairs assigned to us by Him, for this reason we have deemed it necessary to publish a chapter concerning the eradication of oaths.[2]

For all those who are not ignorant of Holy Scripture it is manifestly clear that the Law given through Moses is a shadow of future goodness and not itself the icon of things,[3] on account of the imperfection and immaturity of those who received it. For those who have clung to the sojourn of this age lately could not be made to hear the truth itself.[4] But at the end of days,

1 Irene, *Novels*, ed. L. Burgmann, 'Die Novellen der Kaiserin Eirene', *FM* IV (Frankfurt, 1981), 1–36, with a parallel German translation.

2 Oaths were a central component of Byzantine justice and can be found across these texts. See for instance E.6.4.3, 14.4, 14.7, 17.2; AE.12; NN.2.15, NN.3.12–14; NG. 26–28, 73; NM.8.1, 12.1–2, 13. For the overall importance of oaths in Byzantine society at this time see Nichanian, 'Iconoclasme et prestation de serment à Byzance?' One should also compare the first three paragraphs of this Novel with the rhetoric of the *Ecloga*'s prologue. Both are not only steeped in Scripture but structure their argument around biblical commands.

3 Cf. Hebrews 10:1.

4 This complex opening, couched in biblical language, is an attack on the Iconoclasts in general, and the Isaurian emperors in particular, whose ideology was so dependent on the Old Testament and the Law of Moses. Here, using the words of Hebrews 10:1, that law is declared only the foreshadow of Christ's Grace, which is the true 'icon' of things, that is

He himself, the son[5] of God and our God, shall come to save our race. Bringing in this way the Old Law given through Moses to completion and illuminating all peoples with the knowledge of His truth, He gave to us, we who are to be perfected, knowledge of His perfect law from His grace. Illustrating the whole through an exemplary portion, we say along with the Evangelist: In the past it was said 'Thou shalt not kill', but the Lord, ordering us to cut away the beginnings of sins, tells us not to be angry without cause; [it was said] 'Thou shalt not commit adultery', but we are not to look at a woman in lust; [it was said] 'Thou shalt not swear falsely', but we are not to swear at all.[6]

Concerning which, the present edict has been toiled upon by us, since perjury, which is a denial of God, is brought forth from oaths. But a certain custom, which is not fair and pleasing to the Lord, but may rather be called a mostly Hebrew custom, has prevailed until now, that of resolving the complications of disputes by means of an oath. For since our God and Saviour Jesus Christ, who ordained the Old Law, expressly commands, as has been said, that there should be no swearing at all; since, following him, the Apostle James cries out, 'Above all, my brothers, do not swear';[7] and since, likewise, our glorious and blessed fathers have followed suit and agreed, passing down the injunction to refrain from all oaths, we bow the neck of our rule to this divine legislation and we banish this prevailing, contrary and unlawful custom, deeming it not right that the pollution of oaths should be authorised among the most Christian flock entrusted to us. For if the most grandiloquent[8] prophet Isaiah says, 'Those who cause my people to sin with words shall be destroyed utterly', how much more so [if

the true form of goodness. The only people who could think otherwise were those ignorant of Scripture (i.e. the Iconoclasts), or those who originally received the Law because of their 'imperfection and immaturity' (i.e. the Jews), with whom the Iconoclasts were rhetorically aligned and thereby traduced by the Iconophiles. It is the Iconoclasts, sojourning—*paroikia*, a word used to refer both to the Jews in Egypt but also to Christians in general living in exile in this veil of tears, see e.g. Psalm 120:5, Acts 13:17, 1 Peter 1:17—in this present age who could not be 'made to hear'—*akoutizō*, yet another word and idea with rich biblical connotations, see e.g. Judges 13:23, Song of Songs 2:14—the 'truth itself', that the Law of Moses was not the true icon of Christ. For more on the Iconoclasts' use of the Old Testament and the Iconophiles' response, which labelled the Iconoclasts ignorant and 'Jewish-minded', see Auzépy, 'State of Emergency', 278–84.

5 Some MSS have 'the Word of God'.

6 Matthew 5:21–22, 27–28, 33–34.

7 James 5:12.

8 It is a good measure of the distance between Byzantine and modern mentalities that calling someone 'grandiloquent', today an insult, was deemed high praise in Byzantium.

they do so] with an oath?[9] For Moses himself also explicitly cries out to reject oaths to those willing to examine carefully the Holy Scriptures, for he says, 'Do not swear falsely by the name of Lord your God',[10] and 'Do not take the name of the Lord your God in vain'.[11] Therefore, the concerns of this world and disputes about things are all unjust and vain, for according to the saying of Solomon, 'All is vanity'.[12] But for us, before whom the prize of citizenship in the kingdom of heaven and the company of angels is presented by the evangelists, the laws are similarly lofty.

Wherefore we decree that every case and dispute resolved through use of written or unwritten testimony shall be settled as follows:

In our imperial city, for betrothals, dowries, limited *emphyteusis*[13] of any kind, recording of orphans' property, agreements of all sorts, settlements, gifts, sales, purchases, loans, deposits, wills and manumissions, and any other similar legal matters, seven or five (or, in the case of wills or manumissions and only for these, three)[14] trustworthy witnesses—priests, magistrates, imperial officials, leading citizens of wealth or with a profession, people who manifestly live piously and in reverence—shall be called forward, and in the presence of these shall all kinds of contracts, agreements and documents be produced. And if the author of a document can write, let him write it all, the witnesses adding their signatures—except for betrothals and limited leases, for in these cases let the *taboularioi*, the *nomikoi* and the witnesses do the writing in the normal way, the witnesses who sign belonging to the categories mentioned above.[15]

Whenever a contract made in this way is contested by any of the parties, the witnesses and the documents shall be brought forward, and the witnesses shall be asked about whether the document is genuine. And if they agree, calling upon God as a witness, and say that the document produced is genuine, then the hearing should end, the plaintiff should be fined by the judge the sum included in the document which was produced and should hand it over to his opponent. But if the lawsuit takes place

9 Isaiah 29:20–21.

10 Leviticus 19:12.

11 Exodus 20:7.

12 Ecclesiastes 1:2.

13 *Emphyteusis* was a form of long-term tenure; for more, see E.12.

14 On the number of witnesses being potentially lower for wills, see E.5.4.

15 As discussed at 60 n. 88, a *taboularios* was an official charged with the preparation of documents and part of an organised guild in Constantinople. *Nomikoi* were another form of notary in Byzantium, and in Constantinople were subaltern officials to the *Eparch*. See A. Kazhdan, 'Nomikos', *ODB*, vol. 3, 1490.

after the deaths of the witnesses in the deed which was produced, then the hearing shall end in the same way without further investigation.[16]

But if the man who commissioned the document [which fell] under the headings listed above is illiterate or cannot write because of a disability, he should place a precious cross at the top and have the rest of it written by a *taboularios* or *nomikos* or other scribes. If necessary, the witnesses should sign; otherwise, they should be identified by their names.

This is the procedure to be followed for unwritten agreements: as has been said, seven or five trustworthy witnesses (or, in the case of wills and manumissions and only then, at least three) shall be summoned and in their presence contracts and agreements of all kinds shall be concluded. Whenever a dispute arises from any of the parties, the witnesses shall be found and questioned. And if, while under examination two or three times by the judges, they agree with the plaintiff, let them make a written statement in their own hand and deposit it in a church. If they are illiterate, let them make the sign of the precious cross and let the rest be written by scribes, using this form of words: 'Such and such with occupations or titles. The Lord God be our witness and this holy place in which we stand and deposit this document. We bore true witness and did not lie in any way, and with this testimony of ours we will stand before the fearful tribunal[17] of Christ our God. May we and our children now and forever receive our just deserts for this testimony of ours. If ever we are proved to be false witnesses on any occasion or at any time, then we shall pay for the damages arising from our testimony to the injured party, and we shall be subjected to the penalty for false witness, for as it is written in Proverbs, "A false witness shall not go unpunished for his wrongdoing"'.[18]

If the witnesses do not agree or give testimony for each party, then the judge should make a selection from the witnesses, and let those who are in a majority and are more trustworthy write statements in their own hand (as has been said), and the case be so settled.

Let these procedures be followed in the cities outside [Constantinople] and in the provinces, except when boundaries are at issue. For we decree that disputes about these shall be settled according to the declaration of witnesses holding the holy gospels or the precious cross, as has been the

16 That is, what is said in the document should be followed.

17 The *bēma* was both a judicial tribunal and the sanctuary of a church, and presumably a deliberate play on words here.

18 Proverbs 19:5.

custom prevailing until now, with the obvious proviso that they shall not swear and shall draft the document in the proper manner, as stated above.[19]

Novel II

The same pious emperor

Concerning those who unlawfully contract third or subsequent marriages, and concerning those who marry their own female slaves

Moses, who saw God, said about what is written in Holy Scripture, 'it is not to be added to, nor is it to be taken away from'.[20] Therefore, what was previously said in the second title [of the *Ecloga*], following the divine Apostle Paul about those contracting lawful marriages,[21] quoting him about doing so up to a second union and under no circumstances a subsequent one (as such are unlawful and bestial), is hereby confirmed.[22]

Wherefore we order that all third marriages and subsequent unions shall not take place, as they are alien to the commandment of the divine Apostle and foreign to Christian kinship. Nor indeed shall girls who happen to be household slaves be brought into a legitimate marriage or called a spouse, especially by the pre-eminent and those holding a dignity.[23] If anyone should dare to do this from now on, the union shall be illegal and children born of such marriages shall be bastards.

19 Cf. AE.2; NG.7.
20 Deuteronomy 4:2, 12:32.
21 I Corinthians 7.
22 Cf. E.2.8.
23 Cf. AE.4.1, 4.

BIBLIOGRAPHY

Translated Texts

Appendix Eclogae, ed. L. Burgmann and S. Troianos, 'Appendix Eclogae', *FM* III (Frankfurt, 1979), 24–125.

Ecloga, ed. L. Burgmann, *Ecloga: Das Gesetzbuch Leons III. und Konstantinos V.* (Frankfurt, 1983). Old edition by A. Momferratos, *Ecloga Leonis et Constantini cum appendice* (Athens, 1889); trans. E. Freshfield, *A Manual of Roman Law, The Ecloga* (Cambridge, 1926).

Irene, *Novels*, ed. L. Burgmann, 'Die Novellen der Kaiserin Eirene', *FM* IV (Frankfurt, 1981), 1–36.

Krisis peri gambrōn stratiōtōn, ed. D. Simon, 'Byzantinische Hausgemeinschafts-verträge', in F. Baur, K. Larenz and F. Wieacker (eds), *Beiträge zur europäischen Rechtsgeschichte und zum geltenden Zivilrecht: Festgabe für J. Sontis* (Munich, 1977), 91–128, text at 94.

Nomos Georgikos, ed. I. Medvedev et al., *Vizantiĭskiĭ zemledel'cheskiĭ zakon* (Leningrad, 1984). Old edition by W. Ashburner, 'The Farmer's Law I', *JHS* 30 (1910), 85–108 (edition); 'The Farmer's Law II', *JHS* 32 (1912), 68–95 (commentary and translation).

Nomos Mosaikos, ed. L. Burgmann and S. Troianos, 'Nomos Mosaikos', *FM* III (Frankfurt, 1979), 126–67.

Nomos Rhodion Nautikos, ed. W. Ashburner, *The Rhodian Sea-Law* (Oxford, 1909). See also the new edition of the *Rhodian Sea Law* as it was incorporated into the *Basilica*: G. Rodolakes, *Apo to Nomo Rodiōn sto 53o Biblio tōn Basilikōn: sumbolē stē meletē tou Buzantinou nautikou dikaiou* (Athens, 2007).

Nomos Stratiotikos, ed. W. Ashburner, 'The Byzantine Mutiny Law', *JHS* 46 (1926), 85–109.

Other Primary Sources

Agapetus, *Ekthesis*, ed. R. Riedinger, *Der Fürstenspiegel des Kaisers Justinianos* (Athens, 1995).

Aristotle, *Politics*, trans. S. Everson, *Aristotle: The Politics and the Constitution of Athens* (Cambridge, 1996).

Basil of Caesarea, ed. J.-P. Migne, *In Principium Proverbiorum*, Patrologia Graeca 31 (Paris, 1857), 385–424.

Basilica, ed. H. Scheltema et al., *Basilicorum libri LX*, Series A (Text) 8 vols, Series B (Scholia) 9 vols (Groningen, 1953–88).

Book of the Eparch, ed. J. Koder, *Das Eparchenbuch Leons der Weisen* (Vienna, 1991).

Burgmann, L., et al. (eds), *Repertorium der Handschriften des byzantinischen Rechts: Teil I Die Handschriften des weltlichen Rechts* (Frankfurt, 1995); A. Schminck and D. Getov (eds), *Teil II Die Handschriften des kirchlichen Rechts I* (Frankfurt, 2010).

Collectio Tripartita, ed. N. Van der Wal and B. Stolte, *Collectio Tripartita: Justinian on Religious and Ecclesiastical Affairs* (Groningen, 1994).

The Council in Trullo, ed. H. Ohme, *Das Konzil Quinisextum* (Turnhout, 2006); trans. G. Nedungatt and M. Featherstone (eds), *The Council in Trullo Revisited* (Rome, 1995).

Ecloga ad Prochiron mutata, ed. K. Zacharia von Lingenthal, *Jus Graeco-Romanum* IV (Leipzig, 1865), 49–170.

Eisagoge, ed. K. Zacharia von Lingenthal, *Collectio librorum juris Graeco-Romani ineditorum* (Leipzig, 1852), 61–217.

Grierson, P., *Catalogue of the Byzantine Coins in the Dumbarton Oaks Collection and in the Whittemore Collection, III: Leo III to Nicephorus III, 717–1081*, 2 vols (Washington D.C., 1973).

Heraclius, *Novels*, ed. J. Konidaris, 'Die Novellen des Kaisers Herakleios', *FM* V (Frankfurt, 1982), 33–106.

Justinian I, *Codex Iustinianus*, ed. P. Krüger, vol. 2 of *Corpus iuris civilis* (11th ed., Berlin, 1929); trans. F. Blume, *Annotated Justinian Code*, ed. T. Kearley, http://www.uwyo.edu/lawlib/blume-justinian/.

Justinian I, *Digest*, ed. P. Krüger and T. Mommsen, vol. 1 of *Corpus iuris civilis* (16th ed., Berlin, 1928); trans. A. Watson, *The Digest of Justinian* (Philadelphia, 1985).

Justinian I, *Institutes*, ed. P. Krüger and T. Mommsen, vol. 1 of *Corpus iuris civilis* (16th ed., Berlin, 1928); trans. P. Birks and G. McLeod, *Justinian's Institutes* (London, 1987).

Justinian I, *Novellae*, ed. R. Schöll and G. Kroll, vol. 3 of *Corpus iuris civilis* (6th ed., Berlin, 1928).

Leo VI, *Taktika*, ed. G. Dennis, *The Taktika of Leo VI* (Washington D.C., 2010).

Plato, *Republic*, trans. R. Waterfield (Oxford, 2008).

Prochiron, ed. K. Zacharia von Lingenthal, *Ὁ Πρόχειρος Νόμος* (Heidelberg, 1837); trans. E. Freshfield, *A Manual of Eastern Roman Law: The Procheiros Nomos* (Cambridge, 1928).

The Septuagint, ed. and trans. L. Brenton, *The Septuagint with Apocrypha: Greek and English* (London, 1851).

Strategikon, ed. G. Dennis and E. Gamillscheg, *Das Strategikon des Maurikios* (Vienna, 1981); trans. G. Dennis, *Maurice's Strategikon: Handbook of Byzantine Military Strategy* (Philadelphia, 1984).

Theophanes Confessor, *Chronicle*, ed. C. de Boor, (Leipzig, 1883–85); trans. C. Mango and R. Scott, *The Chronicle of Theophanes Confessor: Byzantine and Near Eastern history, AD 284–813* (Oxford, 1997).

Secondary Literature

Angold, M., 'The Byzantine Political Process at Crisis Point', in P. Stephenson (ed.), *The Byzantine World* (London, 2010), 5–21.

Arjava, A., 'Paternal Power in Late Antiquity', *Journal of Roman Studies* 88 (1998), 147–65.

Auzépy, M.-F., *L'Histoire des iconoclastes* (Paris, 2007).

Auzépy, M.-F., 'State of Emergency', in J. Shepard (ed.), *The Cambridge History of the Byzantine Empire c.500–1492* (Cambridge, 2008), 251–91.

Avotins, I., *On the Greek of the Novels of Justinian* (Hildesheim, 1992).

Barber, C., *Figure and Likeness: On the Limits of Representation in Byzantine Iconoclasm* (Princeton, 2002).

Bartusis, M., 'Solemnion', A. Kazhdan et al. (eds), *The Oxford Dictionary of Byzantium*, 3 vols (Oxford, 1991), vol. 3, 1924.

Bell, P., *Three Political Voices from the Age of Justinian* (Liverpool, 2009).

Berger, A., *Encyclopaedic Dictionary of Roman Law* (Philadelphia, 1953).

Brand, C., *Roman Military Law* (Austin, 1968).

Brandes, W., and Haldon, J., 'Towns, Tax and Transformation: State, Cities and their Hinterlands in the East Roman World, ca. 500–800', in N. Gauthier, (ed.), *Towns and their Hinterlands between Late Antiquity and the Early Middle Ages* (Leiden, 2000), 141–72.

Brubaker, L. and Haldon, J., *Byzantium in the Iconoclast Era, c.680–850: The Sources* (Aldershot, 2001).

Brubaker, L. and Haldon, J., *Byzantium in the Iconoclast Era, c.680–850: A History* (Cambridge, 2011).

Bryer, A. and Herrin, J., *Iconoclasm: Papers Given at the Ninth Spring Symposium of Byzantine Studies, University of Birmingham, March 1975* (Birmingham, 1977).

Burgmann, L., 'Ecloga', in A. Kazhdan et al. (eds), *The Oxford Dictionary of Byzantium*, 3 vols (Oxford, 1991), vol. 1, 672–73.

Burgmann, L., 'Die Nomoi Stratiotikos, Georgikos und Nautikos', *Zbornik Radova Vizantološkog Instituta* XLVI (2009), 53–64.

Bury, J.B., *The Imperial Administrative System in the Ninth Century, with a Revised Text of the Kletorologion of Philotheos* (London, 1911).

Cappel, A., 'Emphyteusis', in A. Kazhdan et al. (eds), *The Oxford Dictionary of Byzantium*, 3 vols (Oxford, 1991), vol. 1, 693–94.

Cappel, A., 'Roga', in A. Kazhdan et al. (eds), *The Oxford Dictionary of Byzantium*, 3 vols (Oxford, 1991), vol. 3, 1801.

Constantelos, D., *Byzantine Philanthropy and Social Welfare* (New Brunswick, 1968).

Crook, J., 'Legal History and General History', *Bulletin of the Institute of Classical Studies* 41 (1996), 31–36.

Decker, M., *Tilling the Hateful Earth: Agricultural Production in the Late Antique East* (Oxford, 2009).

Donner, F., *Muhammad and the Believers at the Origins of Islam* (London, 2010).

Evans Grubbs, J., '"Marriage More Shameful than Adultery": Slave-Mistress Relationships, "Mixed Marriages", and Late Roman Law', *Phoenix* 47 (1993), 125–54.

Flower, R., 'The Insanity of Heretics Must Be Restrained: Heresiology in the *Theodosian Code*', in C. Kelly (ed.), *Theodosius II: Rethinking the Roman Empire in Late Antiquity* (Cambridge, 2013), 172–94.

Fögen, M.-T., 'Arrha Sponsalicia', A. Kazhdan et al. (eds), *The Oxford Dictionary of Byzantium*, 3 vols (Oxford, 1991), vol. 1, 185–86.

Fögen, M.-T., 'Hypobolon', in A. Kazhdan et al. (eds), *The Oxford Dictionary of Byzantium*, 3 vols (Oxford, 1991), vol. 2, 965.

Fowden, G., *Before and After Muhammad: The First Millennium Refocused* (Princeton, 2013).

Garnsey, P., *Social Status and Legal Privilege in the Roman Empire* (Oxford, 1970).

Gero, S., *Byzantine Iconoclasm during the Reign of Leo III with Particular Attention to the Oriental Sources* (Louvain, 1973).

Gero, S., *Byzantine Iconoclasm during the Reign of Constantine V with Particular Attention to the Oriental Sources* (Louvain, 1977).

Haldon, J., *Byzantine Praetorians* (Bonn, 1984).

Haldon, J., 'Military Service, Military Lands, and the Status of Soldiers: Current Problems and Interpretations', *Dumbarton Oaks Papers* 47 (1993), 1–67.

Haldon, J., *Byzantium in the Seventh Century: The Transformation of a Culture* (rev. ed., Cambridge, 1997).

Harries, J., *Law and Crime in the Roman World* (Cambridge, 2007).

Hendy, M., *Studies in the Byzantine Monetary Economy, c.300–1450* (Cambridge, 1985).

Herrin, J., *Women in Purple: Rulers of Medieval Byzantium* (London, 2001).

Honoré, T., *Tribonian* (London, 1978).

Howard-Johnston, J., *Witnesses to a World Crisis: Historians and Histories of the Middle East in the Seventh Century* (Oxford, 2010).

Hoyland, R., *Seeing Islam as Others Saw It: A Survey and Evaluation of Christian, Jewish, and Zoroastrian Writings on Early Islam* (Princeton, 1997).

Humphreys, M., *Law, Power, and Imperial Ideology in the Iconoclast Era, c.680–850* (Oxford, 2015).

Jones, A.H.M., *The Later Roman Empire, 284–602: A Social Economic and Administrative Survey*, 2 vols (Oxford, 1964).

Kazhdan, A., 'Chartoularios', in A. Kazhdan et al. (eds), *The Oxford Dictionary of Byzantium*, 3 vols (Oxford, 1991), vol. 1, 416.

Kazhdan, A., 'Eparch of the City', in A. Kazhdan et al. (eds), *The Oxford Dictionary of Byzantium*, 3 vols (Oxford, 1991), vol. 1, 705.

Kazhdan, A., 'Nomikos', in A. Kazhdan et al. (eds), *The Oxford Dictionary of Byzantium*, 3 vols (Oxford, 1991), vol. 3, 1490.

Kazhdan, A., 'Scholae Palatinae', in A. Kazhdan et al. (eds), *The Oxford Dictionary of Byzantium*, 3 vols (Oxford, 1991), vol. 3, 1851–52.

Kazhdan, A., 'Tagma', in A. Kazhdan et al. (eds), *The Oxford Dictionary of Byzantium*, 3 vols (Oxford, 1991), vol. 3, 2007.

Kazhdan, A., and Cutler, A., 'Notary', in A. Kazhdan et al. (eds), *The Oxford Dictionary of Byzantium*, 3 vols (Oxford, 1991), vol. 3, 1495.

Laiou, A., 'A Note on the Farmer's Law, Chapter 67', *Byzantion* 41 (1971), 197–204.

Letsios, D., *Νόμος Ῥοδίων Ναυτικός—Das Seegesetz der Rhodier. Untersuchung zu Seerecht und Handelsschiffahrt in Byzanz* (Rhodes, 1996).

Lilie, R.-J., 'Die zweihundertjährige Reform: zu den Anfängen der Themenorganisation im 7. und 8. Jahrhundert', *Byzantinoslavica* 45 (1984), 27–39, 190–201.

Maas, M., 'Roman History and Christian Ideology in Justinianic Reform Legislation', *Dumbarton Oaks Papers* 40 (1986), 17–31.

Maas, M., (ed.), *The Cambridge Companion to the Age of Justinian* (Cambridge, 2005).

MacMullen, R., 'Judicial Savagery in the Roman Empire', *Chiron* 16 (1988), 147–66.

Magdalino, P., 'Justice and Finance in the Byzantine State, Ninth to Twelfth Centuries', in A. Laiou and D. Simon (eds), *Law and Society in Byzantium: Ninth–Twelfth Centuries* (Washington D.C., 1994), 93–115.

Magdalino, P., and Nelson, R. (eds), *The Old Testament in Byzantium* (Washington D.C., 2010).

McCormick, M., *Origins of the European Economy: Communications and Commerce, AD 300–900* (Cambridge, 2001).

McGeer, E., 'Camp', in A. Kazhdan et al. (eds), *The Oxford Dictionary of Byzantium*, 3 vols (Oxford, 1991), vol. 1, 369.

Nichanian, M., 'Iconoclasme et prestation de serment à Byzance? Du contrôle social à la nouvelle alliance', in M.-F. Auzépy and G. Saint-Guillain (eds), *Oralité et lien social au Moyen Âge: Occident, Byzance, Islam: parole donnée, foi jurée, serment* (Paris, 2008), 81–102.

Oikonomidès, N., *Les Listes de préséances byzantines des IXᵉ–Xᵉ siècles* (Paris, 1972).

Oikonomidès, N., 'Middle Byzantine Provincial Recruits: Salary and Armaments', in J. Duffy and J. Peradotto (eds), *Gonimos: Neoplatonic and Byzantine Studies* (Buffalo, 1988), 121–36.

Oikonomidès, N., 'Indiction', in A. Kazhdan et al. (eds), *The Oxford Dictionary of Byzantium*, 3 vols (Oxford, 1991), vol. 2, 993.

Oikonomidès, N., 'Titles, Purchase of', in A. Kazhdan et al. (eds), *The Oxford Dictionary of Byzantium*, 3 vols (Oxford, 1991), vol. 3, 2089.

Oikonomidès, N., 'The Role of the Byzantine State in the Economy', in A. Laiou et al. (eds), *The Economic History of Byzantium*, 3 vols (Washington D.C., 2002), vol. 3, 973–1058.

Pieler, P., 'Byzantinische Rechtsliteratur', in H. Hunger (ed.), *Die hochsprachliche profane Literatur der Byzantiner*, 2 vols (Munich, 1978), vol. 2, 341–480.

Prinzing, G., 'Das Bild Iustinians I. in der Uberlieferung der Byzantiner vom 7. bis 15. Jahrhundert', *FM* VII (Frankfurt, 1986), 1–99.

Sarris, P., 'Economics, Trade, and "Feudalism"', in L. James (ed.), *A Companion to Byzantium* (Chichester, 2010), 25–42.

Sarris, P., *Empires of Faith: The Fall of Rome to the Rise of Islam, 500–700* (Oxford, 2011).

Scheltema, H., 'Byzantine Law', in J. Hussey (ed.), *The Cambridge Medieval History Vol. IV* (Cambridge, 1967), pt. 2, 55–77.

Schilbach, E., *Byzantinische Metrologie* (Munich, 1970).

Schminck, A., 'Bermerkungen zum sog. "Nomos Mosaikos"', in *FM* XI (2005), 249–68.

Simon, D., 'Legislation as Both a World Order and a Legal Order', in A. Laiou and D. Simon (eds), *Law and Society in Byzantium: Ninth–Twelfth Centuries* (Washington D.C., 1994), 1–25.

Spatharakis, I., 'The Text of Chapter 30 of the Lex Rhodia Nautica', *Hellenika* 26 (1973), 207–15.

Speck, P., *Artabasdos, der rechtgläubige Vorkämpfer der göttlichen Lehren: Untersuchungen zur Revolte des Artabasdos und ihrer Darstellung in der byzantinischen Historiographie* (Bonn, 1981).

Speck, P., *Ich bin's nicht, Kaiser Konstantin ist es gewesen: die Legenden vom Einfluss des Teufels, des Juden und des Moslem auf den Ikonoklasmus* (Bonn, 1990).

Stolte, B., 'Not New but Novel: Notes on the Historiography of Byzantine Law', *Byzantine and Modern Greek Studies* 22 (1998), 264–79.

Stolte, B., 'Balancing Byzantine Law', *FM* XI (2005), 57–75.

Svoronos, N., 'Notes sur l'origine et la date du code rural', *Travaux et mémoires* 8 (1981), 487–500.

Troianos, S., *Oi Pēges tou Vyzantinou dikaiou: eisagōgiko voēthēma* (Athens, 1986).

Turner, D., 'The Politics of Despair: The Plague of 746–47 and Iconoclasm in the Byzantine Empire', *The Annual of the British School at Athens* 85 (1990), 419–34.

Van Bochove, T., *To Date and Not to Date: On the Date and Status of Byzantine Law Books* (Groningen, 1996).

Van der Wal, N., and Lokin, J., *Historiae iuris Graeco-Romani delineatio: les sources du droit byzantin de 300 à 1453* (Groningen, 1985).

Whittow, M., *The Making of Orthodox Byzantium* (Basingstoke, 1996).

INDEX

abortion 43, 75, 98–99, 101
alienation 41, 61–62, 109
  see also dowry, exchange, gifts, inheritance, sale
animals 28, 31, 42–43, 70, 82, 108, 134–35, 137–38, 141, 149–52, 156, 159
  asses 134–35, 144, 149–50, 152
  bulls 43, 70, 141, 152
  calves 149–50, 152
  dogs 135, 137–38
  horses 42, 67, 70
  oxen 132–35, 139, 141, 144, 152
  pigs 134–35
  rams 43, 70, 134
  sheep 133–35, 149–50
  wolves 132, 134
  see also sexual crimes: bestiality
Antecessores 4, 14, 22, 98, 109–10
apostates 42, 69–70, 95–96
Arabs 5–8
Army 6–9, 18–21, 32, 77–88
  arms 67, 70, 78, 82, 85–88
  camp 43, 66, 70, 81–82, 85–86, 88
  conspiracy 80, 83, 86
  desertion 19, 44, 58, 77, 81, 84, 86
  military pay 66–68, 77–79
  mutiny 80
  officers 77, 80–84, 87–88, 92
  sedition 80, 83, 86
  soldiers 18–21, 42, 62, 66–68, 78–88
  spoils 19, 44, 67, 77
  units 7–8, 21, 80–82
  see also Peculium Castrense
arson 27, 31, 44, 75, 136
  see also fire
Artabasdos 7–8, 23

baptism 40, 46, 58, 73, 93–96, 103
Barbarians 84, 86, 114
betrothal 38–39, 43, 45–46, 74, 109, 154, 166
Biblical figures
  God 1, 6, 10, 15–17, 23, 29–32, 34–38, 48–51, 57–58, 67, 69, 73, 77, 101, 108, 130, 132, 143–51, 153, 156, 160, 162–68
  Isaiah 34, 165
  James 165
  Jesus Christ 32, 34, 37, 165
  Jesus son of Sirach 37
  Maccabees, the 16, 77
  Moses 1, 10, 16, 29–30, 140, 143–44, 146–47, 149, 164–66, 168
  Paul 48–49, 168
  Peter 35
  Pharisees, the 51
  Solomon 1, 10, 16, 36–37, 166
bishops 57, 95
blasphemy 140, 143–44, 166
blinding (non-punishment)
  of animals 133, 135, 138
  of people 115, 119
  see also corporal punishment: blinding
boundary markers 90–91, 108, 130
  see also fences, property disputes
Bulgars 5, 8

capital punishment 69, 80–88, 90, 98, 103, 144–45, 151–52, 154–56, 159–63
  by beheading 83, 88, 91, 94, 96, 100, 103
  by burning 75, 97, 102, 155, 158
  by the sword 74–77
  hanging 76, 86, 134
  sent to the mines 99, 101
  thrown to wild beasts 86, 98, 102
  see also exile, slavery: enslavement
Chartoularioi 61–62, 66–67
Christians 37, 42, 45–46, 69–70, 93, 95–96, 103, 164–65, 168
Church, the 30, 58, 62, 70, 72–73, 92, 96
churches 42, 49, 57, 69, 95, 167
  Hagia Sophia 62
cities 5–6, 30, 75, 81, 94, 107, 121, 145–46, 153–54, 161–62, 167
  see also Constantinople
citizenship 96, 111, 166
clerics 42, 58, 66–67, 69, 71, 92, 95, 141, 155, 162, 166
  see also bishops, churches, the Church, monks
clothing 79, 119, 125, 136, 147–49
  see also silk
confiscation of property 74, 76, 82, 86–87, 91, 93–96, 99, 101–03
Constantine I 15
Constantine V 1, 8–10, 14, 15, 16, 18, 21, 23, 28, 30, 31, 33, 34, 78 n. 1, 80 n. 5
Constantine VI 10, 31, 32
Constantinople 4–9, 15, 35, 57, 62, 92, 102, 166–67
corporal punishment 17
  amputation of
    hand 70–71, 76, 134, 136, 138, 154
    nose 73–74
    penis 75
    tongue 69, 133
  beating 44, 69–76, 83–84, 86, 88, 90, 118, 133, 136–38
  blinding (as punishment) 31, 71, 134, 137
  branding 136
  scourging 102
  shaving of head 71, 74
  torture 63, 76, 86, 118
  whipping 86, 133–34, 136–38

damage
  by or to animals 28, 31, 70, 132–39, 138, 141, 149–51
  to property 75, 81, 120, 123–27, 129–23, 136, 138
  see also injury
damnatio memoriae 86
debt 40–42, 52, 56, 60, 64–65, 89–90, 109, 111, 122, 126, 136, 148
  see also guarantors, loans, security, sureties
delict *see* damage, injury
deposits
  as down-payment 40, 59, 131
  for safekeeping 41, 60–61, 114–16, 121–22, 141, 149–50, 166
  see also freight charge
demons 51, 76, 98
divorce 17, 50–51, 73, 98, 105, 146, 153–54
documents 14, 32, 38–39, 41, 45–47, 49, 52–53, 57, 59–61, 63–65, 111, 115–16, 121–23, 126, 166–68
  see also wills
dowry 39, 46–48, 50, 52–53, 60–61, 93, 105, 154, 166
drugs 97–101, 137

Emperors 4, 6, 9–10, 23, 29, 34–35, 68–69, 78, 86 108, 164, 168
enemies 35, 37, 40, 58, 62, 69, 77, 81–86, 88, 120, 136, 153, 161

estates 63, 93
exchange 41, 62, 129–30
exile 17, 69–71, 73–76, 83–84, 87, 90–91, 96, 98–101, 103
  deportation 87, 102

family
  children 37, 39–42, 45–50, 54–58, 60, 63, 68, 73–76, 93, 95, 97, 104–06, 108, 114, 140, 145, 147, 151, 155–56, 167–68
  concubines 56, 105–06
  cousins 46, 75, 104
  daughters 43, 46, 55–56, 74–75, 93, 96–97, 104, 141, 144, 147, 152–53, 155, 158
  fathers 46, 48, 50, 55–56, 66–68, 73–75, 93, 104–06, 137, 140, 144–47, 153–58
  grandchildren 49, 54–55, 104, 141
  grandparents 55, 66, 104
  husbands 39, 41, 47–52, 60, 73, 76, 98, 109, 146, 153–55
  illegitimate children 105–06, 168
  in-laws 18–19, 46, 78–79, 141, 157
  mistresses 141, 153
  mothers 37, 43, 46–48, 50, 55, 68, 73–76, 97, 104–06, 141, 144–45, 153, 156, 158
  parents 41, 45–46, 48–49, 52–57, 60, 63, 66–68, 74, 93, 98, 105, 108, 140, 145, 153
  sons 46, 55–56, 68, 74–75, 87, 104, 141, 144–45, 147, 152, 157
  stepchildren 46, 74
  stepparents 56, 74, 141, 156, 158
  wives 39, 41, 43, 46–52, 55, 60, 73–76, 88, 95–96, 105–06, 109, 147
fences 135–36
  see also boundary markers
fields 28, 63, 75, 90–91, 107, 109, 114, 129–39, 144, 151, 154
fighting 24, 44, 76, 115, 118–19, 141–42, 154–55, 160
fines 17, 45, 60, 64–65, 72, 75, 81, 83–84, 90, 92–93, 103, 118, 122–23, 126, 131–37, 139, 149–50, 152–55, 166–67
fire 44, 61, 75, 114, 122, 124, 135, 141, 152
  see also arson
foodstuffs 148
  fish 114
  grain 117, 126, 136–37, 152
  milk 133
  olive oil 126
  wine 88, 126, 137
forgery 43, 71
fraud 42, 61, 65, 112, 121, 143
freight charge 116, 122–27
friends 36, 49, 57, 110

gardens 28, 133, 135
gifts 16, 37, 39, 42, 48, 50, 52–53, 64, 67, 78, 93, 109, 143, 166
  betrothal gift 45
  nuptial gift 47
Gospels 69, 114, 167
guarantors 62, 85, 89–90
  see also debt, loans, security, sureties

heretics 11, 22–24, 92–96, 103
  Manicheans 44, 77, 92–96
  Montanists 44, 77, 94
  see also the Orthodox
hiring
  animals 42, 70, 134, 150
  labour 28, 58, 60, 85, 119, 133, 146, 151
  ships 115–16, 120, 122–27
  tools 132
  see also freight charge, leases

homicide 17, 26, 30, 44, 76, 84, 91, 97, 115, 119, 142–44, 150, 154, 159–62, 165

Imperial House, the 62–63, 103, 112
imperial officials 6, 15, 42, 62, 66–67, 92–93, 95, 108, 112, 120, 166
  Antigrapheis 15, 35, 38
  Defensores Civitates 60, 93
  Dioikētai 62
  the *Eparch* of Constantinople 92, 125 n. 38, 166 n. 15
  the *Quaestor* 15, 35, 38
  see also judges, magistrates, *Nomikoi, Taboularioi*
inheritance 22, 39–40, 42, 47–50, 53–57, 62, 66–68, 93, 97, 100, 105–07, 109–11, 147
  see also Peculium, Peculium Castrense, wills
infamy 50, 85, 87, 101–02
infanticide 76 n. 174
injury 54, 58, 107, 161, 167
  insult 53–54, 56, 58, 72–73, 92, 101–02
  personal 44, 53, 84, 87–88, 98, 115, 118–19
  see also fighting
Irene 1, 30–33, 164

Jews 22–24, 93, 95–96, 103, 164 n. 4
jettison 24–25, 115, 117, 119, 123, 125–27
  see also salvage
judges 6, 15–16, 25, 28, 36–38, 41, 58, 63–65, 90, 93, 100, 109, 162, 166–67
  see also imperial officials, magistrates
Justice 17, 23, 31, 35–38, 78, 107, 140, 143
Justinian I 3–5, 7–8, 14–15, 17, 22–29, 34, 46 n. 28, 47 n. 32, 49 n. 41, 62 n. 99, 98 n. 50, 100 n. 58, 109–10, 112, 129

leases 41, 63, 166
  emphyteusis 41, 61–62, 166
  sharecropping 130–31
  see also tenants
Leo III 1, 7–9, 14, 15, 16, 18, 19, 23, 34, 78 n. 1
Leo IV 10, 18, 31, 33
Leo VI 45 n. 24, 80 n. 3
Lex Aquilia 99–100
  see also damage
loans 24–25, 31, 41, 59–60, 109–11, 114–16, 122, 136, 141, 147–48, 166
  see also debt, pledges, security, sureties

magic 100
  amulets 44, 76
  astrologers 102
  diviners 102, 142, 163
  enchanters 92, 142, 163
  magicians 23, 102
  sorcerers 22, 44, 76, 97, 102
magistrates 16, 26, 42, 54–5, 58–9, 61, 65, 69, 72–73, 75–76, 91, 94, 109–10, 130, 134, 136, 166
  see also imperial officials, judges
marriage 17, 22, 32–33, 38–39, 45–52, 73–75, 96–97, 105–06, 168
  see also adultery, betrothal, divorce, dowry
mills 28, 138–39
monasteries 57, 62
  see also monks
money 8–9, 25, 36, 38, 59, 65, 67, 71, 83, 98, 115–16, 122, 147–48, 149, 152–54, 159

Folles 132, 136
gold 49, 74, 92, 93, 103, 114–16, 118–22, 124, 126, 127
Nomismata 72, 81
silver 114, 116, 121–22, 124, 126, 127, 152, 154
monks 11, 58, 95
see also clerics, monasteries
murder *see* homicide

neighbours 28, 129, 131, 133, 138, 141–44, 147–50, 152, 154–55, 160–61
Nomikoi 55, 166–67
notaries *see* imperial officials: *Defensores Civitates*, *Nomikoi*, *Taboularioi*
nuns 23, 72–73
see also monasteries, monks, virgins

oaths 30, 32, 56, 63, 64, 108, 114, 121, 133, 137, 146, 150, 164–68
occupations 63, 166–67
brothel-keepers 96
charioteers 96, 102
doctors 118–19
farmers 42, 129–39
herdsmen 132–33
merchants 113, 115–26
midwives 100
prostitutes 98
sailors 113–28
shepherds 133
ship captains 113–16, 118–27
see also army, bishops, clerics, imperial officials, monks, nuns
Orthodox, the 92–93, 95, 103
orphans 38, 40, 45–46, 57, 140, 146–47, 166
orphanages 57, 62
Pagans 22–24, 95–96, 102–03
partnerships 41, 60, 116, 122–25, 141, 149
passengers 113–15, 117–21, 125–27
Patria Potestas 39–40, 42, 47–49, 53, 66–68, 78 n. 1
see also Peculium, *Peculium Castrense*
Peculium 42, 66 n. 122, 68
Peculium Castrense 53, 66–68, 77–79
perjury 42, 69, 121, 133, 142, 144, 162, 165–67
pirates 115, 121–22
see also robbers, theft
plants and by-products
chaff 136
figs 136
fruits 133
hay 136
straw 133
trees 75, 107, 133–34, 136, 138, 161
vines 131, 136
see also fields, foodstuffs, gardens, vineyards
pledges *see* security
poisoners 44, 56, 76, 92, 97, 99–100, 142, 163
see also drugs, enchanters, sorcerers
prison 88
prisoners of war 40, 53, 58, 108
Procurators 61–62
property disputes 18, 28, 31
illicit use of or encroachment on other people's property 91, 129–32, 136, 138
over boundaries 28, 90–91, 130, 167
over ownership or possession 91, 109–10, 130
use of force 42, 69, 90–91, 110, 136
see also boundary markers, damage, fences

priests *see* clerics
provinces 5–6, 8, 57, 62, 72, 81, 92, 167
public crimes 85, 87, 92
punishment *see* capital punishment, confiscation of property, corporal punishment, exile, fines, slavery: enslavement
purchase 40, 59–61, 79, 93, 108, 111, 141, 151, 166
  see also sale

refuge 42, 69, 160–61
robbers 44, 76, 115, 118, 120–22
  see also pirates, theft
Romans 84, 88, 95, 111

sale 40, 59–61, 71–72, 84–85, 88, 93, 97, 100, 133, 137, 141, 148, 150–53, 108, 120, 166
  see also purchase
salvage 120, 123–28
  see also jettison
Samaritans 94, 96, 103
security 22, 41, 59–60, 109, 111, 136, 141, 147–48
  see also debt, guarantors, loans, sureties
settlements 42, 65, 166
sexual crimes
  adultery 17, 22, 43, 51, 73–74, 87, 98, 144, 155, 165
  bestiality 17, 44, 75, 142, 159
  bigamy 17, 43, 75
  general illicit sex 17, 43, 51, 71–74, 106, 141, 153
  homosexuality 17, 43, 75, 142, 159
  incest 17, 43, 74, 141, 156–59
  rape 17, 73–74, 92
  sex with a slave 72, 97, 168
ships 24–25, 59, 107, 113–27
silk 116, 125–26
sin 10–11, 32, 35–36, 51, 72, 74, 86 n. 49, 87, 94, 144–46, 148–49, 154, 159, 162, 165
slander 44, 56, 73, 77
slavery 40, 57–58, 103, 106, 108, 143
  enslavement 40, 58, 87
  freedmen 40, 58, 63, 96, 105–06, 108, 112
  manumission 54, 57–58, 97, 103, 105–06, 108, 110–11, 166–67
  masters 32, 40, 44, 57–58, 63, 70–72, 76, 90, 103, 106, 121, 134–35, 137
  slaves 28, 32, 40–41, 43–44, 57–58, 63, 70–72, 76, 90, 96–97, 99–100, 103, 105–06, 108, 110–12, 115, 120–21, 134–35, 137, 142, 151–52, 159, 168
social distinctions
  Cohortales 93
  Curiales 108
  dignities 15, 35, 38, 42, 63, 68, 93, 112, 167–68
  the honourable 72, 99, 101, 108
  the more humble 72, 99, 101
  the poor 31, 36, 39, 43, 49, 70–71, 74, 89, 105, 130–31, 140, 143, 146–48
  the powerful 36
  the rich 43, 63, 70–71, 74, 166
  Senators 96
  see also clerics, monks, slavery
state servants *see* imperial officials
subscription
  by making the sign of the Cross 167
  by sealing 54, 122–23
  by signature 53–54, 57, 64–65, 166–67
suicide 21, 87–88
sureties 56, 89–90
  see also debt, guarantors, loans, security

Taboularioi 41, 60, 64, 166–67
tax 6, 8–9, 14, 19, 28, 123, 131
taxpayers 81, 131
tenants 28, 61–63, 110, 130–31
see also leases
testimony 32, 41, 63–64, 69, 108, 121, 124–25, 137, 162, 166–67
see also perjury, witnesses
theft 17, 24, 26–28, 43, 61, 70–71, 82, 84, 86, 102, 115, 118, 121, 126, 130, 132–37, 141, 144, 149–50
cattle-rustling 27, 43, 70, 134–35, 150
see also pirates, robbers
tools 28, 132, 136
treason 17, 69, 86
Treasury, the 8, 38, 49, 52, 55, 63, 68, 72, 77, 96, 106, 131
village districts 6, 28, 75, 130, 138
vineyards 28, 75, 130–32, 134–36, 138–39, 151
virgins 43, 73–74, 96, 153–54

weights and measures 36, 137, 140, 147
wills 39–40, 53–57, 62, 66–68, 97, 109, 166–67
witnesses 22, 32, 37, 39, 41–42, 45–46, 52–57, 63–65, 108, 118, 121, 123–24, 129, 133, 142–44, 162, 166–67
see also perjury, testimony
women 37, 39–40, 43, 45–47, 49–53, 72–75, 96–100, 105–06, 114, 141, 146, 152–59, 163, 165, 168
see also family, nuns, virgins
woods 28, 44, 75, 131–32, 134–36, 161

Printed and bound by CPI Group (UK) Ltd, Croydon, CR0 4YY
13/09/2026
14961097-0001